THE VATICAN BILLIONS

Jesus Christ
is THE WAY
THE TRUTH
THE LIFE

God Bless in His
Holy Name and
may The Grace
of The LORD
Bless You.

BOOKS BY AVRO MANHATTAN

Currently out of print:

The Catholic Church in the 20th Century

The Vatican in World Politics

Spain and the Vatican

Catholic Power Today

The Vatican and the U.S.A.

The Dollar and the Vatican

Religion in Russia

Religious Terror in Ireland

The Vatican in Asia

Terror Over Europe

Terror Over Yugoslavia

Vatican Imperialism in the Twentieth Century

Available from Chick Publications:

The Vatican Moscow Washington Alliance

Vietnam: Why Did We Go?

THE VATICAN BILLIONS

Two thousand years of wealth accumulation
from Caesar to the Space Age

AVRO MANHATTAN

*Where your treasure is, there will
your heart be also.* Matthew 6:21

Published by Chick Publications
P.O. Box 662, Chino, CA 91710
Printed in the United States of America

Copyright © Avro Manhattan 1983

All rights reserved. No part of this publication may be reproduced, stored in a retrieval system or transmitted in any form or by any means, electronic, mechanical, photocopying, recording or otherwise, without the prior permission of the Copyright owner.

Library of Congress Catalog Card No. 83-72654

I.S.B.N.: 0-937958-16-6

CONTENTS

Preface — Page 15

Chapter 1 — 17
THE HISTORICAL GENESIS OF THE VATICAN'S ACCUMULATION OF WEALTH

Historical genesis of the Vatican's accumulation of wealth — The splitting of Christianity accelerated by its policy of acquisition of temporal riches — Christianity expropriates all rival religions — How the Apostolic tradition of poverty was abandoned.

Chapter 2 — 23
THE ORIGIN OF THE CHURCH'S TEMPORAL RICHES

The cult of the Blessed Peter — Sale of the filings from his iron chains — King Canute goes to Rome — Origin of the wealth of the church — The Turnkey of Heaven writes a letter in gold — St. Peter's Throne — Birth of the Papal States — The pontiffs become kings.

Chapter 3 — 32
THE CHURCH AS THE INHERITOR OF THE FORMER ROMAN EMPIRE

She claims the ownership of all the territories of the Roman Empire — Ecclesiastical forgeries and counter-forgeries — The Donation of Constantine and its subsequent profound repercussions for the West.

Chapter 4 — 38
THE CHURCH CLAIMS OWNERSHIP OF THE WESTERN WORLD

Basic policy for the establishment of a universal temporal domain of St. Peter — The Church commands secular rulers to pay her — She claims the ownership of all lands, with all their inhabitants and riches — She "sub-lets" most of Europe to the Kings of England, of Germany and of France.

CONTENTS

Chapter 5 — 45
THE CHURCH CLAIMS THE OWNERSHIP OF ALL ISLES AND LANDS AS YET UNDISCOVERED

A Pope sells Ireland to England — All Irishmen to pay an annual tribute of one penny to the Holy See — All islands the rightful possessions of St. Peter — The Church "lends" the Americas to Spain and Portugal

Chapter 6 — 53
WHEN THE WORLD WAS ABOUT TO END — A.D. 1000

Why the world would come to an end in the year A.D. 1000 — What caused the credence — Reaction of a terrorized Christendom — Believers give all their possessions to the Church. The Church becomes immensely rich — Appearance of a new monasticism based on total poverty — St. Francis and St. Bernard condemn the wealth of the Church — Heretics as a source of more wealth — Anathemas and excommunications as means to extract money — Denounce your neighbor to seize his property — Greed and corruption of the clergy

Chapter 7 — 62
PAY TO BE A CHRISTIAN — WHETHER ALIVE OR DEAD

The Pope who sold a million Italians for 800 ounces of gold — Fines in the confessional — The Exeter farmers' trick — Direct and indirect church taxation — The Church's crushing burden: the tithes — The "second best" — Deadly ecclesiastical economic stranglehold — The Church claims 33 per cent of personal riches of all "dead Christians" — Collects money from lepers, beggars and prostitutes.

Chapter 8 — 70
HOLY MASS TOURISM FOR EACH GENERATION

Holy Mass Tourism for each generation — Origin of the first Jubilee — The Pope's empty coffers prompt him to declare the Jubilee of A.D. 1300 — Monetary considerations behind the reduction of intervals between Jubilee from 100 to 50 and then to 25 years — Popes Boniface,

CONTENTS

Clement, Alexander and Paul as organizers of the Grand Tour — Discounts and reductions from St. Peter — Go to heaven via Rome...but pay first!

Chapter 9   76
MIRACLES, PORTENTS AND WONDERS FOR SALE

Grasshoppers, caterpillars, leeches and snails excommunicated — Florins and vermin — Too many miracles — The saint who had to work a miracle to stop miracles — The blessed, as unending sources of money

Chapter 10   81
STOCK EXCHANGE IN INDULGENCES

Pay for the release of a soul — Buy one million years of indulgences, to avoid Hell and shorten Purgatory with money — Dr. Martin defies the official seller of indulgences

Chapter 11   88
THE CHURCH CLAIMS THE AMERICAS

The Church "leases" the Americas to Spain, "subleases" part of them to Portugal — Testifying to that effect — The Borgia Pope completes the deal — Text of "The Pope's Bull made to Castille, touching the New World" sealed in the year of Our Lord 1493

Chapter 12   95
THE ECONOMIC FACTOR BEHIND THE REFORMATION

Extortions, greed and rapacity — Luxury conclaves and papal extravaganzas — The most beautiful Pope of all — The Borgia Pontiff who could fill the Sistine Chapel with sacks of gold — Honours and dignities to make money — The explosion — The Church loses more than half her immmense temporal wealth

Chapter 13   103
THE CATHOLIC CHURCH AND THE FABULOUS WEALTH OF THE SPANISH COLONIES

The riots of Mexico City — The Bishop who wanted also

to be a businessman — Conflict between the church's temporal revenue and that of the State — Confrontation between Madrid and Rome. Its significance — The Catholic Church consolidates her economic strangle-hold on the Spanish-American Empire. She becomes the owner of half the total wealth of Central and South America

Chapter 14   111
REVOLUTIONS AND THE CHURCH'S REVENUES

The North American, French and South American Revolutions reduce the Church's wealth — The Church discovers new means to make money — The invention of the "miraculous medal" — The promotion of the "greatest miracle" of the nineteenth century; Lourdes — The popes lose their temporal kingdom. The Papal State and Rome are taken away from them for ever

Chapter 15   117
THE CATHOLIC CHURCH IS ONCE MORE DESPOILED OF HER WEALTH IN EUROPE AND THE AMERICAS

The Church and the dawn of the Industrial Age — A new orientation — Anti-clericalism deprives the Church of economic influence in Europe — The Catholic Church again becomes a billionaire in Latin America — Mexico expropriates all her lands — The Church's alliance with the U.S. Oil Corporation — Attempt to involve the U.S. in a war against Mexico to recover her wealth. President Roosevelt foils such machinations

Chapter 16   122
THE CATHOLIC CHURCH WELCOMES THE RISE OF BOLSHEVISM

Secret negotiations with Lenin. She plans to replace the Orthodox Church, and prepares to administer the latter's wealth — Failure of the Vatican-Kremlin deal — Reasons which prompted the Catholic Church to side with Fascism and with Nazism — The Lateran Treaty, or the closure of an old era and the opening of a new — Birth of a new Vatican Financial Empire.

CONTENTS

Chapter 17 — 128
FIRST FOUNDATIONS OF A TWENTIETH-CENTURY CATHOLIC FINANCIAL EMPIRE

The Catholic Church invests her billion lire in real estate, stocks, shares in Fascist Italy — She backs industrial war machinery to make quick profits — Land speculations in Rome and elsewhere — Causes of her spectacular success — Her vast properties on the Iberian peninsula — Millions of acres of land

Chapter 18 — 134
THE TOTAL WEALTH OF THE CHURCH BEFORE AND DURING THE SECOND WORLD WAR

Economic motivations which prompted the Catholic Church to support Nazi Germany — Her general strategy before, during and after the Second World War — She sides with Franco to keep her wealth in Spain — Holder of stocks and shares — Her riches in European countries — Her policy of investment in South America and the U.S. — Approximate total wealth of the Catholic Church at the beginning and at the end of the Second World War

Chapter 19 — 140
THE VATICAN INVESTS MILLIONS IN WAR INDUSTRIES TRANSFERS MOST OF THEM TO THE U.S.A.

The Holy See by-passes closed frontiers — The Church's interest in Italian and German war industries. Two witnesses: the founder of the Italian Catholic Party and General Mirkovich — The General who wanted to bomb the Vatican — Salvage from the Hitler debacle — Gold for the U.S. — The Catholic Church's financial and economic presence in Italy — Her 500-million-dollar Italian portfolio — 2,000 billion lire per year tax

Chapter 20 — 150
WHY THE CATHOLIC CHURCH IS THE RICHEST CHURCH OF AMERICA

Basic characteristics of Homo Americanus — Materialistic idealism and religious intangibility — Money for the

CONTENTS

churches — Three-billion-dollar income a year for organized religion in the U.S.— Why the Vatican sent its millions to the U.S. — The strange case of the U.S. — Vatican gold purchase — One dollar an ounce less for Holy Mother Church — Vatican investment in U.S. banks and industries

Chapter 21 — 156
MEMBER OF THE BILLIONAIRE CLUB OF THE U.S.A.

What is good for the Catholic Church is good for the U.S.A. — The economic miracle — Rough diamonds into millions — Characteristics of American Catholicism — Religious exclusiveness as the main factor for the accumulation of Catholic wealth — Identification of the Catholic Church with U.S. big business — Mutual help — The Catholic Church as a member of the exclusive Billionaire Club of America

Chapter 22 — 162
CARDINALS INTO STOCKBROKERS

The church in the U.S. run by "stockbrokers" — St. Peter and Cardinal Spellman — The Cardinal with 250-million-dollar building assets — Stockbroker of the Holy Mother Church — the 636-million-dollar diocese — The Catholic Church "second" only to the U.S. government

Chapter 23 — 169
CATHOLIC URBAN TAKE-OVER IN THE U.S.A.

The tale of the three clerics — "The Yankee Stadium? That's ours, too!" — The real estate clerical brigade — Catholic urban take-over — Typical unedifying instances

Chapter 24 — 177
THE WEALTHIEST GIANT THEOCRACY OF THE AMERICAS

Catholic financial penetration of the U.S. — Catholic lion's share of public funds — Schools and hospitals financed by taxpayers — Church subsidy: one billion 75 million dollars pay-tax to pay the Catholic Church —

CONTENTS

The Knights of Columbus — Monks and nuns and their untaxed profits — The Jesuits, the Bank of America and their links with the U.S. air corporations — The "poor nuns" with one-billion-dollar assets — American religious orders, the wealthiest in the world — Twelve-billion-dollar income a year — From 80 to 100 billion — The Catholic Church in the U.S., the wealthiest giant theocracy in the Western Hemisphere

Chapter 25 — 190
THE RICHEST AND THE POOREST, THE CHURCH IN AMERICA AND THE CHURCH IN RUSSIA

The Tiara and Cardinal Spellman — The Million Dollars and the "Mendicant Orders" — The clerical-master builders of America — Second only to the U.S. Government — Closed Churches, empty Churches and Church-Museums in Soviet Russia — Lenin in place of Christ — What the KGB said during a service — The Parish Church by the Black Sea — The cross and the star in Moscow Red Square

Chapter 26 — 199
ORIGIN OF THE CURRENT COLOSSAL WEALTH OF THE CATHOLIC CHURCH

Origin of her contemporary wealth — The Vatican invests millions in Turkish securities — Priests protest at the wealth of their Church — The House of Rothschild and Vatican investments — Catholic gold reserves larger than those of France and England — The Jews handle Vatican finances — The Vatican as the richest estate owner in the world — Vatican colossal evasion of taxation — The Vatican milks the German taxpayer — Pay one billion marks, whether you are religious or not — The Vatican investment with the giant corporations — How wealthy is the Church? Only God knows

CONTENTS

Chapter 27 — 208
THE BEST THING TO HAVE HAPPENED SINCE JESUS CHRIST

The Vatican pleads poverty — Sound re-investment of its funds — Secret financial information from the U.S.A. — The Vatican, the Dollar, the Mark, and the Swiss Franc — Pope Pius XI discovers "The best Jew since Jesus Christ" — Investment without theology — Its phenomenal success — Paul VI finds a promising successor

Chapter 28 — 215
THE POPE'S VERY OWN FINANCIAL LITTLE FOX

The Archbishop and the chicory-seller's son — The wealthiest self-made man of Europe — Early business with the Vatican Bank — Financial advisor and solver of imbroglios — He extracts the Church from embarrassing situations — The Pope calls him "his very own little fox" — The Vatican financial advisor's dazzling progress — The Vatican chooses 18 top businessmen to advise its advisor — Buy what the Vatican sells — Phenomenal growth of the Vatican portfolio — European hostility — Move to the U.S.A.

Chapter 29 — 222
THE CATHOLIC CHURCH, NIXON, THE FREEMASONS, AND THE JAILED "VATICAN WIZARD"

The Vatican and one million dollars for the Nixon campaign — Master-minder of the 20th largest U.S.A. Bank — Rumors of million dollar losses — The Church and the Freemason to the rescue — Disaster in Italy — A suit in U.S. Federal Court — Indicted on 66 counts — Secret meeting in Europe with the Pope's Nuncio — Three Cardinals promise to help the Vatican financial advisor — A federal judge is snubbed by the Vatican — The Vatican Bank's director is questioned by the U.S. about a suspected $900 million in counterfeit bonds — The Pope's financial wizard is found guilty on 65 charges — Condemned to 25 years in jail — Brother Masons try to help

CONTENTS

Brother "Michele" — "Even the Church has truly let him down."

Chapter 30
GOD'S BANKER, LODGE P2, AND THE VATICAN

The corpse across a railway line and the Bank of Rome — The Vatican financial advisor discovers a bright pupil — The pupil becomes God's banker — The mystery of P2 lodge — Black robes, black hoods, black friars (brothers) — The riddle of Catholic Masons — The Vatican Bank issues "comfort letters" — 400 million dollars interest to pay — A Vice-president is shot in the legs — God's banker's secretary commits "suicide"

Chapter 31
THE MAN UNDER BLACKFRIARS BRIDGE, THE MISSING 1,400 MILLIONS AND THE DEATH OF A CARDINAL

The "suicide" of God's banker — The verdict of London's jury — Sinister symbolism of the "execution" — Italy, the Vatican, and the missing millions — The losses of 250 major banks — Order for the arrest of the director of the Vatican Bank — The Pope admits responsibility — A mason's attempts to withdraw 60 million dollars — Third suicide at a Catholic bank — The Archibishop and the IOR — Sudden death of a former papal rival —

Chapter 32
THE VATICAN MAFIA OPERATORS AND OPERATIONS

The three wise men and the "shell" corporations — An investigator is killed, before his report — Brother Mason, "Gentleman of his Holiness" — A secret meeting which never took place — The Opus Dei offers to help the Vatican Bank — The IOR is accused of holding numbered Swiss bank accounts — Cannot, or is prevented from withdrawing its alleged millions — Warnings from the chief of the anti-terrorist police — The 100 bullets assassination — The tip of the conspiratorial iceberg

CONTENTS

Chapter 33 — 262
RIDDLE OF AN ENIGMA, THE VATICAN BANK

Six billion in deposits — Money, religion and power — The Pope's and the Vatican Bank's secret funds — Duality of the Vatican Bank's activities — The Borgia seizure of the Vatican's treasury — The Church cannot run only on Hail Mary's — Ideological subversion and financial adventurism — The "Spurious Invention" of a fictitious Holy Year

Chapter 34 — 270
1983-84: THE UNHOLY HOLY YEAR, INDULGENCES, CASH AND POPE-IDOLATRY

Unholy Holy Year, the great money spinner — The Pope and the Roman shopkeepers — Indulgence, cash, pilgrims, and tax exemption — The Black Virgins and money — Pope-Idolatry, the new cult — The youngest Pope in history buys the Papacy — The Pope who invented a "Sacred Commemoration" to pay a 1,000 million dollar debt — Two historical comments

Chapter 35 — **280**
THE INTANGIBLE BILLIONS OF THE CATHOLIC CHURCH

The immense real and intangible wealth of the Catholic Church — The most incalculable art collector in the world — Value of her art treasures; one thousand millions worth of pictures — How much for the Sistine Chapel? — Other imponderable sources of income — Pilgrimages, shrines, masses — Peter's Pence, its origin, history and its contemporary revival; how many million per year? — Enormous wealth of the Protestant and of the Catholic Churches — What would Christ do with it?

Chapter 36 — **293**
ARBITER OF THE WESTERN WORLD

The Catholic Church as the owner of one-third of all the wealth of Europe and of the Americas by the end of this century — Unheeded examples of history — Who shall testify on her behalf?

PREFACE

Christ was born, lived and died in poverty. His "church" is a multi-, multi-, multi-billion concern. How come that although she claims be preoccupied with the riches of heaven, she is in reality one of the most formidable accumulators of the riches of the earth?

When did it all begin? Where? How? What was the Church's economic empire in the past? One thousand, five hundred or one hundred years ago? How vast is it now? Is it true that it is the most powerful financial entity of all times? If so, how many thousand millions does it handle? How much real estate? How much stock, trusts and bonds? How many shares in oil, motors, automation, electronics, hotels, air lines, chemicals, engineering and space corporations? Is it true that she has vast deposits of gold in Swiss, American and other banks? That she has more dollar assets than the most powerful corporations of the U. S. A., larger monetary reserves than France, Belgium, Italy and Great Britain put together? That by the end of the present century she will control at least one-third of the total wealth of Europe and America?

What are her tangible and intangible financial funds in most of the major countries of the world? Such questions have never been answered before. This book answers them. In a vast, up-to-date piece of history, stretching from the time of St. Peter to the Dark Ages; from the Renaissance to the Reformation and the Counter-Reformation; from the French Revolution in the eighteenth century to the Industrial in the nineteenth. From the birth of Bolshevik Russia to the rise of Fascist Europe and to the Second World War. And from there to the landing of the first man on the moon, and thus to the Space Age.

Two thousand years of astonishing wealth accumulation, highlighted by dazzling deeds of private greed and of public philanthropy, of saintly sacrifices and of evil meanness, of individual generosity and of collective usury, carried out by popes, kings, prelates, rebellious churches, fiery reformers, holy men and villains, in the recent past; by revolutions, dictatorships. political parties, national and international banks, inter-continental corporations and global syndicates, in our times.

The whole is supported by names, dates, figures and facts. It is written in a simple, clear, racy style.

This book is a unique disclosure of the most formidable financial empire the world has ever seen, and which is still in full operation. Now!

AVRO MANHATTAN,
London

PUBLISHER'S FOREWORD

Why would Chick Publications, a Christian publishing house, publish the works of a secular writer?

Since the Vatican II Council, the Roman Catholic Institution, while posing as Christ's Church, has grown in power, wealth and political influence beyond your wildest imagination. Christian leaders have been silent about this, placing the true Church in a vulnerable position. The Lord devoted two entire chapters in the Book of Revelation to the Roman Catholic Institution, with loud warnings. He even promised her destruction. There is much blood on her hands, and "Inquisition" is the name of the game.

The head of every Christian family should read THE VATICAN BILLIONS. He should prayerfully teach his family who Rome really is and warn them against this power. God describes her as the enemy of the Church, "drunken with the blood of the saints." (Rev. 17:6)

Avro Manhattan, the world's foremost authority on Vatican politics, is a distinguished writer well-respected for his accuracy on Roman Catholic issues. His book is an eye-opener, as are his other books. To give Christians insight we are publishing more of his writings to open your eyes to what is secretly going on around us.

Enjoy your reading. It's a great book!

Jack T. Chick, President
Chick Publications, Inc.

CHAPTER 1

THE HISTORICAL GENESIS OF THE VATICAN'S ACCUMULATION OF WEALTH

Jesus, the founder of Christianity, was the poorest of the poor. Roman Catholicism, which claims to be His church, is the richest of the rich. Indeed, the wealthiest institution on earth.

How come, that such an institution, ruling in the name of this same itinerant preacher, whose want was such that he had not even a pillow upon which to rest his head, is now so top-heavy with riches that she can rival — indeed, that she can put to shame — the combined might of the most redoubtable financial trusts, of the most potent industrial super-giants, and of the most prosperous global corporations of the world? It is a question that has echoed along the somber corridors of history during almost 2,000 years; a question that has puzzled, bewildered and angered in turn untold multitudes from the first centuries to our days.

The startling contradiction of the tremendous riches of the Roman Catholic Church with the direct teaching of Christ concerning their unambiguous rejection, is too glaring to be bypassed, tolerated or ignored by even the most indifferent of believers. In the past, indeed, some of the most virulent fulminations against such mammonic accumulation came from individuals whose zeal and religious fervor were second to none. Their denunciations of the wealth, pomp, luxury and worldly habits of abbots, bishops, cardinals and popes can still be heard thundering with unabated clamor at the opening of almost any page of the chequered annals of western history.

But, while it was to their credit that such men had the honesty to denounce the very church to which they had dedicated their lives, it is also to the latter's discredit that she took no heed of the voices of anguish and anger of those of her sons who had taken the teaching of the Gospel to the letter and therefore were eager that the Roman Catholic system, which claimed to be the true bride of Christ, be as poor as the one she called master. When she did not silence them, she ignored them or, at the most, considered them utterances of religious innocents, to be tolerated as long as her revenue was not made to suffer.

Whenever that happened the Vatican did not hesitate to resort to the most prompt and drastic coercion to silence anyone capable of setting in motion forces, within or outside her, likely to divest her of her wealth.

The employment of suppressive measures went from the purely spiritual to physical ones; the ecclesiastical and lay machineries were used according to the degree and seriousness of the threat, and this to such an extent that in due course they became so integrated as to operate at all levels, wherever the two partners deemed themselves imperilled.

The result was that finally the religious exertions of the Roman Church became so intermingled with her monetary interests as to identify the former with the latter, so that very often one could see a bishop or a pope fulminate excommunication and anathema against individuals, guilds, cities, princes and kings, seemingly to preserve and defend the spiritual prerogatives of the Church, when in reality they did so exclusively to preserve, defend or expand the territorial, financial or even commercial benefits of a Church determined to retain, and indeed to add to, the wealth it already enjoyed.

This policy was not confined only to some critical or peculiar period of Catholic history. It became a permanent characteristic throughout almost two millennia. This feature, besides causing immense sorrow to the most fervent of her adherents, became the spring of countless disputes, not only with the principalities of this world, whom she challenged with her incessant quest for yet more temporal tributes, but equally with vast sections of Christendom itself.

The splitting of this giant religious system into three distracted portions, Roman Catholicism in the West, the Orthodox church in the Near East, Protestantism in Northern

GENESIS OF VATICAN'S ACCUMULATION OF WEALTH

Europe, to a very great extent became a reality very largely because of the economic interests which lay hidden behind the high-sounding dissensions between the simmering rival theological disputations.

Thus, had the Church of Rome remained apostolically poor, it is doubtful whether the lay potentates would have aligned themselves to the support of the ecclesiastical rebels, since the greed of the former for the possible acquisition of the immense wealth controlled by the Church in Germany, England, and elsewhere would not have become the decisive trigger which made them side with the revolutionary new spiritual forces whose objectives were not solely confined to the curtailment of the spiritual and political might of Rome, but equally to depriving this religious system of the wealth which she had accumulated through centuries of uncontrolled monopoly.

It was the allurement of the immediate potential redistribution of the Vatican's riches among the lay potentates which a successful religious secession would have rendered possible, that became the principal factor ultimately to persuade them to rally to the side of Luther and his imitators.

The dynastic issue of King Henry VIII of England was not as basic as the economic motivation which really led to the final breakaway from Roman authority. The landed gentry who supported his policy did so with their eyes well fixed upon the economic benefits to come. The variegated alignment of the German princes with Lutheranism was prompted chiefly by the same basic economic considerations. It was such concrete, although seemingly secondary, factors which in the long run made the Reformation possible.

Seen in this light, therefore, the Roman Catholic Church's persistent ignoring of the fundamental command of Christ concerning the riches of this world caused irremediable harm to the spiritual interests of Christendom at large; and, even more than that, ignited revolts, provoked revolutions and promoted destructive wars which were to scar the western world for hundreds of years, up to our own days.

That was not always so. The true early Church acted upon, and indeed practiced, the tenets of Jesus Christ, thus putting the accumulation of the treasures of heaven before the accumulation of those of the earth.

But as the Roman Catholic system began to develop, the first tiny seeds of the temporal amassment of wealth were planted. These were eventually to grow into the monstrous giant mustard tree which was to obscure the light of Europe for over a thousand years.

The early Christians, following upon the example of the Apostles and the first and second generations of Christ's disciples, upon conversion obeyed Christ's commandment to the letter and disposed of their possessions. These they either sold or gave to the Christian community, the latter using them for communal benefit, so that all members would partake of them in equal portion. There was no personal attachment as yet to riches thus used, either on the part of the single Christian individual or for any autonomous Christian nucleus. The ownership, possession and enjoyment of any wealth was anonymous, impersonal and collective. There was also the help of the poor, of the slaves, of the sick and of the prisoners.

During the first and second centuries the early Christians, by acting in this manner, retained the innocence of the apostolic tradition; and even during the third, although the Church's wealth had already become substantial, she managed to act in harmony with Christ's injunction about poverty.

Christians, however, by now no longer sold their goods upon being baptized. They had come to harmonize the possession of worldly goods with the teaching of Christ by conveniently quoting or ignoring sundry passages of the Gospels. Also, by following the example of the Church, which as a corporate body had begun to accumulate wealth. Its retention was justified by her help of the destitute, and also by the fact that the habit had started by which many, upon their death beds, left estates or money to her.

It was thus that the apostolic tradition of poverty was eventually abandoned. There was nothing contradictory, so the argument ran, in Christians retaining earthly riches so long as these were used in the "service of religion." The argument seemed a sound one to the individuals, particularly since

GENESIS OF VATICAN'S ACCUMULATION OF WEALTH

Christianity had "turned respectable." The Roman Catholic Church thus gradually became the custodian of wealth passed on to her by her sons, acting as its distributor and administrator.

Until now there had been no indication of the shape of things to come. This was soon visible, however, with the historical event of the utmost importance. The Emperor Constantine, following concrete political consideration, had decided to align the growing forces of Christianity on his side. A pious legend has it that he put upon the Roman standards a cross, with the words "In this sign conquer!" He won against the rearguard forces of the pagan world. Constantine recognized Christianity in A.D. 313.

Thenceforward a new phase was initiated. The Church Triumphant began to vest herself with the raiment of the world. The state became her protector. With this came not only power, but also wealth. Accumulation of the latter was no longer regarded solely for the purpose of helping the poor. It became a visible testimony to her newly found status; a necessity which went with her prestige and mounting strength and power.

This was reflected in the multiplying erection of prestigious cathedrals, the opulence of the vestments of her prelates, the magnificence of her liturgy. Parallel with these grew unchecked worldly pride, also mounting greed for earthly riches. The two begot lack of charity, which turned soon into blatant intolerance.

Pagan temples were either closed, transformed into Christian shrines or demolished. Their properties were summarily added to the Church's patrimony. The wealth of sundry religions was mercilessly expropriated, their clergy dismissed or persecuted, when not civilly or even physically obliterated. This transfer of political might made an easy transition into acquisitional power, the Roman Catholic Church set out in earnest to promote a policy of swift appropriation of real estate, of highly remunerative governmental posts, and even of speculative monetary and commercial enterprises.

Simultaneously with the accelerated growth of prestige, might and wealth, a new factor appeared on the scene amidst the ruins of the classic and the new emerging cultures: the monastic communities. These, the nuclei of which had come to the fore in original obscurity even when the Church was being persecuted, now transformed themselves into vast associations of pious individuals determined to ensure the spiritual riches of heaven by the abandonment of the riches of the earth.

But now, unlike their predecessors the anonymous hermits who sustained themselves solely upon locusts and spring water, their imitators found it increasingly difficult to follow such a strict mode of life. The legacies of the pious, the presents of parcels of expensive lands, estates and goods from newly converted highly placed pagan individuals, and the thanksgiving of repentant sinners, all contributed within a few centuries to make the monastic families in Europe the custodians of earthly riches and thus the administrators of earthly goods. Thus this Church soon found herself not only on a par with the political and military potentates of this world, but equally a competitor with these amassers of wealth, from her high prelates, consorting with the high officials of the imperial court, to the monastic communities, springing up with ever more frequency in the semi-abandoned hamlets of former Roman colonies.

The early apostolic tradition of poverty became an abstraction; at most, a text for sermons or pious homilies. And, while single heroic individuals preached and observed it, the Church Triumphant, congregating with the principalities of the earth, not only ignored it; she shamelessly stultified its injunctions, until, having become embarrassed by it, she brazenly disregarded it, abandoning both its theory and, even more, its practice.

CHAPTER 2

THE ORIGIN OF THE CHURCH'S TEMPORAL RICHES

It was at this stage that another no less spectacular factor, predestined to have profound repercussions upon the development of Roman Catholicism during its first millennium, appeared on the scene.

The tradition was established of pilgrimages to places where the saints had lived, had been martyred and had been buried. Monasteries, nunneries, churches, all had their own. With the possession of the relics of the blessed, with promotion of their legends and accounts of their miracles went not only the spiritual devotions, but also the monetary offerings of the pilgrims. That spelled wealth for those localities where the pious voyagers gathered. The more popular a shrine or a saint, the more abundant the collection of silver and gold coins.

The most fabulous was undoubtedly that promoted by the cult of the Blessed Peter, the Turnkey of Heaven. The cult demanded a journey to Rome, where Peter's tomb lay.

Peter had been crucified there, it was asserted with no more plausible data than a pious tradition, for the Bishops of Rome had no more evidence then than have the pontiffs of the twentieth century. The latter have attempted to substantiate it with doubtful archaeological finds. The process, begun by Pope Pius XII (1939-58), was completed by Pope Paul VI. In 1968 Paul declared officially that "a few fragments of human bones found under the Basilica of St. Peter are the authentic mortal remains of the Apostle".[1]

How the "identification" had been carried out, on a site where hundreds of thousands of bodies had been buried during many centuries, was not plausibly explained, in view also of the fact that there has never been any definite historical evidence to prove that Peter was ever in Rome. The Roman

Bishops, however, cultivated the myth with undiminished eagerness. This they did, not as mere upholders of a devout legend, but as the skillful promoters of a growing cult which had concrete and far-reaching objectives, since its magnification brought them immense authority, and with it, money. For the belief that the tomb of Peter was in the Eternal City induced thousands of pilgrims, beginning with English and Scottish ones, to go to pray over the Apostle's tomb; a source of tremendous revenue. Today we would call it by the more accurate and prosaic name of tourism.

The successors of Peter promoted pilgrimages to his "tomb" in Rome very early, although from the start they showed a special predilection for the richest and most powerful personages of the times - that is, for individuals who could give them costly presents, land and power.

To quote only one typical case, Pope Leo tells us how the Emperor Valentinian III and his family regularly performed their devotions at the tomb of St. Peter, "such practice yielding a *useful* respect for the Apostle's successors" to whom they offered costly *presents* and the *tenure of lands*.

Pope Gregory, on the other hand (590-604), promised Queen Brunhilda remission of her sins. "The most blessed Peter, Prince of the Apostles...will cause thee to appear pure of all stain before the judge everlasting"[2] as long as she granted him, Gregory, what he asked of her, that is, money, real estates, and investitures which yielded abundant revenues to the Church: a practice which became a tradition during the oncoming centuries.

Gregory went even further and sent the nobleman Dynamius a cross containing "filings" from St. Peter's chains, telling him to wear the cross at his throat "which is like as if he were wearing the chains of St. Peter himself," and adding "these chains, which have lain across and around the neck of the most Blessed Apostle Peter, shall unloose thee for ever from thy sins". The gift, of course, was not a free one. It cost money and gold.[3]

Not content with this, Gregory began to send out "the keys of St. Peter, wherein are found the precious filings and which by the same token also remit sins" - provided the recipients paid in cash or with costly presents.[4]

ORIGIN OF THE CHURCH'S TEMPORAL RICHES

Once it became known that the relics of St. Peter, when combined with the spiritual power of his successors, could remit sins, it was natural that most of the Christians throughout Christendom longed to go to the tomb and thus partake of Peter's and the pope's spiritual treasures. The latter invariably involved earthly treasures of money, silver and gold, or deeds of real estate. And that is how the pilgrimage to Rome, called the Pardon of St. Peter, was initiated — curiously enough, mostly by Anglo-Saxons.

In addition to encouraging the belief that Peter's tomb was in Rome and that his successors had "filings" from St. Peter's chains, the popes encouraged the belief that by coming to the Eternal City the pilgrims *could address the Blessed Peter in person*. The Church, far from discouraging such dishonest humbuggery, gave her approval to it: witness for example the notable St. Gregory of Tours, who, in his *De Gloria Martyrum*, gave a detailed description of the ceremony that had to be performed in order to speak with the Prince of Apostles.[5]

The pilgrim had to kneel upon the tomb of St. Peter, the opening to which was covered by a trap door. Then, raising the door, he had to insert his head into the hole, after which, still remaining in that posture, he had to reveal in a loud voice the object of his visit to the saint. Offerings of money were thrown in. Then veneration and obeisance were to be offered to St. Peter's successor, the pope.

The religious and even political results of this practice upon deeply ignorant nations like the Anglo-Saxons, and upon the Franks who imitated them, can be easily imagined. Secular rulers of the highest rank flocked to Rome. At the beginning of the seventh century, for instance, two Anglo-Saxon princes renounced their thrones and passed the remainder of their lives at the tomb of St. Peter.[6] King Canute himself could not resist Peter's appeal. Once in Rome, having paid homage to the pope, he wrote a letter to the nobles of his kingdom, in which he said: "I inform you that I come to Rome to pray for the redemption of my sins... I have done this because wise men have taught me that the Apostle St. Peter received of the Lord great power to bind and to loose, that he is the turnkey of the kingdom of heaven...That is why I thought it most useful to obtain this special patronage before God."[7]

The well-calculated policy of this cult, once widely established, yielded increasingly valuable results for the popes, who were quick to turn the prestige thus gained into a powerful instrument by which to obtain the submission of men of low or high rank, both in the spiritual and in the secular fields.

The accumulation of riches, which had not only begun to be a permanent feature of Roman Catholicism but had started to grow since the times of Constantine, when that Emperor had issued a law concerning the acquisition of land by the Church (A.D. 321), by now had reached such a stage that it had become a kind of patrimonium, owned, controlled and administered by the Bishops of Rome.

The possession of property brought with it inevitable deterioration and indeed corruption of the clergy and therefore of the Church herself, since the former, seeing the latter's eagerness for the things of this world, followed her example. The clergy, for instance, began to ask for money in exchange for their work or made money out of church goods.

Thus, under the pontificate of Gregory, clerics accepted valuables in exchange for burial places. Gregory forbade the practice, "never permitting that anyone should have to pay money for a grave." He issued sundry decrees which prohibited the charging of fees for the induction of clerics into office, for the investment of a bishop, for the drawing up of documents, and so on.

Upon learning of repeated cases in which the clergy were accused of selling church vessels, Gregory began a thorough investigation into the whole question of the Church's wealth. After having been told of how a priest had sold two silver chalices and two candelabra to a Jew, he issued a series of ordinances which decreed that each Christian community should make a correct inventory of all its sacred vessels, land and property. For the first time the census gave precise information of the wealth of the Church. It showed to a surprised Gregory how his Church owned landed property in Sicily, Gaul, Spain, the Balkan lands, the Near East and even many parts of Africa.

These properties included not only lands and farms, but also whole towns. St. Peter's Patrimony, as it began to be called, owned Syracuse and Palermo, besides numerous rich estates all over Sicily, southern Italy, Apulia, Calabria and even Gallipoli, although in ruins. The estates in Campania and those of Naples and the Isle of Capri were all producing large revenues.

All in all, the Roman Church in Gregory's time owned twenty-three estates, whose total area comprised 380 square miles, with an aggregate revenue of over one million dollars a year, a colossal sum at that period.

Gregory himself lived a life of austerity. He was a strong believer in the "ancient rule of the Fathers", that is, in evangelical poverty. When confronted by all this wealth, he called himself "the poor man's treasurer," and tried to live up to the role. He was the first pope to call himself *Servus Servorum Dei*, Servant of the Servants of God.

Yet, while in agreement with the fathers of the early church, such as Origen, Tertullian and Cyprian, that material possessions were not a good thing, the fact remained that Gregory was ruling a religious system which owned vast properties, real estates and riches of all kinds. Gregory justified their retention on the ground that they should be used, as the early Christians had used them, to help the destitute. That he genuinely believed this was proved by the fact that once, having heard how a beggar had died of starvation in Rome, he became so distressed that he shut himself in a cell for three days and nights without food or drink, refusing even to say Mass. He tried to administer the riches with wisdom, by giving to the poor as much as he received.

But the tide of corruption and of the progressive amassment of worldly wealth continued unabated. Indeed, it gathered momentum, notwithstanding Gregory's uncompromising efforts to stem it by every means at his disposal, such as his demands for precise details of how the money had been spent, the scrutiny of bookkeeping and his stern prohibition of "hidden balances of the Greek sort."

It came to pass then that, only 300 years after Constantine, Roman Catholicism had already turned herself into one of the largest land owners of the West. The Patrimony of St. Peter had become, not a modest sum of liquid money to be "distributed to the destitute," but the accumulated wealth of a rich religious system determined to become even richer in the years ahead.

While there were still individuals within the Church who believed in poverty, wealth continued to accumulate, and this to such an extent that at one stage she (or rather some of her leaders) had the audacity to make the Blessed Peter himself "write a letter from heaven."

Before relating how the Blessed Peter wrote such a celestial missive, it might be useful to cast a glance at the events which preceded, and in fact prompted, the deed.

After Pope Gregory's death, the process of adding more riches to the already vast accumulation went on unabated for another hundred years or so. Then, to the horror of the popes, the tide suddenly turned.

In the eighth century, when the papacy had so much that it did not even know how much, the semi-converted Slavs started to despoil St. Peter's Patrimony. This had been bad enough. But then, even worse, robbers appeared on the horizon. They sprang from distant Arabia. And the Arabs, to make things worse, also started to despoil St. Peter's Patrimony, claiming that they were doing it in the name of God. They called Him Allah. In addition, they had the bad habit of pinpricking the pope's subjects with their scimitars, telling them, while taking away all their possessions (or rather the possessions of their papal master) that in addition to having changed landlords they had better change also their religion — which the vast majority promptly did.

In this manner, whole papal dominions were lost. These included Dalmatia, Istria, Spain, the South of France, and the whole of North Africa. To all this, Providence, or rather human greed, added insult to injury when the successors of Constantine, the most Christian emperor of Constantinople, followed suit and deprived Peter's Patrimony of its vast estates in Sicily, Sardinia, Calabria and Corsica. Within a few decades, St. Peter had been robbed of such immense estates that his former boundless dominion was eventually reduced to central Italy, not for away, relatively speaking, from Rome.

ORIGIN OF THE CHURCH'S TEMPORAL RICHES

Notwithstanding such a shrinking of their possessions, the worst devils of all, the Lombards of North Italy, set out to rob the Blessed Peter of this last estate as well. This they were about to do when the pope invoked the help of none other than the Prince of the Apostles, the Blessed Peter himself. He asked him to mobilize the most powerful potentate of the times, Pepin, King of the Franks. Pepin, said the pope, must preserve intact the Church's earthly possessions. Indeed, it might even be of spiritual benefit to him to add some of his own to them.

The Blessed Peter complied! How? Simply by writing a letter. Direct from Heaven. To Pepin. The celestial letter, of course, was first sent to the pope, Stephen, who had plenty of Peter's chains' "filings". Stephen sent it to the king by special papal envoy.

The letter, on the finest vellum, was all written in pure gold. It read as follows:

> Peter, elected Apostle by Jesus Christ, Son of the Living God. I, Peter, summoned to the apostolate by Christ, Son of the Living God, has received from the Divine Might the mission of enlightening the whole world ...

Pepin knelt reverently before the Papal Legate, who went on reading the Blessed Peter's missive:

> Wherefore, all those who, having heard my preaching, put it into practice, must believe absolutely that by God's order their sins are cleansed in this world and they shall enter stainless into everlasting life Come ye to the aid of the Roman people, which has been entrusted to me by God. And I, on the day of Judgment, shall prepare for you a splendid dwelling place in the Kingdom of God.
>
> Signed, Peter, Prince of the Apostles.[8]

The Papal Envoy showed the letter to the whole court and solemnly vouched for the authenticity of Peter's signature. Not only that. St. Peter had gone to the length of writing the letter with his very own hand. Something he had never done before...Or since!

How had the letter ever reached the earth? asked Pepin.

The Blessed Peter in person had come down from Heaven and given the letter to his successor, the pope of Rome, explained the Papal Envoy. Thereupon he showed the king how St. Peter had addressed the celestial letter:

> Peter, elected Apostle by Jesus Christ, to our favorite Son, the King Pepin, to his whole army, to all the bishops, abbesses, monks, and to the whole people.[9]

Pepin, King of the Franks, had no alternative. How could he ever refuse the urgent request of the Prince of the Apostles? The turnkey of Heaven?

The devout Fleury, in his famous *Historia Ecclesiastica*, book 43, 17, cannot contain his indignation at the Blessed Peter's celestial letter, which he bluntly declared to have been nothing else than "an unexampled artifice." Artifice or not, whether written by Stephen himself or by some of his advisors, the fact remained that the letter of the Blessed Peter had the desired effect. In the year of our Lord 754, Pepin the Short, King of the Franks, defeated the rapacious Lombards. Since they had originally wished to rob the lands of Peter, Pepin, besides donating to Stephen what he had just preserved and recovered, added to it the Duchy of Rome, the Exarchate and the Pentapolis. All of these added up to a considerable amount of territory encompassing thousands of villages, forts, cities, farms, and estates — henceforward to be owned by the representative of St. Peter on earth, the pope.

The success of the heavenly missive spurred its authors to new efforts. Soon afterwards, in fact, the Roman chancery produced the throne of the Blessed St. Peter as well — the very chair in which St. Peter sat when in Rome, it was asserted; a further inducement to Pepin and his successors to grant the popes their protection, and additional property, if need be. The inducement was a powerful one, since a king of the Franks, if crowned sitting on the Chair of the Turnkey of Heaven, would be invested with an authority surpassing that of any other temporal ruler, with the exception of the pope.

Pepin, it seems, never heard of Peter's chair, or had not the time, or — what is most probable — died before the scheme was put into full working operation. The chair was never used for its original purpose in his lifetime. His son, the Emperor

Charlemagne, when crowned Emperor in the year 800, did not sit in it either. The throne, however, eventually came into its own. And this so much so that by the following century — during the rule of Charles the Bald (A.D. 875) — it had become one of the most precious relics of Roman Catholicism. Since then it has been venerated as the true chair upon which Peter used to sit, the sacred relic of the Petrine cult for centuries. In 1656 it was put inside an ornate bronze case, on papal command, by the sculptor Bernini.

Some years ago, however, its authenticity was questioned by certain Catholic authorities. Having been put under intense study by a commission of scholars and scientists, following strict carbon 14 and other radiological tests, it was discovered that the chair belonged approximately to the times of Charles the Bald — i.e. around A.D. 875 — and not to the first century A.D.

Pope Paul VI was thus, in the winter of 1969-70, put into another serious quandary. What could he do with Peter's throne after a thousand years of veneration? Put it back where it had been during a long millennium, in St. Peter's Basilica, or put it in the Vatican Museum?[10] But that was the personal problem of a pope of the twentieth century. Those of the eighth had been concerned only with magnifying the cult of the Blessed Peter, so as to enhance their power, no less than the earthly patrimony of the Church.

And so it came to pass that, thanks mostly to the cult of the Blessed Peter, Roman Catholicism, which had collected such vast amounts of temporal wealth prior to Pepin, now crowned her earthly possessions with additional territorial dominions. These, which had originally formed the first nucleus of the papal possessions, theoretically were given legal status by Pepin in A.D. 754. They became a concrete and accepted reality in 756. In 774 the Donation was confirmed by Pepin's immediate successor, Charlemagne. The Papal States had truly come into existence. Here the popes reigned as absolute temporal rulers for more than a thousand years, until 1870, when the Italians, having seized Rome with all the adjacent papal territories, declared the Eternal City the capital of the newly formed united Kingdom of Italy.

CHAPTER 3

THE CHURCH AS THE INHERITOR OF THE FORMER ROMAN EMPIRE

The establishment of the Papal States provided the Roman Catholic Church with a territorial and juridical base of paramount importance. From then on it enabled her to launch upon the promotion of an ever bolder policy directed at the accelerated acquisition of additional lands, additional gold, and the additional status, prestige and power that went with them.

The Emperor Charlemagne had not, in fact, turned his back on Rome after recognizing Pepin's Donation, but Pope Hadrian I in A.D. 774 presented him with a copy of the Donation of Constantine. This was reputed to be the grant by Constantine of immense possessions and vast territories to the Church. It was another papal forgery. Whereas the letter from Peter had been a forgery by Pope Stephen, the Donation of Constantine was one by Pope Hadrian I.[1]

The Donation of Constantine had tremendous influence upon the territorial acquisition and claims of the papacy, and a cursory glance at its origins, contents, and meaning will help to elucidate its importance.

The Donation was preceded and followed by various papally forged documents on the level of the Blessed Peter's missive. Like the latter, their specific objective was to give power, territory and wealth to the popes. Thus, soon after Pepin's death, for instance, a document appeared on the scene which was a detailed narrative put into the mouth of the dead Pepin himself. In it Pepin related, in somewhat extravagant Latin, what had passed between himself and the pope, "the successor of the Turnkey of Heaven, the Blessed Peter". His disclosure was meant as proof that he had donated to the pope, not only Rome and the Papal States already mentioned, but also Istria, Venetia and indeed the whole of Italy.[2]

INHERITOR OF THE FORMER ROMAN EMPIRE

Not content with the Papal States and the new regions acquired, the popes now wanted even more, thus proving the accuracy of the old saying that the appetite increases with the eating. They set themselves to expand even further their ownership of additional territories. They concluded that the newly born Papal States, although of such considerable size, were too small for the pope, the representative of the Blessed Peter. These territories had to be extended to match Peter's spiritual imperium. Something incontrovertible by which the popes would be unequivocally granted the ownership of whole kingdoms and empires had, therefore, become a necessity.

At this point this most spectacular of all forgeries makes its official appearance: the Donation of Constantine. Purporting to have been written by the Emperor Constantine himself, it emerged from nowhere. The document with one master stroke put the popes above kings, emperors and nations, made them the legal heirs to the territory of the Roman Empire, which it granted to them, lock, stock, and barrel, and gave to St. Peter — or rather to St. Silvester and his successors — all lands to the West and beyond, indeed, all lands of the planet.

The document was a sum of the previous forgeries, but unlike past fabrications it was definite, precise and spoke in no uncertain terms of the spiritual and political supremacy which the popes had been granted as their inalienable right. The significance and consequences of its appearance were portentous for the whole of the western world. The social structure and political framework of the Middle Ages were molded and shaped by its contents. With it the papacy, having made its boldest attempt at world dominion, succeeded in placing itself above the civil authorities of Europe, claiming to be the source of all ecclesiastical and secular power, as well as the real possessor of lands ruled by Western potentates, and the supreme arbiter of the political life of all Christendom.

In view of the profound repercussions of this famous forgery, the most spectacular in the annals of Christianity, it might be useful to glance at its main clauses:

1. Constantine desires to promote the Chair of Peter over the Empire and its seat on earth by bestowing on it imperial power and honor.

2. The Chair of Peter shall have supreme authority over *all churches in the world*.
3. It shall be judge in all that concerns the service of God and the Christian faith.
4. Instead of the diadem which the Emperor wished to place on the pope's head, but which the pope refused, Constantine had given to him and to his successors the *phrygium* — that is, the tiara and the *lorum* which adorned the emperor's neck, as well as the other gorgeous robes and insignia of the imperial dignity.
5. The Roman clergy shall enjoy the high privileges of the Imperial Senate, being eligible to the dignity of patrician and having the right to wear decorations worn by the nobles under the Empire.
6. The offices of *cubicularii*, *ostiarii*, and *excubitae* shall belong to the the Roman Church.
7. The Roman clergy shall ride on horses decked with white coverlets, and, like the Senate, wear white sandals.
8. If a member of the Senate shall wish to take orders, and the pope consents, no one shall hinder him.
9. Constantine gives up the remaining sovereignty over Rome, the provinces, cities and towns of the whole of Italy or of the Western Regions, to Pope Silvester and his successors.

With the first clause the pope became legally the successor of Constantine: that is, the heir to the Roman Empire. With the second he was made the absolute head of all Christendom, East and West, and indeed of all the churches of the world. With the third he was made the only judge with regard to Christian beliefs. Thus anyone or any church disagreeing with him became heretic, with all the dire spiritual and temporal results of this. With the fourth the pope surrounded himself with the splendor and the insignia of the imperial office, as the external representation of his imperial status. With the fifth the whole Roman clergy was placed on the same level as the senators, patricians and nobles of the Empire. By virture of this clause, the Roman clergy became entitled to the highest title of honor which the emperors granted to certain preeminent members of the civil and military aristocracy, the ranks of patrician and consul being at that time the highest at which human ambition could aim.

The sixth and seventh clauses, seemingly irrelevant, were very important. For the popes, by claiming to be attended by gentlemen of the bedchamber, doorkeepers and bodyguards (*cubiculari, ostiarii, etc.*) emphasized their parity with the Emperors, as previously only the latter had this right. The same applies to the claim that the Roman clergy should have the privilege of decking their horses with white coverings, which in the eighth century was a privilege of extraordinary importance.

The eighth clause simply put the Senate at the mercy of the pope. Finally the ninth, the most important and the one with the greatest consequences in Western history, made the pope the territorial sovereign of Rome, Italy and the Western Regions; that is to say, of Constantine's Empire, which comprised France, Spain, Britain and indeed the whole territory of Europe and beyond.

By virtue of the Donation of Constantine, therefore, the Roman Empire became a fief of the papacy, while the Emperors turned into vassals and the popes into suzerains. Their age-old dream, the Roman dominion, became a reality, but a reality in which it was no longer the Vicars of Christ who were subject to the Emperors, but the Emperors who were subject to the Vicars of Christ.

The early concrete result of the Donation thus was to give a legal basis to the territorial acquisitions of the popes, granted them by Pepin and Charlemagne. Whereas Pepin and Charlemagne had established them sovereigns *de facto*, the Donation of Constantine made them sovereigns *de jure* — a very important distinction and of paramount importance in the claim for future territorial possessions.

It is very significant that it was after the appearance of the Donation under Pope Hadrian (c.774) that the papal chancery ceased to date documents and letters by the regnal years of the Emperors of Constantinople, substituting those of Hadrian's pontificate.

Although there are no proofs that the document was fabricated by the pope himself, yet it is beyond dispute that the style of the Donation is that of the papal chancery in the middle of the eighth century. The fact, moreover, that the document first appeared at the Abbey of St. Denis, where Pope Stephen spent the winter of 754, is additional proof that the pope was personally implicated in its fabrication. Indeed, although here again there is no direct evidence, it is supposed that the Donation was forged as early as 753 and was brought by Pope Stephen II to the Court of Pepin in 754, in order to persuade that monarch to endow the popes with their first territorial possessions. Once the Papal States came into being, the document was concealed until it was thought that it could be used with his son, Charlemagne, who had succeeded his father.[3]

The first spectacular materialization of the Donation was seen not many years after its first appearance, when Charlemagne, the most potent monarch of the Middle Ages, granted additional territories to the Papal States and went to Rome to be solemnly crowned in St. Peter's by Pope Leo, as the first Emperor of the Holy Roman Empire, in the year 800. The great papal dreams of (a) the recognition of the spiritual supremacy of the popes over emperors and (b) the resurrection of the Roman Empire, at long last had come true.

The subjugation of the Imperial Crown was not, however, enough. If it was true that this put the source of all civil authority — that is to say, the emperor — under the pope, it was also true that the distant provinces could not or would not follow the imperial example. The best way to make them obey was by controlling the civil administration in the provinces, as had been done at its center with the emperor. As the pope had made a vassal of the emperor, so equally the bishops had to make vassals of the civil authorities in their dioceses. By so doing the pope, with a blindly obedient, hierarchical machinery, would control at will the civil administration of the whole empire.

It was to put such a scheme into effect that yet another forgery, complementary to the Donation, appeared little more than half a century later, again from nowhere. In 850 the pseudo-Isidorean Decretals, better known as the "False

Decretals," made their first official appearance. They are a heterogeneous collection of the early decrees of the councils and popes. Their seeming purpose was to give a legal basis to the complaints of the clergy in the empire, appealing to Rome against the misdeeds of high prelates or of the civil authorities. Although some of the contents of the Decretals are genuine, a colossal proportion was garbled, forged, distorted or entirely fabricated. This was in order to achieve their real aim: to obtain additional power for the popes by giving to the abbots, bishops, and clergy in general, authority over civil jurisdiction in all the provinces, thus establishing a legal basis for evading the orders of the provincial secular rulers.

The result was that the Roman Church obtained important privileges, among them immunity from the operation of the secular law, which put her out of reach of the jurisdiction of all secular tribunals. In this fashion the clergy acquired not only a peculiar sanctity which put them above the ordinary people, but a personal inviolability which gave them an enormous advantage in all their dealings or disputes with the civil power.

Thus, thanks to a series of fabrications, forgeries, and distortions, carried out through several centuries and of which the Donation of Constantine was the most spectacular, the popes not only obtained a vantage ground of incalculable value from which to extend their spiritual and temporal power, but rendered themselves practically independent of all secular authority. Even more, they saw to it that the statutes of emperors and kings, no less than the civil law of nations, be undermined, greatly weakened and indeed obliterated by their newly acquired omnipotence.

CHAPTER 4

THE CHURCH CLAIMS OWNERSHIP OF THE WESTERN WORLD

Once rooted in tradition and strengthened by the credulity of the times, the dubious seedling of the Donation grew into a mighty oak tree under the shadow of which papal authoritarianism thrived. From the birth of the Carolingian Empire in the year 800 onwards, the gifts of Pepin, the Donation of Constantine, and the False Decretals were assiduously used by the pontiffs to consolidate their power. This they did, until, with additional forgeries and the arbitrary exercise of spiritual and temporal might, these documents became the formidable foundation stone upon which they were eventually to erect their political and territorial claims, the rock upon which stood the whole papal structure of the Middle Ages.

The Donation was given increasingly varied meanings by the succeeding generations of theologians. Notwithstanding the disparity in their views, however, they all agreed upon one fundamental interpretation: the Donation gave the widest possible power and authority to the papacy. Thus, for instance, whereas Pope Hadrian I stated that Constantine had "given the dominion in these regions of the West" to the Church of Rome, Aeneas, Bishop of Paris, asserted about the year 868 that as Constantine had declared that two emperors, the one of the realm, the other of the Church, could not rule in one city, he had removed his residence to Constantinople, placing the Roman territory "and a vast number of various provinces" under the rule of the Apostolic See, after conferring regal power on the successors of St. Peter.

The popes acted upon this, using the argument as a basis to increase their territorial sway, with the inevitable new accumulation of wealth which went with it. Gregory VII (1073) directed all his energies to that effect. He concentrated spiritual and political jurisdiction in himself, the better to administer the Western Empire as a fief of the papacy. That implied the extension of his temporal dominion over the kings and kingdoms of the earth and therefore over their temporal riches.

Indeed, Gregory had no qualms in openly asserting temporal supremacy over the whole of the Byzantine Empire, including Africa and Asia. He went even further by declaring that his ultimate goal was simply the establishment of the universal temporal domain of St. Peter. Hence his continual exertions to take possession of, in addition to Rome and Italy, all the crowns of Europe, many of which he succeeded in placing under his direct vassalage.

Although his vast scheme only partially materialized during his reign, his successors continued his work. Pope Urban II, following in his footsteps, decided to bring under subjection the churches of Jerusalem, of Antioch, of Alexandria and of Constantinople, with all the *lands* wherein they flourished. Under the pretext of liberating the tomb of Christ, he simply mobilized the entire western world into an irresistible army which, leaving the shores of Europe, plunged into Asia Minor like a tornado, creating the greatest military, political and economic commotion in both continents.

The capture of Jerusalem and the success of this First Crusade gave incalculable prestige to the pontiffs. While the nations of Europe attributed this victory to manifest supernatural power, the Roman Pontiffs were quick to transform the great martial movements of the Crusaders into powerful instruments to be used to expand their spiritual and temporal dominion. This was done by employing them as military and political levers which never ceased to yield territorial and financial advantages throughout the Middle Ages.

Such policies went a step further when, basing papal claims on an even more daring interpretation of the Donation, it was stated that the secular rulers should be made to pay tribute to the papacy. A vehement advocate of this was Otto of Freisingen, who in his Chronicles composed in 1143-6, did not hesitate to declare that as Constantine, after conferring the imperial insignia on the pontiff, went to Byzantium to leave the empire to St. Peter, so other kings and emperors should pay tribute to the popes.

For this reason the Roman Church maintains that the Western kingdoms have been *given over to her possession* by Constantine, and *demands tribute* from them to this day, with the exception of the two kingdoms of the Franks (i.e. the French and German).

Such advocacy was made possible because only a century earlier, in 1054, Pope Leo IX had declared to the Patriarch Michael Cerularius that the Donation of Constantine really meant the donation "of the earthly and heavenly imperium to the royal priesthood of the Roman chair."

From all this it followed that soon Lombardy, Italy, and Germany began to be reckoned, in the eyes of Rome, as "papal fiefs," the popes declaring ever more boldly that the German kings had possessed the Roman Empire, as well as the Italian Kingdom, solely as a present from the pontiffs. Such claims, of course, did not go unchallenged, and they often caused the profoundest political commotion — for instance, the one that broke out in Germany in 1157, when a letter from Pope Hadrian to Frederick Barbarossa spoke of "*beneficia*" which he had granted to the Emperor, or could still grant, and expressly called the imperial crown itself such a *beneficium* — i.e. a feod, as it was understood at the imperial court. Hadrian said, on the strength of the fact that it was he who had placed the crown on the Emperor's head, that the pope was the *real owner* of Germany.

It was not only the princes who rebelled against the papal pretensions. Men otherwise devoted to this religious system spoke in no uncertain words against papal infringement upon civil power. Provost Gerhoh of Reigersburg, for instance, commenting upon the custom (which, of course, rested for support on the Donation of Constantine) of the emperor holding the pope's stirrup, a custom which had prompted the Romans to paint those offensive pictures in which kings or emperors were represented as vassals of the popes, concluded that this, besides causing the embittered feelings of temporal rulers, went also against the divine order by allowing the popes to claim to be *emperors and lords of emperors.*

CHURCH CLAIMS OWNERSHIP OF WESTERN WORLD

A few years later Gottfried, a German educated in Bamburg, chaplain and secretary to the three Hohenstaufen sovereigns, Conrad, Frederick, and Henry IV, building on what Aeneas, Bishop of Paris, had already said, went a step further than Pope Adrian and included France in the Donation. In his Pantheon, which he dedicated to Pope Urban III in 1186, he stated that in order to secure greater peace for the Church, Constantine, having withdrawn with all his pomp to Byzantium, besides granting to the popes regal privileges, had given them dominion over Rome, Italy and Gaul, with all the riches therein.

With the passing of the centuries, the popes, instead of abating their claims, continued to increase them by declaring that, by virtue of the Donation, emperors were emperors simply because *they permitted them to be so,* the sole ruler in spiritual *and temporal* matters being, in reality, the pontiff himself.

Such pretensions were not left to wither in the theoretical field. They were directed to concrete territorial, political, and financial goals which the pontiffs pursued with indefatigable pertinacity. Pope Innocent II (1198-1216), the most energetic champion of papal supremacy, thundered incessantly to all Europe that he claimed *temporal* supremacy over all the crowns of Christendom: for, as the successor of St. Peter, he was simultaneously the supreme head of the true religion and the *temporal sovereign of the universe.* His tireless exertions saw to it that papal rulership was extended over sundry lands and kingdoms. By the end of his reign, in fact, the Vatican had become the temporal ruler of Naples, of the islands of Sicily and Sardinia, of almost all the States of the Iberian peninsula such as Castile, Leon, Navarre, Aragon and Portugal, of all the Scandinavian lands, of the Kingdom of Hungary, of the Slav State of Bohemia, of Servia, Bosnia, Bulgaria, and Poland. A proud list!

He became also the true *de facto* and *de jure* sovereign of England, after having compelled John to make complete submission. During the last years of that king's reign and the first few of Henry III, Innocent governed the island effectively through his legates. That was not enough, however, for Innocent proclaimed himself the temporal ruler of the Christian states founded in Syria by the Crusaders. Indeed, he went even further. Taking advantage of the Franco-Venetian Crusade of 1202, he planned the annexation of the Byzantine Empire. A Latin Empire came into being in the East, and while the Byzantines became the temporal vassals of the pope, the Greek Orthodox Church was compelled to acknowledge Roman supremacy. Later on, such immense dominion was extended by his successors through the conversion to Roman Catholicism of the pagans of the Baltic.

At this time, as in the past, one country more than any other opposed the irresistible ecclesiastical absorption: the powerful German Empire. But the pope, in spite of many setbacks, never recognized Germany as being outside this formidable papal imperium, on the familiar ground that she was an integeral part of the patrimony of St. Peter.

Not content with the Donation of Constantine, Innocent IV asserted that what Constantine gave to the Church had not belonged to him at all, *for Europe had always belonged to the Church*. In an encyclical published shortly after the close of the Council of Lyons in 1245, Innocent expressly stated:

> It is wrong to show ignorance of the origin of things and to imagine that the Apostolic See's rule over secular matters dates only from Constantine. Before him this power was already in the Holy See. Constantine merely resigned into the hands of the Church a power *which he used without right when he was outside her pale*. Once admitted into the Church, he obtained, by *the concession of the Vicar of Christ, authority which only then became legitimate*.

After which, in the same encyclical, Innocent fondly dwelt upon the idea that the pope's acceptance of the Constantine Donation was but a visible sign *of his sovereign dominion over the whole world*, and hence of all the wealth to be found on earth.

Belief in the Donation and in the wide extent of territory which Constantine included in it grew ever stronger. Gratian himself did not include it, but it was soon inserted as *palea*, and thus found an entry into all schools of canonical jurisprudence, so that from this time on the lawyers were the most influential publishers and defenders of the fiction. The language of the popes also was henceforward more confident.

CHURCH CLAIMS OWNERSHIP OF WESTERN WORLD

"Omne regnum Occidentis ei (Silvestro) tradidit et dimisit," said Innocent III (1198-1216)

Gregory IX (1227-41) followed this out to its consequences, in a way surpassing anything that had been done before when he represented to the Emperor Frederick II that Constantine had, along with the imperial insignia, given over Rome with the duchy and the imperium *to the care of the popes forever.* Whereupon the popes, without diminishing in any degree whatever the substance of their jurisdiction, established the tribunal of the empire, transferred it to the Germans, and were wont to concede the power of the sword to the emperors at their coronation. By now, this was as much as to say that this imperial authority had its sole origin in the popes, could be enlarged or narrowed at their good pleasure, and that the pope could call each emperor to account for the use of the power and the riches entrusted to him.

But the highest rung of the ladder was as yet not reached. It was first achieved by Gregory's successor, Innocent IV, when the synod of Lyons resulted in the deposition of Frederick, in which act this pope went beyond all his predecessors in the increase of his claim and the extent of the authority of Rome.

The Dominican, Tolomeo of Lucca, author of the two last books of the work *De Regimine Principum*, the first two books of which were by Thomas Aquinas, went even further and explained the Donation as a formal abdication of Constantine in favor of Sylvester. Connecting with this other historical circumstances, which were either inventions or misconceptions, he thence drew the conclusion that the power and wealth of all temporal princes derived its strength and efficacy solely from the spiritual power of the popes. There was no halting half way, and immediately afterwards, in the contest of Boniface VIII with Philip of France, the Augustinian monk Aegidius Colonna of Rome, whom the pope had nominated to the archbishopric of Bourges, drew the natural conclusion without the slightest disguise in a work which he dedicated to his patron.

The other theologians of the papal court, Agostino Trionfo and Alvaro Pelayo, surpassed all previous claims and declared, that if an emperor like Constantine had given temporal possession to Sylvester, this was merely a restitution of what had been stolen in an unjust and tyrannical way.[1]

Emperors and kings were compelled very often, not only to acknowledge such claims as true, but to swear that they would defend them with their swords; to cite only one example: the oath which the Emperor Henry VII had to take before his coronation. Pope Clement V made this monarch swear that he would protect and uphold all the rights which the emperors, beginning with Constantine, had granted to the Roman Church — without, however, stating what these rights were.[2]

The power given by the Donation to the Roman Church was further enhanced by that inherent in the papacy itself. As the direct successors of Peter, the popes were the only true inheritors of the might of the Church, and hence of whatever and whoever were under her authority. The theory ran as follows:

> Christ is the Lord of the whole world. At his departure he left his dominion to his representatives, Peter and his successors. Therefore the fullness of all spiritual and *temporal* power and dominion, the union of all rights and privileges, lies in the hands of the pope. Every monarch, even the most powerful, possesses only so much power *and territory* as the pope has transferred to him or finds good to allow him.

This theory was supported by most medieval theologians.[3] It became the firm belief of the popes themselves. In 1245, for instance, Pope Innocent IV expounded this doctrine to none other than the Emperor Frederick, saying that, as it was Christ who had entrusted to Peter and his successors both powers, the sacerdotal and the royal, the reign of both kingdoms, the heavenly and the earthly, belonged to him, the pope: by which he meant that the spiritual dominion of the papacy had to have its counterpart also in papal dominion *over all the lands, territories and riches* of the entire world.

Not even the most ambitious emperors of the Ancient Roman Empire had ever dared to claim as much.

CHAPTER 5

THE CHURCH CLAIMS OWNERSHIP OF ALL ISLES AND LANDS AS YET UNDISCOVERED

Following claims with deeds, the popes set about implementing their new, astounding theory by word, diplomacy, cunning, threats, and ruthless action. While appealing for support, armed with all the mystic and spiritual authority of the Church, they went on stating, asserting, and declaring that their rights were based upon the utmost legality, by virtue of the Donation of Constantine.

It was, in fact, a clause in the fabulous Donation (or rather a couple of sentences as interpreted by them) which, although seeming at first sight insignificant, had the most tragic and far-reaching consequences. The words, in the last clause of the Donation: "Constantine gives up the remaining sovereignty over Rome..." and ending: "...or of the western regions to Pope Sylvester and his successors." became the foundation stones upon which the papacy demanded sovereignty, not only over practically the whole of Europe, but over all the islands of the oceans.

As in the case of their claims for Europe, those for the islands grew with the passing of the years and the increase of the political power of the popes. It all began in a rather hazy fashion and with a comparatively small matter. When the popes proclaimed their sovereignty over Naples they included the various small islands nearby, on the ground that they were possessions of the Church. Later on, as documented in the chronicles of the Church of St. Maria del Principio, the popes, after having declared that Constantine gave to St. Peter also all the lands in the sea, said that the papal sovereignty covered the island of Sicily as well.

The use of the forged Donation initiated a new and more definite phase, however, when Pope Urban II claimed possession of Corsica in 1091, deducing Constantine's right to give away the island from the strange principle that all islands were legally *juris publici*, and therfore State domain. When the popes, after having abstained for one hundred and eighty nine years from ruling Corsica directly, became strong political potentates themselves, they had no hesitation in asking for "their island" back. In 1077 Pope Gregory VII simply declared that the Corsicans were "ready to return under the supremacy of the Papacy."

On this notion that it was the islands especially that Constantine had given to the popes they proceeded to build, although nothing had been said in the original document; and with a bold leap the Donation of Constantine was transferred from Corsica to the *far west*, that is, to Ireland, with the result that soon the papal chair claimed possession of an island which the Romans themselves had never possessed.

From then onwards, by virtue of the Donation of Constantine, the popes loudly claimed to be the feudal lords of *all the islands of the ocean*, and started to dispose of them according to their will. Laboring to obtain papal supremacy, they used these rights as a powerful political bargaining power by which to further their political dominion over Europe: (a) by compelling kings to acknowledge them as their masters, (b) by granting to such kings dominion over lands of which the papacy claimed ownership, and (c) by making the spiritual and political dominion of the Church supreme in the lands thus "let" to friendly nations.

The most famous example of such a bargain in transfer is undoubtedly Ireland. Ireland had been for some time the prey of internecine wars which were steadily but surely bringing it to a total state of quandary. By 1170, in fact, she had already had sixty-one kings. It so happened that the popes, having decided to bring the Irish, among whom were "many pagan, ungodly and rebellious rulers," under the stern hand of Mother Church, planned a grand strategy thanks to which they would not only impose the discipline of their religious system, but also tie to the papacy more firmly than ever the English kingdom by conferring upon the English monarch the

CLAIMS OWNERSHIP OF ALL UNDISCOVERED LANDS

sole right to conquer that island and subjugate its people. In this way the popes would achieve several goals simultaneously: they would reimpose their authority on Ireland, strengthen their power over the English kingdom, and thus also reinforce their hold upon France and indirectly upon the whole of Europe.

It so happened that the English kings had entertained similar designs, and also that at the time there was sitting in the papal chair a man by the name of Nicholas Breakspeare, known as Hadrian IV, an Englishman (1154-9), who made possible the English subjugation of Ireland by his "*Anglicana affectione*," as an Irish chieftain declared in 1316 in a letter to Pope John XXII.

King and pope began to negotiate. The pope was ready to confer the dominion of Ireland on the English king, upon the condition that the king accepted the doctrine of papal sovereignty, which implied that, as King of England, he was a vassal of the pope. The king, on the other hand, was ready to accept this upon the condition that the papacy would support him in his military and political conquest of the Irish by using the powerful machinery of the Church.

Fortune seemed to favor the project, for Diarmait, an Irish potentate years before Henry became King of England, had brought him a long-desired opportunity by proposing the conquest of Ireland. Once the pope and the king were in agreement, Hadrian IV granted to the English king the hereditary lordship of Ireland, sending a letter with a ring as a symbol of investiture, thus conferring on him dominion over the island of Ireland, which *"like all Christian islands, undoubtedly belonged of right to St. Peter and the Roman Church".*

The papal grant, made in 1155, was kept a secret until after Henry landed in Ireland in 1172. Thus the English received dominion over Ireland on the grounds that the pontiffs were feudal lords of all islands of the ocean, thanks to the Donation of Constantine.

The Irish conquest, ordered by Pope Hadrian IV, is authenticated by a document popularly called the "Bull Laudabiliter," found only in the Roman Bullarium (1739) and in the Annals of Baronius, but its authenticity has been accepted by Roman Catholic and Protestant historians alike.

The "Bull Laudabiliter" is inserted in the *Expugnatio Hibernica* of Giraldus Cambrensis, published in or about 1188,[1] wherein he asserts it to be the document brought from Rome by John of Salisbury in 1155. He also gives with it a confirmation by Alexander II, obtained, he states, by Henry II after his visit to Ireland. John of Salisbury, the intimate friend and confidant of Pope Hadrian, quotes also the Donation of Constantine, on the grounds of this right of St. Peter over all islands.

In addition to these two documents, there are three letters from Alexander III, which are similarly known to us only at second hand, being transcribed in what is known as the *Black Book of the Exchequer*.[2] In them, the pope expresses his warm approval of Henry's conquest of Ireland, calling his expedition a missionary enterprise, praising him as a champion of the Church and particularly of St. Peter and of his rights, which rights St. Peter passed on to the popes. Especially significant is the fact that the rights claimed by the popes under the Donation of Constantine, *over all islands*, are here asserted, not so much as justifying the grant of Ireland to Henry, but as entitling the papal see to claim those rights for itself.

Such rights were still claimed by the Vatican in an official document as recently as 1645. When in that year Pope Innocent X despatched Rinuccini as Papal Nuncio to Ireland, he gave him formal instructions in which were included a brief outline of past events. In it we find this definite and most striking passage:

For a long period the true faith maintained itself, till the country, invaded by Danes, and idolatrous people, fell for the most part into impious superstition. This state of darkness lasted till the reigns of Adrian IV and of Henry II, King of England.

Henry, desiring to strengthen his empire and to secure the provinces which he possessed beyond the sea in France, wished to subdue the island of Ireland; and to compass this design had to recourse to Adrian, who, himself an Englishman, with a liberal hand granted all he coveted.

The zeal manifested by Henry to convert all Ireland to the faith moved the soul of Pope Adrian to invest him with the *sov-*

CLAIMS OWNERSHIP OF ALL UNDISCOVERED LANDS

ereignty of that island. Three important conditions were annexed to the gift:

1. That the King should do all in his power to propagate the Catholic religion throughout Ireland.
2. That each of his subjects should pay an *annual tribute* of one penny to the Holy See, commonly called Peter's Pence.
3. That all the privileges and immunities of the Church be held inviolate.[3]

These "conditions" were obtained through papal authority and the king's sword. When King Henry seemed to have firmly established himself on Irish soil, the pope strengthened him by mobilizing the Irish Church in his support. Christian O'Conarchy, Bishop of Lismore and Papal Legate, presided at the Synod, attended by the Archbishops of Dublin, Cashel and Tuam, their suffragan abbots and other dignitaries. Henry's sovereignty was acknowledged and consitutions made which drew Ireland closer to Rome than ever. Thus it was one of the ironies of history that Catholic Ireland was sold by the popes themselves to a country destined to become the champion of Protestantism.

But the grant of Ireland had another great repercussion. It provided a precedent to the popes, *not only to claim and give away islands and peoples*, but also to give away a *new world*. For the language of the grant of Hadrian IV and some of his successors developed principles as yet unheard of in Christendom, since Hadrian had declared that Ireland *and all the islands* belonged to the special jurisdiction of St. Peter.[4]

This was not a rhetorical expression. It became a solid reality when daring sailors began to discover lands in the until-then-uncharted oceans. When in 1492 Christopher Columbus discovered the Americas, his finding not only stimulated a keener competition between the two adventurous Iberian seafaring nations, but opened up to both Spain and Portugal tremendous vistas of territorial, economic and political expansion.

As soon as the race for the conquest of the western hemisphere began, the pope come to the forefront, as a master and arbiter of the continents to be conquered. For, if all islands belonged by right to St. Peter, then all the newly-discovered and yet-to-be-discovered lands with all riches, treasures and wealth in any form belonged to the popes, his successors. The New World thus had become the possesion of the papacy. It was as simple as that.

This was left neither to the realm of theoretical claims nor to that of speculative rights. It was promptly acted upon, with full authority. Pope Alexander VI, then the reigning pontiff, in fact, one year only after the dicovery of America — that is, in 1493 — issued a document which is one of the most astounding papal writs of all times. In it Pope Alexander VI, acting as the sole legal owner of all islands of the oceans, granted all the lands yet to be discovered to the King of Spain.

Here are the relevant words of this celebrated decree:

> We are credibly informed that whereas of late you were determined to seek and find certain islands and firm lands, far remote and unknown...you have appointed our well-beloved son Christopher Columbus...to seek (by sea, where hitherto no man hath sailed) such firm land and islands far remote and hitherto unkonwn...
>
> ...We of our own motion, and by the fullness of Apostolical power, *do give, grant and assign to you, your heirs and successors, all the firm lands and islands, found or to be found, discovered or to be discovered.*[5]

But then, since the rivalry between Spain and Portugal threatened to imperil the situation, in 1494 the Treaty of Tordesillas moved the papal line of demarcation to the meridian 370 leagues west of the Azores. This brought Brazil into existence.

Pope Leo, long after feudalism had passed away, upheld as intransigently as ever the conception of earth-ownership. As *world suzerain*, he granted to the King of Portugal permission to possess *all* kingdoms and islands of the Far East, which he had wrested from the infidel, and all that he would in future thus aquire, even though up to that time *unknown and undiscovered*.[6] The pope's will was soon to be infringed by rebellious nations such as Protestant England, Holland, and even Catholic countries like France. Yet it was strong enough to transform two-thirds of the New World into the spiritual domain of Rome.

CLAIMS OWNERSHIP OF ALL UNDISCOVERED LANDS

The Donation of Constantine, therefore, was fraught with incalculable consequences, not only for Italy, France, Germany, England, Ireland and practically the whole of Europe, but also for the Americas and for the Near and Middle East. Indeed, in its full extent found admittance *even in Russia*, for it exists in the Kormezaia Kniga, the Corpus juris Canonici of the Graeco-Slavonic Church, which was translated from the Greek by a Serbian or Bulgarian in the thirteenth or fourteenth century.

Many were those who rebelled against it. Wetzeld, in a letter to the Emperor Frederick, dated 1152, centuries before the English precursor of Protestantism, Wycliff, had no hesitation in declaring:

> That lie and heretical fable of Constantine's having conceded the imperial rights in the city to Pope Sylvester, was now so thoroughly exposed that even day laborers and women were able to confute the most learned on the point, and the pope and his cardinals would not venture to show themselves for shame.[7]

The exposure of the falsity of the Donation proceeded until the middle of the fifteenth century, when three men succeeded, more than any others had done, in exploding the myth on historical grounds, proving without doubt that the *fact* of the Donation, no less than the document, was a fraudulent invention. They were Reginal Pecock, Bishop of Chichester, Cardinal Cusa, and, above all Lorenzo Valla, who proved that the popes had no right whatsoever over any land in Europe and had not even the right to possess the States of the Church in Italy or in Rome itself.

One of the most stubborn opponents of the Donation, a certain Aeneas Sylvius Piccolomini, Secretary to the Emperor Frederick III, in 1443, went so far as to recommend that Emperor to summon a council at which the question of the Donation of Constantine, "which causes perplexity to many souls," should be finally decided, on the ground of the Donation's "utter unauthenticity."

Indeed, Piccolomini went further and proposed that after the council had solemnly proclaimed the unauthenticity of the Donation, Frederick should take possession of most of the territories included in it and openly reject all papal claims of supremacy over rulers and nations. Aeneas Sylvius Piccolomini was afterwards Pope Pius II. A century before him, Dante, who had not hesitated to consign many popes to the hellish flames, uttered his famous lamentation on the Donation: "Ah, Constantine! Of how much ill was mother, Not thy conversion, but that marriage dower which the first wealthy Father took from thee."

CHAPTER 6

WHEN THE WORLD WAS ABOUT TO END-A.D. 1000

But, as if the ownership of immense territorial domains and, indeed, the ownership of practically the whole of the western world were not sufficient, the Roman Catholic Church, prior to, during and after her acquisitions, set out with no less success to despoil of their riches the faithful who lived in them. This she did, via the greed of rapacious priests with their misuse of religion, their abuse of the credulity of multitudes, their exercise of fear and their unscrupulous use of promises designed to extract from these people land and valuables for which they had developed the most insatiable appetite since the times of Constantine.

Thus, while the Church's possessions, identified in the gradual accumulation of lands, buildings and sundry goods, multiplied with the erection of new monasteries, nunneries, abbeys and the like, her treasures in the shape of money, gold and jewels increased as new monastic and ecclesiastical centers arose. These, besides becoming the traditional repositories of the communal wealth became also the collectors, and therefore the users, of the tithes and all other legal, semi-legal and at times forced contributions which believers were compelled to "donate".

When to these were added the voluntary contributions of believers either as a penance for their sins or as a thanksgiving for celestial favors received or on their death-beds, then the total wealth accumulated in the course of the centuries became equal to that of any baron or prince. Indeed, a time arrived when it surpassed the wealth of kings.

During the ninth and tenth centuries, after the time of the Emperor Charlemagne, her riches, already magnitudinous, became even more so by the accidental and planned combination of popular superstitions, genuine misrepresentation of the Scriptures, and the cunning promotion of a credence which in due course was accepted as the fearful reality of the immediately approaching future. This became gradually but steadily identified with belief in the end of all things. How such a prediction came to the fore and was so widely adopted by the Roman Catholic Institution and, above all, by the European populace, has yet to be assessed. Contributory factors of varied character seem to have given solidity to the belief that the world would come to an end with the closing of the first millennium of Christianity.

The Gospels, which spoke of the "present generations" before the coming of the Son of Man, became the main supporters of this belief — at least as interpreted by an ignorant or cunning clergy; for it must be remembered that at this period the masses could neither read nor write. Books or any other form of literature did not exist. The only sections of western society (beside the true Christian believers hiding in the mountains, with copies of Bible manuscripts) which had access to the Scriptures were the monks and certain pockets of the clergy. They were the only sources for the reading, interpreting and explaining of the prophecies, particularly those concerned with the approaching end of the world.

That the credence was a gross by-product of popular ignorance, superstition and fear there is no doubt. That it was fostered, promoted and magnified by certain sections of this religious system is a fact. That what motivated them to do so was the collection of more riches is a certainty. Proof of this was to be found in her behavior before, during, and after the closing of the year 1000.

For, far from minimizing or discrediting the "millennium" prophecy the Roman Church fostered it even if in a negative fashion, by doing nothing! She let the legend grow, helped by many of her clergy and the monastic orders who genuinely believed in its concrete fulfilment. Thus her policy assumed a most sinister character when finally the credence which for a long time had remained somewhat vague, unreal, and distant, began to appear as a fast-approaching reality to the vast Christian multitudes, as the predicted date came nearer and nearer.

WHEN THE WORLD WAS ABOUT TO END — A.D. 1000

When at last panic seized the faithful and when practically the whole of Christendom, particularly its most ignorant and barbaric portion, that of Northern and Central Europe, prepared for the end of the world, the Roman Church, instead of preaching that this was all nonsense or at least preparing herself to meet the Lord, made herself ready to accommodate the terrorized believers who deemed it prudent to get rid of their earthly possessions prior to the Day of Judgment. For, had not Christ said that it was easier for a camel to pass through the eye of a needle than for a rich man to enter into the Kingdom of God?

Many Roman Catholics, in fact, who until then had ignored Christ's teaching about temporal wealth, now took it in deadly earnest. As the year 1000 drew nearer, they got rid of their possessions with increasing speed. How? By donating them to what they were told was Christ's bride on earth, the Roman Church. And so it came to pass that monasteries, nunneries, abbeys, bishops' palaces and the like bustled with activity. Believers came and went, not only to confess their sins, to repent and to prepare for the end of the world in purity and poverty, but also to donate and give to the Roman Catholic Institution all they had. They gave her their money, their valuables, their houses, their lands. Many of them became total paupers, since what would it avail them to die as the owners of anything when the world was destroyed? Whereas, by giving away everything they were gaining merit in the eyes of the Great Judge!

The Church, via her monastic orders and clergy, accepted the mounting offers of earthly riches. This she did by duly recording them with legal documents, witnesses and the like. Why such mundane precautions? To prove to the Lord on Judgment Day that Smith in England, Schmidt in Germany, Amundsen in Scandinavia, MacLaren in Scotland and O'Donovan in Ireland had truly got rid of their earthly possessions? Not at all! To prove with matter-of-fact concreteness that the possessions of all those who had given were, from then on, the possessions of the papacy.

For that is precisely what happened.

When, following the long night of terror of the last day of December 999, the first dawn of the year 1000 lit the Eastern sky without anything happening, many Roman Catholics, whether they believed that the Lord had postponed the Day in response to prayers or that they had made a mistake, gave an audible sigh of relief throughout Christendom. Those who had given away their property made for the ecclesiatical centers which had accepted their "offerings," only to be told that their money, houses, lands, were no longer theirs. It had been the most spectacular give-away in history.

Since the Church returned nothing, she embarked upon the second millennium with more wealth than ever, the result being that the monasteries, abbeys and bishoprics, with their inmates and incumbents, became richer, fatter and more corrupt than before.

To believe, however, that the accumulation of wealth ended with the *grand coup* of the millennium prophecy would be a mistake. The faithful, although spared the collective confrontation of Judgment Day in the year 1000, were still dying singly as individuals. That meant that to gain merit in heaven they had to give away solid goods down on earth. The tradition was never abandoned. It survived the shock of the year 1000. And this to such an extent that it is still flourishing in our very day as we fast approach the close of the year 2000, the wealth of the Roman Catholic system today in Europe and in the U. S. being the best witness to the veracity of this assertion.

Believers continued to give; and since believers have died, generation after generation, their gifts have continued to increase in the bosom of a religious system which never died, which indeed continued to expand and to prepare for new temporal contributions, not only from generations as yet unborn, but equally from territories as yet un-Christianized.

The consequences of this uninterrupted process of wealth-gathering became so blatant after the first two or three centuries of the second millinnium that an increasing number of the most austere sons of Romanism revolted against it. And so it was, that Christianity witnessed the phenomenon of Francis of Assisi, whose initial steps to sainthood were the renouncing of even the very clothes he wore, which he returned to his own father; after which, having thus openly signified his total renunciation of worldly goods, he dedicated himself to a life of total poverty by asking the protection of the bishop, stark naked. The episode was a rebuff to the Church of his time, since St. Francis, following this symbolic gesture with practical concreteness, founded a new monastic order, that of the Franciscans, and saw to it that the most striking feature of such order was the total renunciation of the riches of this world.

St. Francis, however, was not the only figure reacting against the papacy's barefaced and brazen concern with wealth. Other individuals came to the fore in sundry lands. Bernard of Clairvaux appeared to the north, in France. Like Francis, Bernard had renounced all earthly riches as an individual. He enjoined such repudiation upon his new monastic order as well. He not only gave new life to a corrupt and rich western monasticism, he enforced his rule of total poverty outside the monasteries' walls whenever he could. To do so he did not spare ecclesiastics of low or high rank, thundering against the wealth and opulence of the Church Militant.

He fulminated again and again against a religious system with a voracious appetite for earthly goods, accusing her of worshipping Mammon instead of God. He spared neither priests, bishops nor even popes. In his *Apologia* he attacked "excessively rich prelates." In his treatise *On Customs and Duties of Bishops*, he thundered against bishops who "grew fat on the revenues from bishoprics." He did not hesitate to castigate the Papal Legates themselves. "Those rapacious men" who "would sacrifice the health of the people for the gold of Spain", going so far as to declare that the Curia in Rome was nothing but "a den of thieves." He even compared any pope who took pride in his office and riches to a monkey "perched high on a tree top" - this although the pope of that period had formerly been one of his monks and lived, like him, a most austere life.

If St. Bernard did not spare the Church, he was also a ruthless denouncer of heretics. Many he had arrested and imprisoned. Hundreds were pitilessly burned at the stake in public squares. He became the terror of any dissenter. The Roman Church turned him into another tool to strengthen herself in matters of this world: that is, in wealth, for she saw in the denunciation of heretics another important source of revenue.

St. Bernard had not been the first; he was one of many in a series of extirpators. But he gave a renewed impetus to the practice, since, with the increase of varied heresies and the even more varied measures to suppress them, the very profitable method of expropriating their property and levying crushing fines came increasingly to the fore. Thus the burning of heretics soon brought with it two visible benefits - the elimination of dangerous, devil-inspired people, and the addition of ever-increasing wealth to the Church.

From the sporadic denunciations of the early periods and the relatively mild punishments that followed, a time came when the charge of heresy transformed the ecclesiastical structures into a ponderous and terrifying machinery at the service of fanatical or corrupted monks and prelates. No one was safe from its tentacles. It could crush the humblest dwellers in the poorest burgh or the mightiest head of any clan, be he in the wilderness of Scotland or a Prince of Sicily, Portugal or Germany, with equally arrogant ease.

Bishops and cardinals themselves were not immune. This became so because the desire to preserve the Faith in all its purity, the concern of monks, ultimately became so intertwined with greed for wealth in anonymous denunciators that in the long run the two became inseparable. So it came to pass that the fulminations of the popes, for instance, launching anathemas, interdicts or excommunications, in addition to arrest, torture and the death penalty, led also to the expropriation of all the goods, money and property of those who had been denounced.

This became a source of untold wealth for prelates, bishops and popes who practised or pretended orthodoxy, so that very often no one knew with certainty whether the accused had been arrested because of their deviation from the Faith or because of greed for their wealth on the part of their anonymous denunciators. The authorities, lay or ecclesiastical, were compelled under pain of excommunication "to seize all the heretic's property, goods, lands and chattels, to arrest him and throw him into prison."[1]

Pope Innocent III issued specific instructions concerning this. The *Corpus Juris*, the official law book of the Papacy, gave details: "The possessions of heretics are to be confiscated. In the Church's territories they are to go to the Church's treasury".[2]

This papal injunction was carried out everywhere the Roman Catholic Institution ruled. Thus, for instance, following the edict to the authorities of Nimes and Narbonne, in 1228, Blache of Castille ordered that any person who had been excommunicated "shall be forced to seek absolution *by the seizure of all his property.*"[3]

This order became so general that, in a collection of laws known as the *Etablissement*, it is commanded that royal officers, whenever summoned by the bishops, shall seize both the accused and his property.[4]

Sundry French kings eventually enacted similar decrees — Philip III and Louis X for instance. Church councils did the same. Popes strengthened them. To mention one example the pontiff in 1363 ordered that any heretic "should be arrested, imprisoned, *and all his property seized.*"

When Pope Honorius crowned Emperor Frederic II in 1220, he hurled a solemn excommunication against anyone "infringing the privileges of the Church." He declared that, among others, "Bishops could excommunicate any Prince or Secular Ruler who refused to persecute heretics..." They were to be reported to the pope himself, who would then "deprive them of their ranks, power, civil liberties, followed by the seizure of all *their temporal possessions.*"[5] Thanks to such decrees the Church could obtain vast estates and substantial wealth merely by accusing a rich man of heresy.

This practice was not, however, confined to wealthy individuals. As it became more common it degenerated to such an extent that it was turned into the most blatant pretext for collecting money, often in connivance with secular rulers. To cite only one case: witness the Regent, Blache of Castille, who in 1228, besides, as already mentioned, decreeing the seizure of any heretic's property, ordered that "to quicken the process a fine of ten livres would be exacted on all those excommunicated who had not entered the church within forty days."

The clergy, high and low, then began to practice another money-extracting device. They forced the faithful, when these were beyond reproach and could not be accused of heresy, *to purchase escape* from excommunication. This yielded tremendous sums to the clergy throughout Christendom. Prelates, cardinals and popes used their position to make money, not only for the Church, but also for themselves. Bishops became notorious for their greed. There was the case of the Bishop of Cyfeiliawg, for instance. The bishop excommunicated his king. When the latter asked for the excommunication to be lifted, the bishop agreed — but at a price. This price? A plate of pure gold the size of the bishop's face.[6]

Besides such trivia for extracting money, more serious abuses became common practice. Thus, for example, if during a quarrel one single drop of blood was shed in a cemetery, an interdict was automatically proclaimed. The latter was not lifted unless the people collected the sum of money demanded by the clergy. Refusal to pay meant that the *corpses* for which the necessary fine had not been paid were dug up and thrown off consecrated ground.

If a priest was killed, a whole district would be put under an interdict until the crime had been *paid for* with money or its equivalent in goods.

Greed for money went even further. The clergy began to *excommunicate the neighborhood* of the man who had been originally excommunicated; this with the specific objective of seizing the properties concerned.

The anathemas, interdicts, and excommunications employed by popes, cardinals, bishops, and minor clergy, for motives of the basest avarice became so frequent, so wide-spread and so scandalous that many genuinely religious individuals, no less than lay authorities, began openly to revolt against the abuse.

The scandal was not confined to any limited period or country. It became universal, and it lasted for centuries. Indeed, with the passing of time the greed for worldly riches ultimately permeated the whole system to such an extent that the cry of the Diet of Nuremberg, uttered in 1522, expressed the anguish of countless individuals throughout Christendom: "Multitudes of Christians are driven to desperation whenever their properties are confiscated, thus causing the utter destruction of their bodies no less than their souls." The Verdict of the Diet of Nuremberg was *not* a gross exaggeration. It was a most accurate assessment of the Roman Church's insatiable thirst for the riches of this world.

CHAPTER 7

PAY TO BE A CHRISTIAN — WHETHER ALIVE OR DEAD

At the close of the first millennium A.D. the accumulation of wealth by the Roman Church had been carried out in a somewhat haphazard fashion, since, apart from the extensive territorial gifts which she had received from sundry kings during the seventh, eighth, and ninth centuries, her wealth had grown mostly thanks to the piety of her members.

From the tenth and eleventh centuries, however, the accretion of her riches gathered momentum. That is, it became systematized. Indeed, it became a fixed feature of her administration. Whereas in the past the money had come from the humble and the poor who donated because of religious motives, from now onwards such "donations" became compulsory. It was no longer the humble folk or the Princes who gave for "favors received." Hence forward they were *all made to give* for favors *not yet received*. That is, they had to give to the Church by the mere fact that they were members, the principle being that the children who were cared for by the mother should give her part of their riches as a compensation for her love. The tenet was not new. Its novelty was that now it became systematized, an integral part and parcel of the Vatican's vast machinery.

The popes were anything but slow to incorporate the practice in the expanding structures of ecclesiasticism. They promoted well-planned money-collecting operations throughout Christendom, directing them from the top. The most notorious of these pontiffs, and one of he first creators of Caesaro-Papism, as it was rightly labelled, was Pope Gregory VII, who in 1081 gave orders to his legates in France that *every house* inhabited by baptized persons in that country should pay an annual tribute of one denarius to the Blessed Peter.

How did the pope justify such a monetary injunction or, to be more precise, taxation? Once more, by virtue of that most rewarding of all letters, the missive which the Blessed Peter wrote with his own golden pen to Pepin. For, said Gregory, a yearly donation to the Blessed Peter (that is, to the pope) was an ancient custom first imposed by the son of Pepin the Short, whom we have already encountered, that is, by the Emperor Charlemagne, who, having overcome the ferocious Saxons, had offered his territories to St. Peter and hence to his successors. Anyone inhabiting the territories thus donated, therefore, was duty bound to give such contributions, because, explained Pope Gregory VII, using the appropriate feudal juridical terms of the times, he, Gregory, considered France and Saxony as belonging to the Blessed Peter. As a result, the denarius which every one of the inhabitants gave was nothing less than a *fealty contribution* to the Roman See — an argument which was eventually to be confirmed and practiced by subsequent popes, such as Gregory IX, Innocent III and others; Pope Martin IV, for instance.

Martin interdicted King Pedro of Aragon, after that king claimed his hereditary right to Sicily following Sicily's rising in 1282 against King Charles. Martin, using the papacy's immense spiritual pressure, deprived King Pedro of his Kingdom. Thereupon, what did the pope do? He presented the whole kingdom to somebody else, namely, to Charles of Valois, but on one important condition: Charles had to pay yearly tribute to the coffers of the Blessed Peter — that is, of the papacy.

Pope Clement IV, in 1265, had done even better. He had, in fact, sold millions of South Italians to Charles of Anjou, for a *yearly tribute of 800 ounces of gold* — again, to the Blessed Peter's holy coffers; neglect of payment carrying with it, of course, excommunication and interdict, with all that they implied.

Pope Sixtus IV very often caused a notice to be nailed to he door of a church. When the clergy and the faithful went to see what the papal message was, they discovered that unless a certain sum was forthcoming at *once* that church would be under an "interdict" and furthermore, that its clergy would be suspended. This financial expedient proved abundantly productive with other popes and hierarchs for long periods.[1]

Such measures, although frequent, were not, of course, sufficiently methodical to yield a regular and steady income. Hence the creation of regulations, the enforcement of which resulted in a steady flow of riches into St. Peter's coffers. Some of the most common were the "oblations" or offerings at mass or during certain feast days. These oblations were at first voluntary. With the passing of time, however, they became a kind of unwritten contribution to the clergy, until, in the thirteenth century, they were insisted upon as a right. The canonical tenets which the clergy invoked for their justification were those implying that if an ancient custom is honorable and praiseworthy it acquires the binding force of law. And what habit could be more praiseworthy than that the faithful should offer the Lord some of their money for his Apostle, his Vicar on earth.

This custom eventually became so widespread that the clergy treated the collection of oblations, not only as a *duty* on the part of their parishioners, but as a *right* of the clergy, to such an extent that ultimately the oblations were extorted from the faithful with the utmost disregard, indeed, with such cynicism that many Councils attempted to check the Hierarchy's rapacity. This came about when it was discovered that many priests were putting pressure to bear even in the confessional. In fact, round about 1210, church councils were compelled to inflict penalties on some of their clergy who had gone so far as to refuse to administer the Sacrament to those who had not given their oblation or who were in arrears with their Easter offerings.

The result was not only growing resentment but also avoidance of payment. Many, so as not to pay the oblations, began to stay away from mass. The clergy retorted by making it punishable for them to do so. Indeed, they fined their own parishioners if the latter frequented churches in other parishes. Fines were enforced on those who omitted confessions or communion, at Christmas and Easter, for instance; upon those who neglected church fasts. The higher clergy also imposed fines, both upon lay folk and the lower clergy, for every act of immorality, a system which became the cause of frequent extortion by unscrupulous high prelates, the immorality of clergymen having thus been turned into a regular and constant source of revenue for those above.

The most efficient and steady method of extracting money, as well as the most widespread, was certainly that of the tithes, which were a direct and indirect tax on the faithful. The latter had to give to the Church *one tenth* of all they produced. This applied not only to cottagers and farmers, but equally to merchants, shopkeepers and even to the poorest artisans. The laws, both ecclesiastical and temporal — which, of course, had been interlinked in such a manner as to make the custom compulsory — were considered to include even the down of his wife's geese, pot herbs in the gardens of laborers, and grass cut by the roadside.

Farmers were compelled to cart their tithing sheaves to the very houses of the priests. They had to bring also the milk which they owed, not as milk but in the form of cheese, since cheese was more durable. This last injunction so incensed many farmers that they resorted to some most un-Christian habits to spite both the ecclesiastic recipients and the Church! Since the priest said that all their offerings were to God, they took such words literally, "So that," wrote an English bishop, Bishop Quivil, at the end of the thirteenth century, many farmers in the Exeter diocese, instead of following "the ancient and approved custom in our diocese, namely that men should bring their tithes of milk in the form of cheese ... some maliciously bring the milk to church in its natural state, and," adds the good bishop with genuine horror, "what is even more iniquitous, finding none there to receive it ... pour it out before the altar... in scorn to God and His Church."

The spirit which prompted the Exeter farmers to act thus was, of course, widespread, particularly in times of scarcity, so that it was common for farmers, laborers and others to think of all kinds of subterfuges to avoid paying. Many of these subterfuges, complained another hierarch Archbishop Stratford, addressing the Synod of London in 1342, "were of excessive malice ... to the manifest prejudice of ecclesiastical rights".

In addition to giving tithes while they were still alive, the faithful had to give more while they were dying and after they were dead. Thus a man who had his will written was bound to give tithes in his legacy. "A legatee is bound to give tithes in his legacy, even though it have been already tithed by the testator," as a fourteenth-century manual for parish priests, the *Pupilla Oculi*, asserted, and since it was realized by the Church that even the most devout of her members might fail at times to give her her dues, she made of such an omission nothing less than a *mortal sin*; after which her clergy invented a yet more profitable device: that of the mortuary.

The mortuary fell with the weight of a millstone upon the estate of every dead Roman Catholic. The claim consisted of taking over the *second best* animal from the stock of anyone who had died possessed of *not less than three*, a claim which was not only regulated but also legalized. It was imposed by Archbishop Winchelsey about 1305 and confirmed by Langham in 1367. As a result the mortuary became a kind of tax, amounting to succession duty of thirty-three percent on the personal property of the defunct Roman Catholic. It was soon turned into a set custom, acknowledged by both spiritual and temporal authorities in practically every country of Christendom. In this manner the Church began to appropriate *one-third of a dead man's personal estate*.

Many people, like the Exeter farmers, tried to avoid payment. A typical case is that found among the many pleas to the English Parliament in the year 1330. One Thomas le Forter had paid what he claimed to be a just mortuary on the estate of William le Forter; this in his capacity of executor. The deceased's parson, however, the Abbot of Wenlock, sued him in the episcopal court, claiming a full third of the deceased's property, saying that this was the usual mortuary. Thomas appealed to the king, who decreed that "exactions of this kind . . . manifestly redound to the oppression of the realm." He therefore forbade the bishop to side with the abbot. Parliament intervened and set up a kind of commission, presided over by three abbots, These, invoking a statute of Edward I to the effect that no prohibition could avail to stop proceedings in the episcopal court on a question of tithes or mortuary, compelled the heir to pay in full.

The rapacity of the Church and her clergy reached unprecedented lengths. Suffice it to state that, following Thomas Aquinas, the Doctor Angelicus, theologians came to the

PAY TO BE A CHRISTIAN — ALIVE OR DEAD

learned conclusions that the Church *had the right to collect tithes* even from *lepers and beggars*, who were under an obligation to pay *one-tenth* of their collections. What of prostitutes? Following a modest hesitation and few clerical blushes, the battalion of theological bachelors decided that Holy Mother Church must refuse the prostitutes' contributions to her chaste coffers. *But*, they added (and here is the theological gem) so long as they were *unrepentant*, lest she, the Church, would give the impression that she *shared in their sins*. Should, however, the prostitutes repent of their sins, or should their sins *remain secret* to the average burgh or burghers, although the Church knew about them, then, yes, "the tithes may be taken".[2]

In addition to the oblations, tithes, and mortuaries, there were other means by which to replenish the Church's treasuries with individual sizeable amounts — from the heretics.

The Inquisition was very precise about it. Listen to Diana. In his 43rd *Resolutio* he put the question: "Are the possessions of heretics turned over to the Inquisitors?" — "I speak not," answers Diana, "for other countries, but the Spanish custom is to confiscate to the royal treasury (*fisco regio*) all the possession of heretics (*omnia bona haereticorum*) because our King, who is a pillar of orthodoxy (*columna fidei*), generously supplies the Inquistors and their agents with whatever the Holy Office requires." (*Inquistitoribus et eorum ministris abunde suppeditat quidquid necessarium est ad conservationem sanctae Inquisitionis.*)

Thanks to this principle, the Church could obtain vast estates or substantial wealth when prosperous individuals were, as happened often, accused of heresy and condemned — sometimes in collusion with the temporal authorities. Witness, for instance, the case of Philip II (1556-98). Two-thirds of the income of the Inquisition went to him, the rest to the Roman Catholic institution.

Further to the Inquisition were the weapons of interdiction and excommunication. These were used with increasing frequency to compel the faithful to pay under practically any pretext. Thus, for example, church and temporal powers would often use excommunication for their mutual benefit as they used the Inquisition. Witness Regent Blache of Castille, who in 1228 issued an edict addressed to the authorities of Nimes and Narbonne, directing that the excommunicated who remained unreconciled for a whole year should be forced to seek absolution by the seizure of their property. To quicken the process, a fine of ten livres was exacted on all those excommunicated who had not entered the church within forty days.

To make money, the clergy — as already mentioned — forced the faithful to *purchase escapes from excommunication.* Their threats often related to the most trivial matters. For instance, at vintage time the tithers forbade, under pain of excommunication, the gathering of grapes until they could choose the best, so that very often the peasants, owing to frequent delays, saw the ruin of their crops.

Some popes, besides thundering on behalf of the Church as a whole, did so in their own personal interest. Pope John VIII, for example, who reigned from 872 to 882, left on record at least 382 epistles, no less than 150 of which referred to excommunication. And, it is interesting to relate, almost all dealt with temporal possessions of the Church — some with worthwhile substantial solid affairs like the transfer or promise of a whole kingdom, but some with the most ridiculous and petty concerns. To mention one: the excommunication hurled by good Pope John against those miscreants who stole ... what? Nothing other than the papal horse on which the pope was traveling through France. Or that other papal bolt against those "knaves" who had pilfered his plate while he was staying at the Abbey of Avigny. And, said the pope, to add insult to injury, "probably with the connivance of the Abbey's monks".[3]

But one of the grossest abuses of excommunication was that perpetrated by bishops and even by hierarchs who began to excommunicate the *neighbors* of the orginally excommunicated person, the result being that when finally the family of the latter was exiled and his *whole property* confiscated, dozens of others, his neighbors, were placed under the same ban and hence the same penalties; that is, their properties could be, and as a rule were, confiscated.

The excommunications employed by the popes down to the lowest priest, for motives of the basest avarice, became so frequent and scandalous that many individuals and temporal authorities, including numerous genuinely devout persons, complained bitterly about them. Owing to such abuses, multitudes were driven to desperation, as the Diet of Nuremberg stated in 1522.

The immense wealth thus collected finally reached such proportions that her economic stranglehold upon all and sundry was no less massive than her spiritual dominion, and almost paralyzed whole countries. During the reign of Francis I (1515-47), for instance, a mere six hundred abbots, bishops and archbishops controlled so much land throughout France that the income they derived from it equalled that of the French state itself.[4]

France was not an exception. Practically every other country in Western Europe was in the same situation. The economic dominion of Holy Mother Church had become a collective stranglehold that was slowly but inexorably paralyzing the most vital structures of the land tenancies, commerce and finance of Christendom. She had become such a dead weight that the revolt which her practices provoked, after simmering below the surface for hundreds of years, in due course exploded with the violence of an earthquake. It came, disguised in theological garb, when the hammer of a rebel monk, nailing some theses upon a church door, made Rome totter on her foundations for decades, indeed, for centuries to come.

CHAPTER 8

HOLY MASS TOURISM FOR EACH GENERATION

It all happened in the year 1300 of the Incarnation of our Lord, when the most Blessed Peter's Vicar on earth, Pope Boniface VIII, proclaimed that from the previous Christmas to the next and on every hundredth year following, Roman Catholics visiting the basilicas of St. Peter and St. Paul in Rome would have the fullest pardon for all their sins. What believer could resist such unheard-of and immense spiritual bounty?

And so it was that Burgher Mackirken from Scotland, Manfredo Domino from Sicily, Count Stanislav from Poland, the Knight von Arnhem from Saxony, Senor Olivero from Spain, Olla Olafson from Scandinavia, Sgr Maerigo Bernini from Florence, Charles Montfroid from Paris and thousands of others suddenly departed, all in the same direction and towards the same goal. Rome, the Holy City.

What had prompted Pope Boniface to create such a precedent so unexpectedly? What arcane revelation had induced him to fling wide open the gates to the treasures of heaven? The answer is but one: the allure of the treasures of earth.

For, truly, devotion to the Blessed Peter, which in the early golden days had made the naive Saxons flock to his tomb in Rome to ask his pardon, had greatly diminished. Coin offerings had dwindled to next to nothing. The sad fact was that, whereas the local hierarchies in many parts of Christendom were becoming fat and rich, the Holy Father in the heart of Rome was becoming increasingly poor. St. Peter's coffers, he was being repeatedly told by his treasurers, were very low; indeed, they were well-nigh empty. Something had better be done to replenish them.

HOLY MASS TOURISM FOR EACH GENERATION

And thus it came to pass that one day Providence provided Pope Boniface with a truly "providential" inspiration. This he had, after a man reputed to have reached the ripe old age of 107, had kissed his feet, saying that in the year 1200 his father had come to Rome to offer a coin to St. Peter in order to receive an indulgence for the remission of his sins. Hearing this, Boniface needed no further providential prompting. He thanked God that he had been told about it just at the beginning of the year 1300. Better late than never. Being a man of action, he speedily proclaimed the Jubilee on 22nd February, 1300, to the amazement, surprise and delight of many, particularly in Rome.

The good children of the Church, most of whom did not believe that they could emulate the vigorous old man of 107, but realizing that so wholesome a remission of sins was truly the chance of a lifetime, did not hesitate. They left their villages, cities and countries by the thousands. Europe saw a mass movement the like of which had never before been experienced, and all compressed within a single calendar year. A contemporary, Villani, declared that there were at least 200,000 pilgrims *daily* in Rome. G. Ventura, another contemporary eye-witness, said that crowds were so great that he saw men and women trampled underfoot. The poet Dante could find no better comparison for the multitudes of the damned in his Inferno than the crowds which congregated in Rome during this Jubilee.

But if the pilgrims went to Rome to gain the total remission of their sins, they had to show their gratitude to the Blessed Peter and Paul, not only with prayers, but also with a more tangible token of their reverence, that is, with money; and this they did. Cardinal Gaietano, nephew of the pope, admitted that his uncle Boniface received more than 30,000 gold florins, offered by pilgrims at the altar of St. Peter alone, and over 20,000 at that of St. Paul. He was in a position to know.

In addition we have the description of an eye-witness who took part in the same Jubilee pilgrimage, the historian Ventura. Ventura has assured us that the tribute received by Pope Boniface on this occasion was "incomputable". Then, to prove that his estimate was not exaggerated, he gives a glorious description. At the altar of St. Paul, he says, where he went to pray himself, there stood, by day and by night, two clerks "raking in infinite money" — his very words![1] Pope Boniface's Jubilee had proved a tremendous success. The Blessed Peter's coffers were replenished, and Rome prospered once more for a while.

Boniface's successors, however, brooded. Some of them could never hope to see the beginning of the next century, since the lives of the popes in those days were very often shortened not only by age but also by dagger, poison or greedy nephews. And so, one bright day in January in the year 1343, Pope Clement VI issued a bull declaring that, in view of the shortness of human life, he had reduced the Jubilee's span from one hundred to fifty years.[2] Then, to make sure that the pilgrims would come in multitudes as on the first occasion, he offered them a further spiritual inducement. In June 1346 he issued another bull in which he asserted that he had complete control and, indeed, power over the future life. And, proceeding to exact details, he told the prospective pilgrims that he could order the angels of heaven to liberate from purgatory the souls of any of them who might die on the road to Rome.

Pope Clement's additional spiritual inducements proved a tremendous success, for it must be remembered that traveling in those days was the most hazardous occupation anyone could undertake. Traveling was mainly on foot; horse-riding was only for the few. There were no hotels, hardly any real roads, no food provisions or banks or police; but, on the contrary, robbers all along the way, starvation, sleeping in the open, disease. About the time of this second Jubilee there also appeared the Black Death, which truly decimated the population of Europe. To realize how hazardous an enterprise it was, suffice it to remember that during the first and second Jubilees, only *one out of ten* pilgrims returned home alive.

Yet, in spite of all this, during the Easter of the Jubilee it was estimated that there were more than a million pilgrims in Rome. Many people were trampled to death at the tombs of the Apostles, Once again, the concrete gratitude of the pilgrims replenished St. Peter's coffers beyond Clement's wildest dreams.

Many others throughout Christendom, however, could not or would not come. Either the Black Death had killed their families or had ruined them or the survivors had to attend to important business or were too feeble to undertake such a risky journey. But their piety and their longing for remission of their sins, with the added privilege of liberating a soul from the flames of purgatory, were no less sincere than were these feelings in the fortunate ones who had gone to Rome in person. The pope listened, agreed, and in his paternal consideration for the spiritual welfare of those far-away children, he decreed that they, too should partake of the privileges of the indulgences of the Jubilee.

He began with Hugh, King of Cyprus; Edward III and Henry, Duke of Lancaster in England; Queen Isabella of France; Queen Philippa of England and Queen Elizabeth of Hungary. These all responded with regal oblations: that is, with generous, solid payments of gold.

But if kings and queens had been thus favored, why not lesser folk, as good Roman Catholics as their majesties? The pope agreed, and he promptly instructed his representatives outside Rome to exempt the would-be pilgrims from undertaking the journey — provided, of course, that they did not forget to show their gratitude to the Blessed Peter with a *little offering*. The Papal Nuncio in Sicily was one of the first to carry out the instructions. He exempted thirty persons from undertaking the pilgrimage, provided they paid *what the pilgrimage would have cost them* had they actually gone to Rome. And so the practice of collecting from penitents at home sums equivalent to the cost of the pilgrimage was born.

The advantages for both sides were too obvious to miss, and so hierarchs in other countries decided to imitate the pope. In 1420 the Archbishop of Canterbury proclaimed a Jubilee with the same "pardons" as those of Rome. This precedent, however, was too dangerous. Supposing it spread to other countries? Martin V, the reigning pope, called it "audacious sacrilege", threatened excommunication, and the enterprising archbishop had to be content with local revenues.

The Jubliee of 1450 was again an immense success. The amount of gold collected from the pilgrims was so huge that Pope Nicholas V struck a coin known as "the Jubilee". This coin was of such unusual size that it equalled three of the ordinary gold pieces issued at that time by the royal mints of Europe.

One of Pope Nicholas' successors, Pope Paul II, in 1470 reduced the interval of the Jubilee to twenty-five years, and, to prompt the pilgrims to come to Rome instead of benefiting from the Jubilee's privileges at home, he suspended all other indulgences. Notwithstanding such measures, however, the Jubilee of 1475 was not a great success.

Nevertheless, even on this occasion the Church as a whole benefited in so far as the payment of specific sums continued increasing. The sums thus paid, of course, varied according to the status, wealth and dignity of the "exempted pilgrims." From archbishops, bishops and nobles down to counts, four gold florins had to be paid; abbots and barons paid three gold florins; lesser nobles, doctors, notaries: two florins; all others, one gold florin.[3]

During the Jubilee of 1500, Pope Alexander VI, whose love of money was notorious, decided to add something new, and initiated the first ceremony of the Opening of the Holy Door. What the Holy Door should have been, or was, was never clearly understood — except that it was a device to entice the pilgrims to Rome. However, pope and architects looked in vain for such a Holy Door in St. Peter's Basilica. The Door could not be found; so one was prepared in haste, so as not to disappoint the oncoming penitents.

To make even more money, Pope Alexander VI charged his representatives, most of whom were called *penitentiaries*, with authority to reduce the days to be spent on the pilgrimage *on payment of one-fourth of the expense thus saved*. In addition to this they were also authorized to compound for "irregularity" — for instance, on a charge of simony — on payment of *one-third* of the sums acquired by it. In this manner the Basilica of St. Peter was soon transformed into a veritable market-place where pardons, indulgences, merits, dispensations and suchlike religious privileges were sold, exchanged, re-sold and marketed over the papal money chests.

Not content with that, Alexander in 1501 began to collect additional money throughout the rest of Europe by dispatching his legates everywhere, selling the indulgences at a discount: that is, for one-fifth of what a pilgrimage to Rome would have cost the potential pilgrim buyers. More than one Catholic king, no less business-minded and no less in need of money than the pope, considered the idea an excellent one — to mention the most notorious of them, Henry VIII of England, who came to a cordial understanding with the Papal Legate as to the royal share of the proceeds.

This was the last Jubilee before the Reformation. Indeed, it was the Jubilee which, unnoticed almost by all, had planted the seeds which were eventually to blossom into the portentous trees that were ultimately to make the monolithic structure crack into two mighty halves and bring about the emergence of Protestantism.

CHAPTER 9

MIRACLES, PORTENTS AND WONDERS FOR SALE

Since the ecclesiastical practice of commercializing miracles could be turned into a most gratifying source of money, it soon appeared that the more spectacular the miracle the more spectacular the profits to its promoters. Miracles thus became a kind of religious investment yielding a steady, if uneven, flow of revenue. Their profitability depended, not only upon the spectacular nature or uniqueness of the portents, but also upon the advantages gained by those who believed in them, the combination of these ingredients being the cement with which both Church and its faithful could identify themselves in partaking of the visible results of God's generosity.

If the selling of indulgences was a most lucrative method of amassing wealth, the exploitation of the individual and collective gullibility of Roman Catholic people was no less profitable. God's generosity could be dispensed, distributed and manifested on numberless occasions by the most diverse means and in the most contrasting and inappropriate situations and circumstances.

During the Middle Ages and later, miracles, portents, wonders, and God's interventions were of a variety never seen or experiencd before or since. They reflected in no uncertain terms the nature, credulity and mentality of those influenced by them — not to mention the spirit of the religious system, through which as a rule they were made to work. We shall content ourselves with reporting some of the most characteristic; this will indicate not only their nature but also how they were tuned into events by which the papacy profited through the collection of yet more revenues.

One day the people of Aspe in France carried out a sudden raid upon their neighbors of Saint-Savin. To prevent them from succeeding, the Abbot of Saint-Savin climbed a tree, said the appropriate prayers, and so paralysed them that they were all slaughtered without resistance. The pope, informed of the massacre, cast an interdict upon Saint-Savin, with the result that for seven years it was cursed with sterility in its women, cattle and fields. To gain absolution, Saint-Savin agreed to pay an annual tribute of thirty sous.[1]

In 1120 the Bishop of Laon excommunicated the caterpillars which were ravaging the diocese. This he did with the same formula as employed the previous year by the Council of Rheims in cursing a priest who insisted on marrying. The Bishop of Laon was given money and offerings by the grateful peasants.[2]

Similarly St. Bernard when preaching at Foigny, was interrupted by a swarm of most un-Christian flies. Losing his saintly patience, he excommunicated them. Next morning the flies were all found dead. He recieved offerings, which he gave to the nearest monastery.[3]

In 1451 William Saluces, Bishop of Lausanne, ordered the trial of multitudes of leeches which threatened the fish of Geneva. The leeches were ordered, under pain of excommunication, to gather in a given spot. The people concerned made *abundant offerings* to the Church.

The ecclesiastical court of Autun in 1480 excommunicated an army of caterpillars and ordered the priests of the region to repeat the anathema from the pulpit until the caterpillars had been exterminated. The following year, 1481, and again in 1487, a most irreligious multitude of snails at Macon were duly excommunicated. In 1516 the clergy excommunicated the too numerous grasshoppers at Milliere, in Normandy. In 1587, at Valence, a formal trial was terminated with a sentence of banishment against another multitude of caterpillars.[4]

Bartholomew Chassanee, who wrote a large volume recording such trials, declared that besides being lawful they were also useful in so far that the Church, whenever successful in such actions, was rewarded *with flourins and more abundant tithes* than would have been the case had the vermin never arrived. When such miracles, excommunications, trials and the like were multiplied by the thousand, the florins multiplied with even greater rapidity than swarms of mayflies.

This manner of collecting money, however, although rewarding, did not yield as much as when authentic saints were brought into action. Thus, at the command of St. Stanislaw, one Peter, who was dead, rose from his tomb and went into a law court to certify the sale of an estate — after which, of course, the local church was amply rewarded by receiving a portion of such estate.

In the thirteenth century St. Anthony was told when in Italy that his father, in Lisbon, had been accused of murder. An angel transported him from Italy to Lisbon. Once there, Anthony asked the murdered man: "Is it true that my father is guilty of thy death?" "Certainly not," replied the corpse, and Anthony's father was acquitted. Thereupon Anthony was taken back to Italy by the same angel. A basilica was built over Anthony's body. Pilgrimages have been going on ever since, to this very day, with stupendous money offerings, mostly from North and Latin America.

St. Vincent Ferrier (1357-1419) did even better. For when, frequently in the midst of his preaching, he *grew wings and flew into the air*, he went to various places to console some dying individual. Once when in Pampeluna he told a dying woman that if she consented to confess her sins he would give an absolution from heaven. The woman having assented, St. Vincent wrote a letter as follows: "Brother Vincent beseeches the Holy Trinity to grant to the woman sinner here present absolution of her sins." The letter flew instantly to heaven, and after a few minutes flew back. Upon it was written: "We, the Saint Trinity, requested by our Vincent, grant to the woman sinner of whom he has told us the forgiveness of her sins, and if she confesses she will be in heaven within the next few years. Holy Trinity."[5]

To satisfy the cynicism of the incredulous, the event was attested to by none other than the pope's chamberlain, who gave copious evidence of this "fact", as he called it, in addition to giving the names of fourteen highly placed prelates who vouched for it.[6]

The precedent created an epidemic of heavenly letters. They fetched tremendous prices. Curiously, heaven always sent them to the clergy. The number of miracles worked by St.

Vincent was truly miraculous. During an inquest held in Avignon, Toulose, Nantes and Nancy, it was revealed that the official list totalled eight hundred. "If we reckon only the small number of eight miracles per day during his twenty-five years," says Msgr. Guerin, his biographer, "we have 58,400 miracles." And he adds, with understandable prudence: "Here we deal, of course, with *public* miracles only."

The beneficiaries of such portents, or course, showed their gratitude with solid, matter-of-fact coins. Vincent worked so many miracles that, as was officially related, "it *was a miracle when he did not work miracles*, and the greatest miracle which he worked was when he did not work any."[7]

In Salamanca there was a miracle bell, which rang to warn the people of an oncoming miracle.[8] This happened mostly when the collection in the cathedral had not been too good. And since we are dealing with bells, we might as well recall the case of Pope Alexander IV. When he removed the ban of excommunication, all the bells of the church of Avignonet began to ring of their own accord; not only so, but they went on pealing all night and all day, although they had not been heard for the previous forty years. This "fact" was attested to by a declaration of the inhabitants of Avignonet in the year 1293. The "fact" was furthermore included as such in an *Acte Notaire*, dated January 29th, 1676. On what authority? Not only on that of the inhabitants of Avignonet, but indeed on that of the pope himself. For, truly, none other than Pope Paul III mentioned the "fact" in a Bull of 1537.[9]

All these manifestations, when they "occurred," were taken for solid, concrete events. They happened thanks to the power which the Church vested in those who were in true communion with her — namely, the saints. The result, of a most practical nature, was that shrines were built over their bones; and since the saints went on multiplying with the passing of generations, their shrines did likewise. A shrine is a place of devotion, hence a sure magnet for pilgrimages; a kind of local, regional or even international Jubilee. Shrines like that of St. James of Compostella in Spain, for instance, became almost as famous as the tomb of the Blessed Peter in Rome. Pilgrims congregated there from all parts of Europe, and they included princes and kings, who never went empty handed. The poorest folk always left money at the altar. Magnificent gifts of solid gold, silver, precious stones and the like still adorn the place.

Now it must be remembered that the whole of Europe was dotted with shrines, and that pilgrimages were the order of the day for centuries. This brought a continuous flow of revenue as we have already seen in a previous chapter, with the result that the accumulation of riches continued unabated, ranging from money to land and real estate.

The devotion to the saints, therefore, ultimately became an immense, steady source of continuous wealth for the Roman Church as a whole, and for her clergy in particular.

CHAPTER 10

STOCK EXCHANGE IN INDULGENCES

Miracles, portents and wonders, although they produced a remarkable volume of income, could not be relied upon with confidence by a clerical administration which, like its modern counterpart, was burdened by the ever-mounting flow of a concrete and steady expenditure. The income derived from them was too haphazard and unpredictable, and hence too unreliable. Something of a more consistently dependable nature, therefore had to be devised for the collection of revenues. This was near at hand; the pope's power to bind and to loose.

Such power was, in the eyes of all Roman Catholics, capable of indefinite and indeed of infinite application. When made to work, it brought forth, amidst other things, the practice of buying and selling indulgences. Indulgences, like so many other privileges, were eventually much abused; so much so in fact, that they became one of Christendom's most regrettable scandals.

Originally an indulgence was one of the most innocuous instruments in the spiritual armory of the papacy. Initially it was designed to help the penitent, since it was nothing else than the remission of the penance imposed on confessed sins. The peril of leaving such power in the hands of a notoriously rapacious clergy was too obvious. So the pope reserved the granting of indulgences to himself.

Like many other church institutions the practice of granting indulgences did not come to the fore all at once. At the beginning it was granted with the utmost parsimony, and even then, only during exceptional circumstances. The "real" indulgence began to appear during the eleventh and twelfth centuries, in a very unobtrusive manner, and at this period it was truly a tremendous event if a pope granted an indulgence of even seven days. Later on, a one-year indulgence was still a rare event.

It was the Crusades which eventually pushed indulgences to the forefront. To induce people to enroll under the banner of the Cross, the popes began to grant indulgences with generosity. As the ardor for the Crusades diminished, so the issue of indulgences increased proportionately.

From the liberation of the Tomb of Christ, the indulgences turned to the extermination of the Church's enemies in Europe. Later, they degenerated into "crusades" of all kinds, mostly of a religious-political character. Pope Urban VI, for instance, ordered England to fight against France because France had taken the side of Pope Urban's rival, Pope Clement VII. To encourage volunteers, Urban promised indulgences to anyone who would thus take up arms. Pope John XXIII did the same when he announced a crusade against Naples-again, because Naples happened to support John's rival, the Anti-Pope Gregory. From this to an increasing number of sundry causes the steps quickened. Indulgences were granted with ever increasing facility to places, to people, to saints, to monastic orders, and so on, *ad infinitum*.

This process occurred not only because individuals, orders and places wanted such privileges to enhance their spiritual status, but above all because the privilege in most cases resulted in substantial and steady monetary gains. The fiscal possibilities were seen from the earliest period. By the later Middle Ages the practice of selling indulgences for money became general, until it was abused.

The sale of indulgences took sundry shapes and forms. If the privilege of granting indulgences was accorded to the shrine of some saint, it resulted in the increase of pilgrims, and since, after each visit, numerous coins were invariably left behind, the indulgence became *ipso facto* a money-spinner of considerable importance. This reached such absurd proportions that at one time no less than 800 indulgences-plenaries, accompanied by appropriate offerings, were attached to St. Peter's in Rome.

The small Church of the Portiuncula, where Francis of Assisi had a vision, was enriched with a novel form of indulgence called the *toties quoties*, which meant that anyone visiting it in August during a special holy day gained one plenary indulgence *each time* he entered the little church. The novel indulgence was too good to be restricted to Portiuncula, and in no time Franciscans everywhere wanted a similar privilege, with the result that soon every Franciscan church in every country had its Portiuncula Day. Other monastic orders, of course, could not resist so good an opportunity, and the Dominicans, the Carmelities and countless others followed suit in due course.

Then there was the privileged altar. The pope promised that if a mass was said at a given altar, the soul on behalf of whom the mass had been said would be released instantly from purgatory. Every church was ultimately endowed with such an altar.

If the Crusades opened the flood gates to indulgences, the money-making nature of the multiplying indulgences, of course, brought a veritable flood of indulgences as means of accumulating riches, particularly when they were applicable to the dead, thus tempting, as it were, members of families *to pay* for the release of the souls of their beloved from the flames of purgatory. The absurdity to which this went can be gathered by the fact that no less than 9,000 years, plus 9,000 quarantines for every step of the Scala Santa in Rome, were transferable to the souls of the dead.

This was granted by the authority of Pope Pius VII and even of Pope Pius IX. Why such incredible indulgences? Because the Scala Santa is supposed to be the stairway to Pilate's house, which Christ ascended at His trial. The Stations of the Via Crucis, also in Rome, were so rich in indulgences that, according to an eminent authority on the subject,[1] a Roman Catholic could, within one single year, gain forty-nine plenaries and more than *one and a half million years* of partials.

An English account which appeared round the year 1370 enumerated the widespread indulgences offered by the 147 churches of Rome, the following being but a typical sample:

We learn, for instance, that at St. Peter's, from Holy Thursday to Lammas (August 1st), there was a daily indulgence of *14,000 years*, and whenever the Vernicle (*Sacro Volto*) was exhibited, there was one of *3,000 years* for citizens, 9,000 for Italians, and 12,000 for pilgrims from beyond the sea. At San Anastasio there was one of 7,000 *years* every day, and at San Tommaso one of 14,000 *years*, with one-third remission of sins for all comers.[2]

The indulgences grew in number and power with the passing of time, until finally they became so unlimited that even the most pious began to have doubts about their efficacy. Gerson suggested that they were thus exaggerated owing to "*the avarice*" of the pardoners, "that is, the people *who were selling them*" and declared, incidentally, that as so many dealt with thousands of years they could not have the authority of the popes, since purgatory would end with the end of the world.[3]

On the other hand, another no less devout authority, Lavorio, declared that the indulgences of 15,000 or 20,000 *years* were proof of the extent of purgatorial suffering which hardened sinners might expect, while Polacchi argued that such indulgences should not seem absurd or incredible when we reflect that a single day in purgatory corresponds to many years of the fiercest bodily anguish during life.[4]

The extravangance of the indulgences continued. In 1513, for instance, Pope Leo X granted to the Servite Chapel of St. Annunciata at Florence that all visiting it on Saturdays should obtain *a thousand years* and as many quarantines, and double that amount on the feasts of the Virgin, Christmas, and Friday and Saturday of Holy Week.[5]

Even after the council of Trent had enjoined moderation in dispensing the treasure, Pius IV in 1565 granted to the members of the confraternity of the Hospital of St. Lazarus, besides several plenaries and the indulgences of Santo Spirito in Saxia and the Stations of Rome, the jubilee and the Holy Land, a year and a quarantine for every day, 2,000 years on each of the feasts of the Apostles, 100,000 *years* on Epiphany and each day of the octave, 3,000 years and as many quarantines with remission of one-third of sins on every Sunday, 2,000 years and 800 quarantines of Christmas, Resurrection and Ascension and each day of their octaves, 8,000 years and 8,000 quarantines of Pentecost and each day of the octave, 2,000 years and one-seventh remission of sins on Corpus

STOCK EXCHANGE IN INDULGENCES

Christi and each day of the octave, 30,000 years and 3,000 quarantines on All Saints and each day up to St. Leonard's (November 1st to 6th).[6]

The immensity of the riches which indulgences brought to the papacy during the centuries is incalculable. Their use, abuse and misuse should not make us lightly condemn them as unimportant, nor their absurdity induce us to underestimate the tremendous power they had — or rather, the tremendous power of the cummulative effect of their employment by both the Church and the popes.

For, more often than not, they served their purpose in the mobilization, control and use of the vast masses of men, armies and nations, none of which might otherwise have been mobilized with such ease and fluidity by successive popes. In the struggles of the papacy with the temporal powers, for instance, which was the dominating fact of medieval history, they played a paramount role. This they did, not only by creating renewed zeal, but by putting men, riches and armies at will into the hands of the popes.

It was, thanks to the weapon of indulgences, for example, that Pope Innocent III was able to crush for good the menacing heresy of the Cathari, a heresy which at one time seemed about to engulf half Europe; and, for that matter, that Pope Clement IV was able to humiliate the German emperors and reduce them to quasi-impotence politically, an event which profoundly affected the subsequent course of European history. For by the mere fact that the popes could proclaim a crusade at will with all the indulgences invariably involved, princes, kings and emperors were made to think twice before opposing the papal path in territorial disputes or political or dynastic matters.

Explorations, conversions and domination of known and unknown lands and races were greatly accelerated by the power and use of indulgences. We quote only one typical case, that of the Teutonic Knights, who were spurred chiefly by indulgences in conquering and thus Christianizing North-East Germany and most of Hungary and finally in erecting an impregnable barrier against the invading Islamic armies of the Turks.

Indulgences, therefore, played a paramount part in the shaping and creation of capital events in the history of Europe. Yet, if they were positive factors in certain spheres of the Church's activity, they also contributed mightily to her mounting corruption and decadence. Their trading for money became such a scandal that it turned, as already hinted, into a universal, well-organised abuse, which operated at all levels, its chief exponent and proponent being the papacy itself. Papal dynastic and personal greed was at the bottom of such gross profiteering. The corruption of the clergy, ever ready to make money by selling their offices, was a contributory factor.

Christians everywhere, who for decades had frowned upon the practice, finally came boldly to the fore in open protest. The chief exponent was a troubled monk, Dr. Martin Luther. Following many tergiversations, on the 31st October 1517 he nailed his famous ninety-five Theses to the door of the church in Wittenberg, Germany. It was a fateful day for the whole of Roman Catholicism: for on that day the German monk, acting as the spokesman of untold millions of believers, defiantly challenged the practice of selling documents and offering money payments for penance, that is, rejecting indulgences.

Like many others, he had seen the degradation and abuse of such commerce. He had openly shuddered at the theory that by buying a papal indulgence Roman Catholics could shorten and indeed cut out altogether their time in purgatory. He considered the belief that the souls of the deceased could be released from the flames by the purchse of indulgences on their behalf a theological monstrosity.

The brazen buying and selling of indulgences to make money had become so open as to disgust the most tolerant of Christians. This was being done not only by the pope, who traded them throughout Europe, ostensibly for religious purposes, but equally by lesser dignitaries. To mention only one among many, the Pope Leo X in 1517 gave permission to the Archbishop of Mainz, to sell indulgences on a grand scale in order to pay his debts, which he had contracted in buying the dignity of archbishop. In Germany this type of trade in indulgences was promoted by the pope's delegate himself,

Dominican J. Tetzel, who operated near Wittenberg. The reaction and counter-reaction of Luther's indignation in due course provoked what finally became a historical inevitability-the Reformation.

CHAPTER 11

THE CHURCH CLAIMS THE AMERICAS

Pope Alexander VI (1492-1503), Servant of the Servants of God, as incumbent of the throne of the Blessed Peter, was the heir, not only to the accumulated authority of all his papal predecessors, but also to their decrees, tenets and beliefs, dominated by the portentous Donation of Constantine — the foundation stone upon which the papacy, and thus the Catholic Church, had erected all its claims to territorial sovereignty. To Pope Alexander VI, like all the popes before him, the spirit and the letter of the Donation had to be observed, maintained and practised by all and sundry, starting with its chief custodian, the Roman Pontiff.

Pope after pope throughout the centuries, from the appearance of the Donation, had always unhesitatingly and firmly done so. The precedents, illustrious and well-known, which Alexander could invoke were many. These rested upon the principles enunciated with such clarity by the most significant words of the Donation, which we have quoted elsewhere, to be found in its last clause, namely: "Constantine gives up the remaining sovereignty over Rome..." and ending: "and of the *Western Regions*, to Pope Sylvester and his successors." It was on the strength of such tenets that Pope Hadrian IV in 1155, as we have already seen, gave Ireland to the English king, as "like all Christian islands, it undoubtedly *belonged* of right to St. Peter and the Roman Church."

Pope Boniface VIII declared that "temporal authority is subject to the spiritual,"[1] whereas Pope Gregory asserted that "the pope stands to the Emperor as the sun to the moon." This prompted sundry theological pillars of the Church to state that "the Supreme Pontiff, by divine right, has the fullest powers *over the whole world.*"[2]

THE CHURCH CLAIMS THE AMERICAS

Pope Gregory IX invoked Constantine himself to support such claim. "It is notorious that Constantine thought that he to whom God had confided the care of heavenly things, should *rule earthly things*," he declared.[3] To clarify this he elucidated the matter. "Constantine, to whom belonged universal monarchy," he said, "wished that the Vicar of Christ and Prince of Apostles...should also possess the government of *corporeal things in the whole world*,"[4] that is, territorial possessions, with all their riches and wealth.

In virtue of this, Pope Hadrian compelled King John to pay a yearly tribute to him — that is, a tax — in token of the subjection of England and Ireland.

The successors of the Blessed Peter eventually claimed as their property all islands and lands as yet undiscovered.

Relying on this, they demanded nothing more nor less than "sovereignty" over the newly discovered lands of the Americas. In modern parlance, they claimed that the Americas, with all they contained, were their absolute property.

Were these decretals put forward and maintained only centuries before Columbus actually set foot on the Americas? Not at all. They remained the full-blooded claims of the popes when America was actually found, so much so that when the reigning pontiff heard about the discoveries, he apportioned the New World, on the basis that he, the pope, had the *legal right* to do so, since it was his property and no one else's.

This celebrated document was written only one year after the discovery of the New World; that is, in 1493, by Pope Alexander VI, not so much to re-assert in the plainest possible terms the papal right to its ownership, since that was taken for granted, but to prevent Spain and Portugal from taking over the new lands without these having first been apportioned to them by their owner, or, rather, their landlord, Peter's successor.

The pope in this case was acting not only as a pope but also as a Spanish pope. He wanted his Spain to have all the Americas. To that effect he decreed that the Vatican's new property — that is, the Americas — would be let to Spain. No one else, therefore, could get hold of any portion of it without the permission of the Americas' legal landlord, the pope. To leave the position in no doubt whatsoever, the Pontiff decreed that all lands and islands, discovered and to be discovered, would be leased to Spain. Not only that; but he told King Ferdinand where the new boundaries would be drawn, namely, "towards the West and South, drawing a line from the Pole Arctic to the Pole Antarctic, from the North to the South".

The original papal document, besides its extraordinary intrinsic importance, is a fascinating study which deserves to be better known. The English version is from the original (englished and published by R. Eden in 1577) to be found in *Hakluytus Posthumus*, printed by William Stansby for Henrie Fetherstone, London, in 1625:

Of the pope's Bull made to Castille, touching the New World. Alexander Bishop, the Servant of the Servants of God, to our most dear beloved Son in Christ, King Ferdinando, and to our dear beloved Daughter in Christ, Elizabeth, Queen of Castille, Legion, Aragon, Sicily and Granada, most Noble Princes, greeting and Apostolical Benediction...

We are credibly informed that whereas of late you were determined to seek and find certain Islands and firm lands, far remote and unknown (and not heretofore found by any other), to the intent to bring the inhabitants...to profess the Catholic Faith...

This last phrase, "to the intent to bring the inhabitants...to profess the Catholic Faith," throws the clearest light upon the basic motivation of the whole enterprise. All other factors, no matter how important, were subsidiary to this.

The pope's assumption, which he takes for granted and which he regards as the sole primary driving force for the daring sea voyage, must not be regarded as papal self-deception or wishful thinking or a mere ancillary rhetorical formula. It must be taken in its literal sense, since that is precisely how the true inspirer and launcher of Columbus's adventure, the queen, saw it.

It must be remembered that the queen was not only a very devout person; she was what by modern standards would be called bigoted. She believed implicitly and absolutely in the dogmas and mission of the Roman Catholic Church. She was under the thumb of her confessor, a man responsible, no doubt, for many of her decisions, like the one which dismissed Columbus's first petition, or that which unleashed the horrifying hunting down of heretics, with the resulting burning and torturing, by the Holy Inquistion.

To say that her sponsoring of Columbus was motivated only by her zeal to serve the Roman Church would be inaccurate. The prospect of finding new territories, gold and riches to replenish her empty coffers was no less important. Yet it was in all probability her religious motivation that tipped the scales in favor of financing his expedition. Here again, therefore, that "intangible" religious factor to which we have already referred played a paramount, even if an imponderable, role in the preliminary exertions which were to lead to the discovery of America.

In any case, supposition or fact, the reality of the matter was that this was taken for granted by the pope himself, who talked and acted on that assumption. Following his preliminary introduction, Alexander continued thus:

You have, not without great Labor, Perils and Charges, appointed our well-beloved Son Christopher Columbus (a man certes well commended as most worthy and apt for so great a Matter) well furnished with Men and Ships and other Necessaries, to seek (by the Sea, where hitherto no man hath sailed) such firm Lands and Islands far remote, and hitherto unknown, who (by God's help) making diligent search in the Ocean Sea, have found certain remote Islands and firm Lands, which were not heretofore found by any other: in the which (as is said) many Nations inhabit, living peaceably, and going naked, not accustomed to eat Flesh...

We are further advertised that the fore-named Christopher hath now builded and erected a Fortress, with good Munition, in one of the foresaid principal Islands...

After which the pope, speaking as the master, lord and owner of what the explorers had already explored and would explore in the future, came to the point. Here are his memorable words:

We greatly commending this your godly and laudable purpose...We of our own motion, and not either at your request or at the instant petition of any other person, but of our own mere liberality and certain science, and by the *fullness of Apostolical power, do give, grant and assign to you, your heirs and successors, all the firm Lands and Islands found or to be found, discovered or to be discovered, towards the West and South, drawing a Line from the Pole Arctic to the Pole Antarctic (that is) from the North to the South*: Containing in this Donation whatsoever firm Lands or Islands are found, or to be found, towards India, or towards any other part whatsoever it be, being distant from, or without the foresaid Line, drawn a hundred Leagues towards the West, and South, from any of the Islands which are commonly called DE LOS AZORES AND CAPO VERDE. All the Islands therefore and firm Lands found and to be found, discovered and to be discovered, from the said Line towards the West and South, such as have not actually been heretofore possessed by any other Christian King or Prince, until the day of the Nativity of our Lord Jesus Christ last past, from the which beginneth this present year, being the year of our Lord a thousand four hundred ninety three, whensoever any such shall be found by your Messengers and Captains...

Thereupon His Holiness once more reasserted his authority, indicating the source of such authority, in order to justify the grant he was making to the King of Spain in virtue of and as a derivation of the same.

We (continued the pope) by the Authority of Almighty God, granted unto us in Saint Peter, and by the Vicarship of Jesus Christ which we bear on the Earth, do for ever, by the tenor of these presents, give, grant, assign unto you, your heirs and successors (the Kings of Castile and Legion) all those Lands and Islands, with their Dominions, Territories, Cities, Castles, Towers, Places, and Villages, with all the Rights and Jurisdictions thereunto pertaining; constituting, assigning, and deputing you, your heirs and successors, the Lords thereof, with full and free Power, Authority and Jurisdiction: Decreeing nevertheless by this our Donation, Grant and Assignation, that from no Christian Prince, which actually hath possessed the foresaid Islands and firm Lands, unto the day of the Nativity of our Lord beforesaid, their Right obtained, to be understood hereby to be taken away, or that it ought to be taken away...

Having duly decreed, donated, granted and assigned all the above, Pope Alexander hurled a potential excommunication against anyone who might dare to disregard his decision:

We furthermore straightly inhibit all manner of persons, of what state, degree, order or condition soever they be, although of Imperial and Regal Dignity, under the pain of the Sentence of Excommunication which they shall incur, if they do to the contrary, that they in no case presume, without special Licence of you, your heirs and successors, to travail for Merchandizes or for any other cause, to the said Lands or Islands, found or to be found, discovered or to be discovered, towards the West and South, drawing a Line from the Pole Arctic to the Pole Antarctic, whether the firm Lands and Islands, found and to be found, be situate towards India, or towards any other part.

Alexander then indicated the actual demarcation of the explorations and possessions mentioned earlier in this same document, and said:

Being distant from the Line drawn a hundred Leagues towards the West, from any of the Islands commonly called DE LOS AZORES and CAPO VERDE: Notwithstanding Constitutions, Decrees and Apostolical Ordinances whatsoever they are to the contrary.

In Him from whom Empires, Dominions, and all good things do proceed: Trusting that Almighty God, directing your Enterprises...

Finally, he concluded his deed of gift by threatening anybody who might dare "to infringe" his will:

Let no man therefore whatsoever infringe or dare rashly to contrary this Letter of our Commendation, Exhortation, Request, Donation, Grant, Assignation, Constitution, Deputation, Decree, Commandment, Inhibition, and Determination. And if any shall presume to attempt the same, let him know that he shall thereby incur the Indignation of Almighty God, and His Holy Apostles, Peter and Paul.

Given at Rome at Saint Peter's, in the year of the Incarnation of our Lord 1493. The fourth day of the Nones of May, the first year of our Popedom.

After Catholic Spain there came rival Portugal. As a result, the following year — that is, in 1494 — the Treaty of Tordesillas moved the papal lines of demarcation to the meridian 370 leagues west of Azores. This caused yet another visible effect of the papal decision upon the New World: the existence of Brazil. For, by pushing the line so far west, a great portion of the soon-to-be-discovered Brazilian bulge was included in the Portuguese dominion.

Meanwhile, sundry daring navigators, spurred by the Columbian epic and the allure of immense riches, began to explore the unknown oceans with renewed vigor. Vasco da Gama took the eastern route, the original inspirational concept of bypassing Constantinople by rounding Africa, and in 1498 he reached India, only six years after Columbus discovered America. In 1500 Alvarez Gabral discovered what later was known as Brazil. The following year, 1501, Corte Real sailed north and landed on Greenland. Joao Martins in 1541 set foot on Alaska.

The devout sons of the Church, Spaniards and Portuguese, having caught the fever for incessant exploration, continued to criss-cross the oceans. They became the original pioneers who landed in China, the Moluccas, Japan and even Australia, while, as early as 1520, Magellan was the first man ever to sail around the globe. When the Isthmus of Panama was crossed and the Pacific Ocean discovered, a priest, a member of the expedition, rushed into the waves holding a crucifix and shouting: "I take possession of this ocean in the name of Jesus Christ!" — and hence in the name of His Vicar on Earth, the Roman Pontiff. The New World had become indeed, by divine and legal right, the absolute property of the popes, from the north to the south, from the eastern to the western coasts. A New World was added to the old one, already under the triple crown.

CHAPTER 12

THE ECONOMIC FACTOR BEHIND THE REFORMATION

The cries of anguish, anger and defiance of all the saints, rebels and reformers who chided the Church for her ways, had echoed never-endingly during the past millennium, to the acclaim of true believers, to the indifference of the multitudes and to the deafness of the succeeding reigning pontiffs. Their repeated demands for the renovation of papal Christendom had all been in vain, or, if momentarily effective, had been extinguished with fire. The ashes of all those who had been burned in the public squares of the medieval cities of Europe could testify to that. St. Francis, St. Bernard of Clairvaux, John Huss, Savonarola, and the legions of others no less illustrious and as zealous, had all gone, after crying in vain to the wilderness — not, however, without prophesying unending woes and disasters to come.

When, therefore, the explosion promoted by the forces which had been simmering underneath the monolithic ecclesiastical edifice finally erupted with primeval violence, most of those who were scattered by it were not taken by surprise. Indeed, many of them marvelled that the explosion had not occurred much earlier.

The phenomenon of Martin Luther, consequently, was not unexpected. The German monk, without even realizing it, had become the spokesman, not so much of himself, his doubts and the corruptness of Roman Catholicism when seen in the light of the Scripture, but of a sullen and resentful populace who could no longer suffer with their ancient passivity the mammonic degeneracy of this religious system, ruled as she was by depraved miscreants, by legions of opulent libertines and by hordes of lay and ecclesiastical parasites, all living upon the immense vested interests of a papal Christendom oversaturated by an ever more insatiable thirst for the material possessions of this world.

For truly, the Church could hardly own more than she did — or be more corrupt, or alienate herself more from the spirit of the Apostolic tradition. Monasteries, nunneries, abbeys had become the parasitical landlords of vast estates throughout Europe. Thousands of their inmates had replaced the old landed gentry and had proved to be harsher masters of the laborers tilling the fields than the old ones had been. Free labor, tithes, taxation of all kinds, had helped to fatten the lazy populations of the multiplying monastic orders, while simultaneously impoverishing the rural fold of the semi-abandoned hamlets and the abysmally poor plebs of the cities. Episcopal palaces had become the opulent abodes of luxury-loving prelates whose main concern was the revenue which each diocese yielded. Cardinals openly bought and sold or "let" the incomes of rich abbeys, most of which became bargaining assets whenever an ecclesiastical appointment had to be made. In France and in Germany, as in England, the leadership of monasteries and nunneries had become the domain of the sons or daughters of the wealthy and the powerful.

The popes themselves had set an example of loose living, corruption and of brazen selling of anything sacred to make money. Indeed, prior to the death of a pope, the most scandalous bargaining took place between the cardinals who had to elect the next pontiff — at times even before the dying pope had finally expired. Money flew from the hand of one cardinal to that of another. Ambitious candidates made promises, offered gold and bought votes with brazenness which would seem incredible if it were not true.

In addition to the cardinals buying and selling to the highest bidder their votes for the papacy, the agents of princes, kings and emperors penetrated openly into the conclaves with offers of vast sums of gold or real estate to induce the cardinals to vote for the candidate preferred by the royal bribers, with the result that very often popes were elected according to how many bribes they or their protectors had been able to offer to the voting cardinals.

For centuries the conclaves were nothing but bargaining places where the papacy was bought or sold to the highest bidder. Cardinals, and therefore the popes, thus became the inevitable financial pawns in the sacrilegious game in which simony, corruption and dishonorable bargaining were the principal factors.

It must be remembered that at this period cardinals were not only princes of the Church. More often than not, they were also lay princes, or held positions of power equivalent to that of a prince of the realm. Witness Cardinal Wolsey, who became chancellor and cardinal in 1515. Wolsey wielded almost unlimited power and was the virtual ruler of England from 1514 until 1529. All the affairs of state passed through his hands, as did most of its revenue. He lived in regal splendor. He built himself Hampton Court, which eventually excited the envy and greed of Henry VIII. Cardinal Wolsey was twice on the verge of being elected pope. Had that occurred, in all probability the Church of England would never have been born.

Wolsey was the prototype of the prince of the Roman Church throughout Europe, wielding unlimited ecclesiastical and temporal power, with immense wealth basking in opulence, splendor and glory. Cardinals of this kind, therefore, when gathering together for the election of a new pope, brought with them their temporal pomp, pride, vices, greed, luxury and lust for money. They acted as potentates who came to elect another potentate, a pope, from whom they could derive yet more benefits.

During the fourteenth and fifteenth centuries, most of the cardinals, prior to entering the conclave, brought into its precincts, not a simple straw mattress, bread and water and fervent prayer to the Holy Spirit. Many of them brought into it the luxuries of princes, a secretary or secretaries, servants, three conclavists, a sacristan with his clerk, a confessor, two doctors, a surgeon, a chemist with several attendants, two masters of ceremonies, plus a carpenter, a barber, a mason with his sundry apprentices, and a number of general servants to attend to His Eminence's needs. That was not all. During the greater part of such conclaves Rome used to watch processions of gala coaches carrying the cardinals' meals in boxes which were painted with the coat of arms of each Eminence. These were surrounded by butlers, majordomos, servants and footmen, all dressed in gorgeous liveries and driving in state to the conclave from the sundry cardinals' palaces. This, it must be remembered, while the cardinals were supposed to be leading a life of austerity, penance and prayer for help to make the right choice.

The popes who were elected by such luxury-loving cardinals were worthy of their electors. To mention only a few:

Pope Paul II (1464-71). As soon as he was nominated, the former cardinal announced to the Sacred College that he had taken the name of Pope Formoso the First (*formoso* means beautiful), on the grounds that he was the handsomest man who had ever worn the papal crown. The cardinals objected, fearing too open a scandal with the populace, so he became Paul II instead. Pope Paul revelled in sumptuous clothes, expensive perfumes and fabulous jewels. The papal court was crowded with beautiful women and youths. His greatest weakness — or, rather, disease — was his love for precious stones. He was in the habit of playing with handfuls of them, not only in private but also during public functions. They gave him a sensuous delight, and he gazed at them with fascination for ininterminable hours. He never went to sleep unless the most splendid gems had been put under his pillow. He became so spellbound by jewels that he had the papal crown encrusted with precious stones. The tiara cost an immense sum. Its weight was such that the pope could hardly wear it. Indeed, the first time that he wore it (for longer than he had anticipated) it gave him an apoplectic fit, and he died, a victim of his own vanity, greed, love of luxury, and voluptuary revellings, and a spender of fabulous riches.

The pope who followed him was no better. Sixtus IV (1471-1484) waged perpetual warfare. All ecclesiastical honors were for sale. He granted benefices to the highest bidder. He imposed the most exorbitant taxation upon the populace, hanging and torturing anyone who did not pay. He levied taxes upon everything, including the houses of prostitutes. Indeed, to make money he went so far as to grant absolution of all crimes, with plenary indulgence. He threatened with Hell those who did not pay. In fact, he did not hesitate to threaten Venetian prelates themselves that he would sell them as slaves to the Turks for a fair price.

THE ECONOMIC FACTOR BEHIND THE REFORMATION

Pope Innocent VIII (1484-92) openly bought the votes of the cardinals. His only interests were women and his countless illegitimate children. The Vatican became a vast establishment over-run by his progeny (it was estimated he had more than 100 known illegitimate children). The cost of maintaining his sons, daughters, grandchildren, nephews, and relatives of all kinds was enormous. Through his gross self-indulgence, he grew immensely fat, by the summer of 1492 he had become a mass of flesh "incapable," as the contemporary historian Valore related, "of assimilating any nourishment but a few drops of milk from a young woman's breast."

Innocent VIII was succeeded by an even more notorious cardinal, Cardinal Borgia. Rodrigo Borgia became Pope Alexander VI (1492-1503).

As a cardinal and then again as pope, he indulged whole nights in the wildest revels. He was the father of the legendary Cesare and Lucretia Borgia, besides many other illegitimate children. He spent immense sums of money and received and gave enormous bribes. He sold his influence first as cardinal and then as pope, to anyone who paid him, and this with such brazenness that when pope he used openly to boast that he could have filled the Sistine Chapel with sacks of gold. The Borgia bought his cardinalate by openly bribing all and sundry while still a youth. As a young cardinal he led a life of such intrigue that, having spent enormous sums of money to buy most of the other cardinals over a period of decades, he was finally elected pontiff. He became a legend in his own time, and while many of the stories about him have no more solid foundation than the fervid imagination of the writer of novels, yet a vast amount of what has come down to us is true. It was his open use of the immense riches of the papacy as bribery which evoked the ire of Christendom.

Alexander, it must be remembered, was the pope who claimed that he owned the newly discovered continent of the Americas as the trustee of the Church, which, in her turn, owned them in the name of the Blessed Peter.

Alexander sold or bought or otherwise put to auction abbeys, bishoprics, and cardinalates, appointing abbots, bishops, and cardinals according to how much gold they were able to give him. He leased the Americas to Spain and

Portugal, following secret bargaining for treasures from the Spanish and Portuguese crowns. Such practices, already current, became so widespread that the Vatican finally became nothing but an open auction market where anything, sacred or profane, could be bought for money.

When, therefore, another pope, the Medici Leo X, was elected in 1513, the custom whereby the papacy transacted such commerce was well established. That Leo was an agnostic, if not an atheist, and that he had contracted syphilis in his twenties, did not shock the Vatican. What made him immortal in the annals of Christendom was his blatant selling of indulgences, ostensibly to build St. Peter's Basilica, which set off the spark that ignited the Protestant conflagration.

Christendom was split into two halves. Forces which had been gnashing their teeth for centuries boldly came to the fore and ranged themselves against the papacy. Whereas the primary motives which inspired the Reformation were theological, forces of no less import gave it the impetus, the strength and the opportunity to be the success that it was. These forces were embryonic nationalism, a veiled racial antagonism and a conflict of diversifying cultures. Underneath and behind them all, however, was perhaps the most important: greed. Had this been absent, it is doubtful whether the Reformation could have been born, let alone have survived.

It must be remembered that the Reformation was not the first; it was the latest of many which failed. The Reformation became "*the* Reformation" because it succeeded. Had it not, it would have been nothing but another half-forgotten footnote in the annals of Christian history. Its success was due not so much to the ripeness of the times or the corruption of the Church or the zeal of the movement's leaders (many reformers, as zealous and as brave as Luther, ended at the stake), but to the fact that behind them rallied powerful lay elements desirous of *getting hold of the immense wealth of the Church.* Princes, the nobility, burghers, not to mention kings, were motivated mainly by the allure of the distribution of vast estates until then owned by a church which they wanted to dispossess. The theological disputes were to them providential justification for seizing the lands which had been held for centuries. The opportunity had to be grasped, for it might never come again.

The economic motivation, however, was not confined exclusively to the nobility of Germany, England, and other countries. It existed at all levels of society. It could not have been otherwise, since the fiscal exactions of Roman Catholicism, as we have seen so often, affected everyone. During the fourteenth and fifteenth centuries these had become exceedingly burdensome. They had become a kind of perpetual strangulation which, when added to the taxation levied by the king or local princes or town, became unbearable.

The Church, instead of showing fiscal leniency, became increasingly greedy, both for power and for money. Her right of "visitation" was extended. The system of appeal was developed, the practice of patronage by means of *provisions* became more common. In her direct pressure to secure revenue, she pressed on, regardless of the economic situation. This she did by her *annates*, by sundry tributes, by numberless tithes, and, above all, by the ever-present Peter's Pence. And so it came to pass that the theological disputations which in ordinary circumstances would have interested only a limited section of society became the rallying focus for forces which saw it as a timely opportunity for getting their hands upon riches which they had eyed for a long time. The German princes succumbed to the temptation, as did sundry potentates in Austria, Switzerland, France, and most of the North European countries. In England the battle for the dispossession was headed by the king himself.

Henry VIII, for all his coarseness, animal lust, and excuse of wanting an heir to the throne, ultimately became motivated by the grand prize of wealth he could take through the Reformation, the real mother of Anglicanism. The English nobility who rallied behind him were no less greedy than Henry. Their support yielded vast landed domains, estates, and money, all of which came from the Church which they now so conveniently repudiated. The Reformation was for them nothing but a vast business transaction in which they became the main beneficiaries.

The economic spur thus played a major, if not the major, role in the success of the Reformation as such, not only in

England, but also in Germany — it should never be forgotten that Luther's strength, and therefore success, came through the support of the majority of the German princes who stood by him so as to gain by the "secularization" of the Church's property. It was the allure of the immense material possessions which gave impetus, strength, and the will to succeed to those who had rallied against her. Had such possessions not existed, it is doubtful whether the lay elements which tipped the balance in favor of the protestant reformers would have supported them solely for theological reasons, since few were genuinely interested in these. Material wealth, therefore, ultimately became one of the major factors for the loss of this same wealth which the Roman Church had made it her primary purpose to accumulate and indeed to aggrandize throughout her existence.

It must be remembered that the papacy at this period was the greatest, the wealthiest and the most powerful landlord in the whole of Europe. She was far richer, and owned far more land, real estate, financial interests and gold than any prince or even king. In England alone then, she owned, directly and indirectly, more than half of all the *arable land of the realm*; in fact, her aggregate wealth was such that she exceeded all the nobility and the crown put together. The same went for France, and for the German states, not to mention Spain, Italy, and other countries.

Rome's stubborn accumulation of temporal riches ultimately became one of the main causes, if not *the* main cause, responsible for the spiritual and material losses she was made to suffer via the Reformation, so that the warning of the writer of Ecclesiastes (5:13) that "there is a sore evil which I have seen under the sun, namely, riches kept for the owners thereof to their hurt..." became something more than the foreboding warning of an ancient voice of wisdom, became indeed the verdict against, and the condemnation of, the most corrupt, the most materialistic, the least religious, and, above all, the richest institution on earth, busying herself with Mammon and with all the principalities of this world, instead of consorting with the spiritual children of the One she claimed as her Founder, and acting as their protector, their comforter and their provider.

CHAPTER 13

THE CATHOLIC CHURCH AND THE FABULOUS WEALTH OF THE SPANISH COLONIES

The ways of Providence are inscrutable and the pattern of the future incomprehensible to the finite minds of men. For, while the latter will mourn losses of seemingly apocalyptic proportions, schemes of tremendous import will be set in motion without their being even aware of their significance in the days to come.

With Catholic Europe split asunder into two hostile camps, the seeds of the Roman Church's spiritual and temporal aggrandizement were replaced almost simultaneously in the west, there to grow with a power undreamt of even in the restless Europe of the sixteenth century, since to the pontiffs the newly discovered Americas, besides being a timely portent, were also a most wonderful omen of the shape of things to come. So that when, only a few decades after Columbus set foot on new soil, and Europe, having let loose the Reformation, almost made the old Catholic world crumble, the popes set out in earnest to conquer the boundless fresh horizons.

One year only after the discovery of the Americas, the pope took the first step in that direction. He issued a famous document, which we have already seen, the Bull made to Castile, Touching the New World, 1493, in which he assigned the Americas exclusively to two Catholic countries, Spain and Portugal. The following year, 1494, in the Treaty of Tordesillas the papal line of demarcation between the two countries was moved to the meridian 370 leagues west of the Azores. The concession to the two Iberian nations was soon transformed into what it was really meant to be: namely, a monopoly for the exclusive evangelization of the continent via the two Catholic nations.

The papal move was a spectacular success, for within a century the papal emblems had been planted from the most northerly tip of California down to the most southerly corner of South America, and also along the eastern and western coastal lines of practically the whole of the western hemisphere. Divine Providence had certainly compensated the papacy for the losses it had suffered in Europe only a short while before. The Americas were truly being converted into an immense papal fief, many times the size of the Old World.

The task, however, could not be completed without the full co-operation of the temporal rulers, with the result that from the very beginning church and state became interdependent. Their collaboration, while immensely beneficial to both, led to the inevitable conflict which had so stubbornly bedevilled their relationship back in old Europe; that is, church and state found themselves at loggerheads as frequently as they had done in the old world — indeed, at times more often. For since the Reformation even Catholic kings had become more daring in their claims to royal independence from the papal yoke, with the result that, to the utter stupefaction and anger of the popes, such rulers, while they fought for the Church, at the same time seldom let an occasion go by without putting the interests of the crown before those of the papacy, so that the American colonies soon came to be buffeted by two mighty conflicting and greedy authorities: the ecclesiastical and the secular.

But whereas in Europe the Church then was on the losing side, here she was on the winning side, since she had managed to transform practically the whole American continent into a vast Catholic imperium where her writ was supreme. Because of this, she was determined not to loose her hold, as she had done in Europe. As long as the Spanish crown co-operated, well and good. When it did not, then war between the two ensued.

War broke out whenever the economic interests of the Catholic Church were endangered. Her possessions, which were increasing with greater rapidity even than they had done in Europe, were closely interlinked with her religious power, generally identified with her hierarchy. High prelates grabbed lands, real estates and commercial interests, not only for the Church at large, but equally for their dioceses or, indeed, for themselves. Such activities more often than not were tolerated by the civil authorities, in so far as the latter benefited as much as the clergy from the *status quo*, with solid monetary awards and the prospect of a general stability stretching indefinitely into the future. When, however, the benefits were not reasonably shared and the Church or her hierarchs became too greedy, then conflict ensued. Sometimes it would remain localized, but often its repercussions reached both Madrid and Rome.

It might be useful to illustrate this by a characteristic case which, while typical of the nature and relations of the ecclesiastical and civil economic interests on a local scale, nevertheless became identified with the general economic and financial state, the co-operation and conflict that existed between Rome and Madrid — at that time the two most influential powers on the American continent. The case is especially significant since it shows a situation which was widespread throughout the vast Spanish colonial empire. Because of its extent, the economic factors were equally of immense import to both the religious and the civil partners.

We refer to the great riots that took place in Mexico City in 1624. The spark which ignited them, although trivial in itself, was nevertheless a significant one. Prez de la Sena, Archbishop of Mexico City, in addition to tending the spiritual welfare of his flock, spent a not inconsiderable amount of energy in furthering his own financial and commercial interests. Among sundry businesses, he ran a private slaughterhouse in the very precincts of the archiepiscopal palace. Its establishment was illegal, and the viceroy requested him to close it. The archbishop refused, saying that the viceroy had no power over the head of the hierarchy; after which he launched a furious attack upon the colonial government.

While this was going on, a well-known food profiteer was found guilty of running a grain trust. This was one of the most serious offences against the state, as by hoarding stocks of staple corn he had purposely made prices soar to such an extent that the poorer section of the population suffered real hunger and near-starvation. The merchant was heavily fined and the police were despatched to arrest him. It so happened, however, that the accused was an intimate friend of the archbishop's, and the latter encouraged him to resist arrest. The merchant attacked the police, fled to a Dominican monastery, and asked for sanctuary.

The viceroy dared not trespass into the monastery; but, although careful not to infringe upon the religious privileges of the Roman Catholic Church, he was determined to punish the culprit, and threw an armed guard round the premises. The archbishop, further to stultify the viceroy's orders and thus undermine his authority, went ostentatiously to the monastery every day, where he visited his friend and advised him to continue to resist, going so far even as to plan his escape. The viceroy, however, remained unmoved and kept the monastery under continuous surveillance.

Realizing that he could not bend the viceroy's will, the archbishop then turned the whole issue into a question of religious versus temporal authority. The viceroy, he asserted, by throwing a cordon of guards round the monastery, was violating the right of sanctuary and hence the right of the Roman Catholic Church, and his action was a direct threat to his, the archbishop's, religious authority. The government continued to refuse the release of the accused. Indeed, it arrested one of the archbishop's notaries for incitement to violence. As a reprisal, the archbishop excommunicated the viceroy, the judges, the soldiers, the guards, and the whole government.

Faced with such religious fulmination, the civil authorities found themselves helpless. The matter was no longer a judicial one, but had become the old issue of church versus state. The viceroy, to avoid worsening the situation, appealed to the apostolic judge, who ordered the archbishop to withdraw the excommunications. The archbishop, however, not only refused but locked up every church building in the capital and laid the whole city under interdict. All sacraments and religious services were suspended. The clergy hurled anathemas, and the bells of all churches, monasteries and convents were made to toll incessantly by day and night, as if to announce a most frightful disaster. At such an astounding, never-ending din, the people began to crowd into the streets in a state of semi-terror, asking the cause of such alarms. The answer was given in the form of long processions of priests carrying candles, singing hymns, led by a huge cross draped in black, stopping at the house of each person excommunicated to affix to the door the archbishop's condemnation placing him outside the Church. No one must speak to, help or befriend any whom the archbishop had condemned.

At such a sight the ignorant populace grew even more alarmed, an alarm which increased when they were told by the priests that they, too, would eventually be condemned to the eternal fire of hell. This while the slow and awful tolling of the bells continued unbroken throughout the day and the following night.

When finally the terrorized mob could no longer endure this, the archbishop, having made sure that they were ready to follow him and do anything he ordered them to do, in the hope of avoiding excommunication, told them to make ready to march with him against those who had compelled the Roman Church to use her anathemas against the city. Thereupon he actually marched to the Supreme Court with the mob at his heels, in an attempt to intimidate the civil authorities. The Court, instead of being intimidated, ordered him to sign a juridical warrant. The archbishop, instead of complying, burst out into insults and incited the mob to use violence. Thereupon the Court had him arrested, heavily fined and officially banished from Mexico City.

Once in the suburbs, however, the archbishop excommunicated the whole government anew and "blasted the city with a new interdict." This was the beginning of an open rebellion. The mob, fearing that they, too, might be put outside the pale of the Church for not helping the archbishop, rose to defend religion against the king. The viceregal building was besieged, nearby heaps of bricks used for the construction of the cathedral were hurled against the palace. When these had gone, the people took to tearing up paving stones. Thereupon, led by a priest on horseback and shouting "Long live Christ! Death to the heretic!" they went to the assault of government headquarters, while another priest, seated on a chair placed on a table and holding the gospels in his hand, "absolved of blame and penance all those who took part in the assault on the palace."[1]

The violence lasted until the next day, when the populace finally stormed the building, set it on fire and opened the jails. The viceroy's guards opened fire, and many were killed. The viceroy, to save his own life, had to escape in disguise and took refuge in a Franciscan convent. Having defeated those who defied the power of the Church, the archbishop "made his triumphant entrance into the city at night, accompainied by more than four thousand men on foot and on horseback, many of them holding aloft lighted torches so that it seemed in the midst of day."[2]

In distant Spain, the riots created a commotion. The king despatched a royal investigator, charged with finding out who was guilty and publishing an official report. Five priests were sentenced to the galleys. The viceroy was completely acquitted.

While the issue was settled by the authority of the king, the real controversy between church and state in Mexico — and, in fact, throughout Spanish America — continued to smolder under the cinders of an uncomfortable truce between the papacy and the most Catholic kings of Spain.

The riots of Mexico City, far from being a local dispute, had once more indicated to the civil authorities that it was far wiser to share the government with the Church than to govern without its consent. The state, represented either by the colonial authorities or by the king, generally gave way to avoid the worst, with the result that in the long run the papacy, by turning the screw upon the civil authorities, threatening them either with revolt, Mexico City type, or forcible surrender to her claims, managed to acquire an ever-increasing influence in American society until finally she came to control the social, economic and hence political life of the Spanish colonies and thus keep a tight stranglehold upon the state itself.

The repetition of such tactics in the course of a few centuries gave such power to the Roman Church throughout Spanish America that it can be said without fear of exaggeration, that the popes had become the real masters of the new continent. This power was exerted, it should be noted, not merely via the control of political instruments: to have gone too far in that direction might have meant a complete breakdown of the relationship between the Spanish monarchy and the Roman Church. Rome, although ruthless, was too subtle not to understand that means could be employed by which to exert *de facto* control without depriving the government of the belief that it was the civil authorities who ruled. Consequently, while it exerted pressure for political control, at the same time it carried on a no less ruthless campaign for the total control of the colonial society in *the economic field.*

The colonial hierarchies were encouraged by Rome to utilize their religious authority for economic ends, using the populace according to circumstances to bring pressure against the colonial government, as in the case of the Mexico City riots. This policy in the long run proved even more effective than the bid for political control. With the result that, whereas in early colonial days the weight of the Church in political matters rested mainly upon religious pressure, particularly through use of excommunication, later on it shifted to the pressure she could exert by sheer *economic wealth.*[3]

This economic wealth was accumulated by sundry devices and the simultaneous use of the spiritual, social and political privileged status of the Church, emphasized by the fact, for instance, that the Catholic clergy were an economically privileged class from the beginning and that they received "large grants of land from the crown" while "many monasteries, cathedrals and individual prelates were given generous *encomiendas.*"

In addition to this, the Church was enriched through her tithes and frequent "gifts and bequests of money and property, parochial fees for marriages, funerals, baptisms, confessions, and for masses, both ordinary and requiem, special collections in honor of some patron saint, alms gathered by the monasteries, dowries given to convents of nuns, and so forth."[4] Tithes and bequests more than anything else, in fact, tended to enrich the Church as time went by, so that an increasing proportion of colonial income and colonial capital came under ecclesiastical control. In addition to this, it should be remembered that "ecclesiastical capital was free from taxation, legally in the early days, virtually always."[5]

That was not all. Church buildings, monasteries, ecclesiastical residences, and anything else belonging to the Roman

Church had to be erected free, the state as a rule having to furnish one-third or one-half of the funds required, while the population furnished the remainder. The Indians always offered their labor without any payment whatsoever, as part of their contribution. This was not confined to the construction of church buildings; it became the rule in the Church's vast tracts of land. The result was that the Church, in the long run, became one of the main instruments through which the impoverishment of the native races continued, until these were reduced to complete destitution. This caused endless riots, one of the most notable of which was the one ignited by the famished and frenzied Mexican masses, again in the Mexican capital, in 1692.

The economic influence of the Roman Church thus continued to grow until in some regions she came to control more of the national wealth than did the government. By the end of the colonial period, the she owned an estimated *one half of the total wealth* of Mexico, Peru, Colombia, Paraguay and Ecuador, and almost that proportion in all the other Latin American countries, while most of the remaining half was "*controlled by the clergy through mortages.*"

The Catholic Church, having lost more than half of the old world, in this way had not only regained what had been taken from her. She had become the undisputed mistress of the souls, and with them of the immense wealth, of the new world.

CHAPTER 14

REVOLUTIONS AND THE CHURCH'S REVENUES

At the close of the eighteenth and opening of the nineteenth centuries, three major hurricanes made the Catholic Church totter upon her grandiose re-accumulation of wealth within the space of just one generation: the North American Revolution, the French Revolution and the Spanish-American War of Independence.

These were not only portentous landmarks in the history of western civilization. They were also three major milestones in the history of Christendom. For, while the revolt of the North American colonies ushered in the United States of America, it simultaneously brought to the fore one of the principles most hated by the Roman Catholic Church: namely, that of the separation of church and state.

The principle, having been incorporated within the framework of the fundamental legislation of the new American states, and, even more, being an integral part of an independent new Protestant nation, became a beacon for nations old and new, to apply to such novel tenet, in theory as well as in practice. Indeed, it was destined to exert a most tremendous influence upon the Roman Catholicism throughout the western hemisphere from its first inception, since it contributed more than anything else to the substantial curtailment of the unchallenged economic aggrandizement of the Church in the western regions. This it did, not so much within the U.S., where the Roman Church at that time was a subdued minority, but outside it.

The French Revolution, on the other hand, by adding even more drastic tenets, set old Europe on fire with doctrines which were still more vigorously hostile to established religion. Besides causing the toppling of thrones resting upon the sacrosanct formula of the Divine Right of Kings which the papacy had blessed for so long, they equally promoted the dispossession of thousands upon thousands of estates and lands owned by the Vatican since before and after the Reformation.

The message of the North American and French Revolutions could not but affect the most monolithic and backward portion of the new world, i.e. the Spanish American Iberno-Catholic enclosure which stretched from California to Tierra del Fuego in the extreme South. From there the Spanish colonies, once stirred by the North American and French revolutionary principles, shook off the European yoke with retarded success. But, whereas they rid themselves of a monarchy, they could not rid themselves entirely of the Roman Church. And, although in their original enthusiasm they managed to divest the Church of most of her former power as well as of her immense possessions, nevertheless the influence and power of Romanism could not be annihilated. She could only be neutralized, and that but temporarily.

For, in spite of the ecclesiastical dispossessions which the new Central and South American Republics carried out, the fact remained that the Roman Church, after lying low for a few decades, began to recuperate at an ever more accelerated pace. And this to such an extent that towards the end of the nineteenth century she had become the owner of more lands and real estates than she had in colonial times.

In Europe the process of Church land seizure was, perhaps, more efficiently drastic than anywhere else. The French Revolution dispossessed the Blessed Peter of the greater part of his immense wealth. Countless monasteries, abbeys and bishoprics were either reduced to the bare minimum or suppressed altogether. Their vast holdings of buildings and land reverted to the state. When it is remembered that prior to the storm the Roman Church in France was the greatest land-owner of the country, her losses there can be gauged in all their dimensions. Napoleon, once he became Emperor, softened this policy, since his political and dynastic ambitions required the Vatican's support. The result was that the Church, notwithstanding many quarrels, began to recuperate, and reached her zenith with Napoleon III, a caricature of Napoleon I.

REVOLUTIONS AND THE CHURCH'S REVENUES

The Church's recovery was made possible, not so much by the brilliant incompetence of Napoleon III as by the religious gullibility of his wife, the Empress Eugenie. For the papacy by now had embarked upon another policy in order to collect vast fortunes, or rather, she re-adopted an old policy which we have already examined: i.e. the creation of massive religious involvement via the planning of miracles, apparitions, the setting up of shrines and the organization of profitable pilgrimages, the revenue from which went to fill her partly depleted coffers — a striking repetition of the practices she had promoted more than one thousand years before, with the cult of the Blessed Peter and the like. In this manner, the revenues she lost from the expropriation of most of her estates during the French Revolution, were recovered in the long run with a hundred per cent profit through the collection of the millions of francs which the pilgrims who went to French shrines left behind as concrete mementoes of their visits.

The policy of promoting miracles and of profiting by them with the matter-of-fact collection of francs, dollars, sterling and any other good currency, a policy which had fallen into disrepute for some centuries, was now revived. Some efforts in this direction were pathetic failures and yielded next to nothing. Others, however, were sound religious and financial successes. One of these is worth recounting, for it was a typical pilot-scheme for others yet to come. It was organized only a couple of decades after the Church lost most of her revenues from the expropriated lands and real estate of France.

A nun called Catherine Laboure one sunny day of June, 1830, saw the Virgin Mary "inside an oval frame." Following this vision, the frame "reversed itself." and, lo and behold: upon its other side there appeared the hearts of Jesus and Mary. Thereupon the Virgin asked practically-minded Catherine to have medals struck with those hearts on them. The incentive? Anyone who wore them would be specially protected by her. Who would be so mean as not to spend a few centimes or a few francs to secure such wonderful protection?

And so it came to pass that, in June 1832, 1,500 such medals were struck. One or two religious Orders, having perceived the vast financial profits to be made, became the sponsors of the miraculous medals. The Daughters of Mercy and the Lazarist Fathers set out for all they were worth to promote the cult.

The result? Within the first four years two and a half million medals had been sold in Paris alone and over eleven million in France. By 1836 the engraver was making three thousand medals a day — this, it must be remembered, in a Europe whose population was minute compared to the overcrowded Europe we know today. The business (for there is no other word for it) of the Miraculous Medal, as it is called, goes on to this day, not only in France, but wherever there are Roman Catholics. Uncover the necks of thousands of American citizens, and you will see the medal, in addition to scapulars, and sundry adornments.

The Miraculous Medal, however, was only a rehearsal for a truly astounding "coup" engineered a few decades later.

One misty day two or three sickly, bare-footed children said that they spoke to or heard or saw the Virgin. Following the usual happenings, with the inevitable villains, suffering, humiliation, incredulity and finally acceptance, the Virgin's appearance and miraculous real presence were officially recognized. The crowds were organized and their religious fervor coolly calculated and weighed. The papacy decided that this had the makings of a truly astounding permanent silver collection. Compared to it the Miraculous Medal was child's play.

The cult of the Virgin was promoted at first upon a local scale, then upon a national one. The latter would have taken time, had not Providence, in the guise of a very gullible lady, come to the fore. The lady, prompted, persuaded and guided by her confessor and sundry persons in her entourage, one day expressed a strong desire to possess a bottle of water from a spring which, Church authorities assured believers, had sprung up suddenly from the dry, hard floor of the cave where the Virgin had appeared and spoken to the little girl who had initially started the story. It seemed that somebody already had one, there for the asking. The lady thereupon let it be known that she was receiving mighty spiritual and physical comfort from the miraculous water of the bottle. Her friends decided to follow her example. The holy water from the cave was suddenly in great demand. It became fashionable, with the result that, instead of a new perfume, the Parisian ladies now asked for holy water collected from the spring in the foothills of the Pyrenees.

Of course, the water did not arrive in Paris for nothing. It cost a little sum. But when the little sums multiplied by the thousand, they became a considerable sum. From then onward, the water, the spring, the cave, the Virgin and the place where she appeared, were put on the map. For the lady was none other than the Empress Eugenie, wife of Napoleon III; and the miraculous place was no other than Lourdes.

Not long afterwards Napoleon lost his throne. The Church suffered another tremendous setback in France, since Napoleon's empire was succeeded by the agnostic-atheistic, Church-hating French Republic. But who cared? Lourdes, the miracle worker and hence the million dollar-spinner, had been successfully launched. It is still with us today.

Lourdes thus became a steady, ever-growing source of immense revenue. Millions of dollars were invested, and are still invested, in its promotion by church and state and by commercial and touristic enterprises. Nobody has ever known how much wealth the Vatican has amassed via the Lourdes cult, particularly since it has been promoted upon a world scale and therefore duly turned into a global money-making machine.

While the Lourdes cult was being promoted in a business-like way, an event of the greatest consequence occurred in nearby Italy. The territorial provinces — i.e. the Papal States — which the popes had received from Pepin and his successors back in the eighth and ninth centuries via the tricks of false documentation, ceased to exist. They were incorporated into a newly united Italy. Sundry attempts during the precious decades to save their inevitable incorporation had all ended in failure, e.g., that in 1848, when the Roman people deposed the pope from being their king and proclaimed a republic, and the pope in reply appealed to the Catholic nations "for an armed intervention to free the states of the Church from the faction of rogues."

In 1870, however, Napoleon III, having gone to war with Prussia, was soundly defeated. The popes, having lost their main protector, could do nothing but shut themselves within the walls of the Vatican, where they remained, without ever "officially" coming out until after the Second World War (1939-45). The Papal States thus vanished from the map of Europe, and from history, for ever. The Roman Church at last, with the exception of the tiny Vatican City, 109 acres, which eventually came into existence in 1929, had no longer any earthly dominion to rule.

Yet in that same year, while the papacy was being reduced to next to nothing in terms of temporal status, prestige and territory, the dispossessed pontiff, having convened the first Vatican Council, used his spiritual puissance to elevate himself above all men and, indeed, above human reason itself, with one single stroke. He did so by declaring himself infallible — something which no man had ever dared to do.

CHAPTER 15

THE CATHOLIC CHURCH IS ONCE MORE DESPOILED OF HER WEALTH IN EUROPE AND THE AMERICAS

The Dogma of Infallibility, by elevating the pope beyond human regions, enabled the papacy, by such a timely masterstroke, to lay the foundations of a novel structure directed at amassing the riches of the world with more efficiency than ever before. For if it is true that the loss of the territories of the Papal States had seemingly left the Church a beggar, it is nevertheless equally true that in a society which was rapidly transforming itself, territorial losses meant much less than in the previous centuries, since the western world by now had embarked upon a road where wealth was no longer confined to the ownership of land. The Industrial Revolution was transforming the west into an Aladdin's cave. Its treasures now were the multiplying factories, the opening of industrial markets, the appearance of embryonic empires based upon the goods produced by industry, science and the organization of labor, the three new deities bent on the opening up of new countries, on the exploitation of new materials, and on the shepherding of the working masses, all of which could be enthusiastically, ruthlessly and profitably exploited.

Seen in such a light the loss of the Papal States and of the immense territories which the Catholic Church had owned in the past, was almost providential, for it forced the papacy to take cognizance of this tremendous shift in the evaluation, production and amassing of a new type of wealth.

The process which had deprived her of her material wealth had not ended in 1870; far from it. The advent of "pestilential" theories, such as Liberalism, Democracy, and, worst of all,

Socialism, had created a universal anti-clericalism. Many nations in the west set up governments, one of whose chief aims was to continue the process of church impoverishment. Liberal, Democratic, agnostic and openly hostile administrations did this throughout Europe. In Germany, Bismark and the *Kulturkamf* paralyzed the Church, while in France the semi-atheistic Republican regimes did not hesitate to carry out further despoliation. All this was in addition to the Vatican's crushing financial debilities and the almost total exclusion of her influence from state, schools and the army. In the newly united Italy inimical governments humiliated her in all fields, restricting her activities in the very regions where once she had ruled unchallenged as a spiritual and temporal power.

European anti-clericalism swept quickly into the western hemisphere, though whereas in the north it was hardly noticed, thanks not only to the fluidity of North America society, to the predominance of Protestantism, and above all, to the effective enforcement of the abhorred principle of the separation of church and state, in Central and South America it caused a devastation of cataclysmic proportions, since anti-clericalism there was like a time bomb, ready to explode at the slightest tremor. It was a natural enemy of clericalism, which had indeed brought it into being, perhaps more violently than in Europe. For whereas in Europe those civil liberties and religious standards which chiefly prevent excess, were protected by the state and by society at large, in South America such limitations were practically non-existent.

The Church, notwithstanding the setbacks suffered during the Latin-American War of Independence at the end of the eighteenth and at the beginning of the nineteenth century, by now had recovered, and this to such an extent that her power, both religious and temporal, had again become almost unparalleled. With this went her stranglehold upon the wealth of the nations. Her properties, represented by the ownership of land, real estate, agricultural and commercial establishments, not to mention her grip upon the banking system and on the governments themselves, had made of her the true ruler of South American society, directly and indirectly. She had become a *de facto* government behind the sundry oligarchies of the various Central and South American republics.

The explosions eventually came — none so potent as that which occurred in Mexico during the first decade of the twentieth century. Most anti-clerical South American administrations came to power as a result of the popular reaction against the Church's stranglehold on the life and wealth of the nation. The Church was thoroughly disestablished; her suffocating monopoly of education and politics was broken. Above all, her immense wealth was confiscated and re-distributed among the land-hungry peasants.

The Church cried to heaven and accused the revolutionary forces of persecuting religion — religion consisting in this case, as so often in the past, of the solid, concrete and profitable ownership of more than a third of all the wealth of Mexico. For the Church conveniently soft-pedalled the fact that, until then, she had controlled more wealth than all the wealthiest Mexicans put together, and not only so, but directly or indirectly, she controlled more estates and money than the Mexican government itself; even worse, her manipulation of her wealth had become so detrimental to the already immensely poor Mexican peasants as to act as a veritable bar to any initiative, collective or individual, on the part of the Mexican people. With the aid of her lay partners, the great landlords, she had, in fact become the great paralyzer of the agricultural and commercial energies of the entire Mexican nation.

The Church reacted to the expropriation of her wealth, with something more than lamentations. She engineered a most destructive civil war which tore Mexico apart for several years, marking a whole decade (1920-30) with risings, mutinies, assassinations and massacres. Catholic bishops, priests, monks and even nuns took active part — witness the assassination of President Alvaro Obregon (July 17th, 1928) by a Catholic sent by the Mother Superior of a Mexican Convent.

She went even further, seeking to engineer the intervention of Protestant U.S. Catholics in the U.S. were duly mobilized, and almost succeeded. Certain "creatures" of the Catholic Church demanded a "preventive" war against Mexico. The call was not a rodomontade. It had a most sinister significance, for behind it there was a second power which the Mexican government had badly hurt: certain giant corporations of the U.S. which had recently penetrated very deeply into the economic life of the nation, many sectors of which they influenced and controlled almost at will.

When, therefore, Mexico, after hitting at the wealth of the Church, took the next step and enforced the 1927 Constitution by declaring that all the natural wealth of the sub-soil was national property, the North American oil, copper, silver interests uttered a cry which reached heaven and Wall Street with simultaneous echoes. The great corporations, which if they were exploiting Mexico, at least gave back some of their riches in royalties and revenues, became the natural allies of the Vatican; rather, the two — tacit partners until then — now came out into the open, so that there was seen the curious spectacle of Holy Mother Church fighting for the interests of the U.S. corporations, while the latter, whose only and unique God was the sound, solid, silver dollar, began to fight for "the spiritual values of true religion," i.e. of Catholic Church.

This unholy alliance brought the U.S. almost to the point of intervention. The great corporations planned to involve the U.S. in a war of intervention to defend their own present and future sources of wealth, just as the Catholic Church wished to defend, not only the spirtitual riches of her children, but also her solid, concrete and profitable riches here on earth.

The two partners left no stone unturned in their efforts to bring about a preventive war. Thus, while the Roman Church used the religious zeal of a Catholic to assassinate the President of Mexico, as already mentioned, the great U.S. corporations used political intrigues and monetary corruption on the most spectacular scale imaginable. One of their "creatures," the main spokesman for "preventive" war against Mexico, was Senator A.B. Fall, whose efforts were investigated by the American Government, with the result that the "superpatriotic" senator was officially convicted of accepting a $100,000 bribe from American oil interests. He was despatched to a penitentiary.

Notwithstsnding the double pressure of the Vatican and the U.S. Catholic hierarchy and the interested corporations, which had managed to bring public opinion almost to boiling point, the U.S. had the good sense not to intervene, but how near the Catholic Hierarchy and the oil corporations had been to their ultimate objective of involving the nations in an armed conflict can be gauged by the fact that definite military steps were taken by the U.S. Army. Some contingents were put on the alert and were ordered to be ready to cross the U.S. — Mexico border, under the pretext of annual military maneuvers at the Mexican frontiers. The possibility of military intervention had become so real that war correspondents were warned to be in readiness.

Their joint campaign for armed intervention to save their interests went on unabated until the first term of President Roosevelt. Roosevelt, putting first the interests of the U.S., and indeed, of the whole western hemisphere, was not only repelled by the colossal self-motivation of the two partners, but, more important still, he became convinced that the U.S. could not interfere in the internal affairs of Mexico without alarming the already suspicious Latin American countries, and, worse still, without imperilling his "good neighbor" policy — a policy intended to diminish South American suspicions of the U.S., to help in the creation of a political and economic partnership between the North, Central and South American nations. The Catholic Church's clever intriguing to plunge two American countries into a savage war, with the object of recovering her wealth in Mexico, thus ended in failure: yet from such failure there was initiated — or, rather, there came to the surface — an alliance, still very much in the making, between two seemingly inimical, or at least neutral forces: the Catholic Church and the enterprising and vigorous American corporations.

In the successive decade such a partnership became so massively integrated as to influence the course of the political, economic and ideological character, not only of the U.S. and of the western hemisphere, but also of Europe — indeed, of the whole western world.

CHAPTER 16

THE CATHOLIC CHURCH WELCOMES THE RISE OF BOLSHEVISM

The unseemly partnership between the Catholic Church and the energetic commercial colossi of the U.S. during the Mexican "despoliation," a phenomenon generated by their mutual determination to defend, preserve and expand their interests, had not been merely a local alliance but the reflection of a phenomenon of immense proportions which had already occurred outside the western hemisphere — that is, in Europe. For there, out of the grandiose folly of European monarchies engaged with dreams of anachronistic grandeur, prompted by nationalistic jingoism and commercial greed, which had plunged that continent into the sanguinary First World War (1914-18), there had emerged the most infernal aberration seen for millennia: Bolshevism.

This monster, which during most of the previous century had existed only within the confines of puny circles of impractical schemers and bohemian dreamers, had suddenly appeared in the devastation of Europe as a concrete, solid, terrifying colossus, seemingly without brains and without vision, determined to smash everything that belonged to the old order, to the old culture, to the old economy, and to the old religion. It had the strength of a primeval cyclops, but instead of one head proportionate to its size, it sported thousands of little ones — uncultured, all filled with odium and with numberless impossible schemes for a new society, a new man and a new future. Its thousands of little brains were all reeling with the fumes of opiate-like hatred and drawn in every direction. Because of their incoherent anarchy, the giant threatened all and sundry with annihilation.

CHURCH WELCOMES RISE OF BOLSHEVISM

Had this curse from the deep appeared in a small country, it would have been terrifying enough, but it identified itself with an immense one, Russia; and besides annihilating everything and everyone within its home frontiers, stretching from Japan to Poland, from the North to China, it threatened the whole of Europe with its pestilential red bacilli.

Following an initial stupor, Europe, while attempting to rebuild upon its ruins, began to set up its defences against Russian and international Bolshevism. Organized Christianity led the assault, for Bolshevism had defiantly declared itself atheistic. The smashing of religion was going to be one of its chief targets. That brought established Christianity with all its vested interests and temporal wealth, swiftly on the side of all those other establishments which had everything to lose. Individuals, organizations, churches, parties, governments and groups of nations united in a common front to destroy the Reds.

Democracy proved a total failure in several victorious, as well as defeated, countries. The Catholic Church set up Catholic parties to dominate the democratic machines, but since these were unable to stem the Red tide, she finally abandoned them and they were disbanded.

Meanwhile a violently energetic movement had appeared amid the general confusion: Fascism; and curiously enough, it came out of a Roman Catholic country: Italy. The first Fascist dictatorship, in fact, ruled from Rome, next to the throne of Peter.

The Catholic Church was quick to see its potentialities, and she soon came to terms with it; for Fascism had been set up to fight Bolshevism, at home and abroad. Imitators follow suit. In Germany the Nazi party made its first moves in Catholic Bavaria. The Catholic Church blessed that as well. She blessed and supported anyone or anything that would stop Bolshevism. All her religious and diplomatic exertions beween the first and second world wars were inspired and promoted by such grand strategy.

Her motives for so doing seemed logical. Bolshevism was preaching atheism, the total annihilation of organized Christianity. The Catholic Church had the right and the duty to fight back to preserve herself as a religion, as a church, and, above all, as a paramount entity of vested interests. For Bolshevism, besides wanting to destroy religion, wanted to abolish property and to re-distribute wealth. That meant that the Catholic Church in common with other churches, would have been divested of her riches if Bolshevism had conquered Europe. For, notwithstanding all the sundry despoliations of the past, she still held a colossal amount of property throughout Europe and the Americas.

Her partnership with Fascism, therefore, when seen in this light, was as natural as the alliance with the U.S. oil corporations in the Mexican venture. The fact that the Catholic Church cared more for her earthly possessions than for her spiritual treasures was demonstrated by her behavior, or rather activities, *vis-a-vis* Bolshevism. These would seem almost unbelievable were they not concrete and well documented, since the truth of the matter is that she actually secretly welcomed the Bolshevik Revolution.

This seems the most absurd contradiction, in view of the Catholic Church's immediate, uniquivocal, and stubborn condemnation and opposition to Red Russia during almost half a century. Yet, while her anti-Bolshevik exertions were genuine and effective, her secret activities in welcoming Bolshevism were no less real. Such double policies, conducted simultaneously at all levels during a period of years, were the result of the two most basic urges which have always bedevilled her conduct throughout her long existence: insatiable greed for ecclesiastical aggrandizement and an equally insatiable appetite for any prospect of potential earthly wealth.

With the fall of Czarist Russia and the advent of atheistic Bolshevism, the Catholic Church saw a vast panorama of such double conquest open before her eyes. The Bolsheviks, it must be remembered, true to their word, had annihilated the Orthodox Church. That Russian Orthodox Church, having identified herself with the Czars, was second only to the crown in prestige, power, and possessions. Her wealth was colossal, the parasitism of her clergy incredible. The overthrow of the Czarist system, therefore, brought with it the inevitable overthrow of the established Orthodox Church.

To the Vatican, which had waged war against the Orthodox Church since the eleventh century, the downfall of her millenarian rival was too good to be true.¹ The evil of Bolshevism could in this manner be accepted in view of its having destroyed the Orthodox Church — with one proviso, however; that it would give Rome a free hand to finish the task of eliminating Orthodoxy in Russia once and for all.

The deal was accepted, and so it came to pass that while the Vatican was publicly fulminating against Bolshevism, the Bolsheviks in the Kremlin and the Vatican's diplomats in Rome began secret negotiations. Lenin agreed with the pope. Machineries were set up. Papal commissions, some headed by American prelates, were despatched to Bolshevik Russia, disguised as famine-relief missions and the like. In Rome and elsewhere Catholic priests were given accelerated instruction in Russian Orthodox theology and ritual. Grandiose schemes were blueprinted for taking over the Orthodox Church, lock, stock, and barrel, including the claims for her former wealth and lands; these to be put forward at a later stage, once Catholicism had taken over. However, Lenin first, and his successors afterwards, became aware of the extent of the Vatican's game. He grew difficult, and the Kremlin-Vatican secret honeymoon was abruptly cut off round about 1925. It had lasted almost since the beginning of the Bolshevik Revolution in 1917-18.

In 1922 Mussolini became Prime Minister of Italy. The Vatican, who was still flirting with Bolsheviks, coldshouldered him. Indeed, she launched a new Catholic party to fight Fascism. In 1925, however, after the Vatican-Kremlin secret negotiations were cut off, the Vatican reorientated her policy and adopted Fascism. She made a secret deal with Mussolini. The pope would support Fascism provided Mussolini supported the Vatican and fought Bolshevism. The following year, 1926, the Leader of the Catholic Party was ordered by the pope himself to disband the party.² Its former members were advised to support Fascism. In 1929 the pope signed the Lateran Treaty and a Concordat with Mussolini. The Vatican-Fascism betrothal became a formal and official marriage.

The Fascist-Catholic union was an event of the utmost import for Europe and the West, for it created two precedents, or, rather, it laid the foundations for two basic Catholic policies. The first of these was the one by which the Catholic

Church identified herself with the two extreme political embodiments of Western right-wing conservatism — i.e. Fascism and Nazism — whose main objective became the containment and ultimate destruction of Bolshevism, Russian or otherwise.[3] The second, and the one which is of paramount interest to our present scrutiny, was the signing of the Lateran Treaty.

The Treaty was the official seal to the ending of the temporal possessions of the Church, which she renounced once and for all — that is, the gift which Pepin had handed back to her in the eighth century, known as the Papal States.

When in 1870 the Italians had wrenched the Papal States from the popes, the latter "immured" themselves within the walls of the Vatican in protest against the "theft," obdurately refusing to set foot outside the Vatican. Pius IX, Leo XIII, Pius X, Benedict XV and Pius XI, once inside the Vatican never came out of it. With the treaty, however, the popes recognized their former papal territory as an integral part of Italy. In exchange for such recognition, they demanded and received a payment for what had once belonged to them.

It was a solid one. The Catholic Church, a religion which concerns itself with the things of heaven, bargained in the business-like manner of a good, go-ahead modern cocern. She did not give anything for nothing. She asked and bargained for sound, solid, earthly investments in the form of money, bank credit and government bonds. No nonsense about evangelical poverty here; even less about selling all one's riches and giving the proceeds to the poor.

The Treaty was signed in February 1929. Italy recognized the sovereignty of the Holy See, based on the Vatican State, covering in all an area of under a square mile. The pope, within that area, is absolute ruler with religious, judicial and legislative power. The vast territories which the Church had misruled, misappropriated and ruined during a whole millennium, were thus reduced to the microscopic state of the present day. The Church, however, while resigning herself to her loss, insisted on her pound of flesh, and she tried to get as much as she could from the sale. Fascist Italy paid her 750 million lire and Italian 5 per cent bonds to the nominal value of 1,000 million lire.

Physically the Vatican had been reduced to the tiniest state in the world — an independent ecclesiastical machine and working theocracy poised on a speck of dust. The sum she received, although seemingly a large one, was small in view of the thousands of square miles she had to surrender.

Yet the millions she got as "compensation" were the seeds of the billions she was to collect in the following decades. She had almost discarded her traditional ways of collecting the riches of this earth; from now on she would multiply her millions in the same ways as contemporary society — that is, she was going to beat the great industrial and financial concerns, trusts and corporations of the world at their own game, and thus become a mammonic colossus in her own right.

The years 1929-30, therefore, became a milestone in the annals of the Catholic Church, for if the Lateran Treaty closed an era, it also simultaneously opened another. It was the beginning of a period when the wealth of the future would surpass beyond imagination the riches of the past.

CHAPTER 17

FIRST FOUNDATIONS OF A TWENTIETH-CENTURY CATHOLIC FINANCIAL EMPIRE

Following the Lateran Treaty of February 1929, the then reigning pope, Pius XI, set up a special agency to administer the 100 million dollars which Fascist Italy had put into the Vatican coffers. With this agency the Catholic Church initiated a brand-new policy which has characterized her exertions ever since: that is, one of international investments. It was a step which, although taking her along the dangerous road of international speculation, financial somersaults, and political risks, nevertheless within an astonishingly short time yielded rich dividends. The year 1930 can be said to have been the beginning of such a new era.

The agency was not entirely a novel one, being the offspring of an elderly parent, the Administratrion of the Goods of the Holy See, orginally established by Pope Leo XIII as far back as 1878. This had been instituted to deal with the financial affairs of the transformed and battered papal economy after the loss of its temporal dominions in 1870.

The papacy now set out in earnest to devise schemes for the investment of the millions now at her disposal. This she did by promptly investing a large proportion of them in Italy itself. Thanks to this, Vatican money soon found its way into the sinews of Italian high finance, commerce, industry, real estate and the like. The process was greatly facilitated by the Vatican's favorable political relations with the Fascist dictatorship, but if this was an important factor, it was by no means the only one. Others, no less important, contributed to the launching of the successful financial operation. They were of varying nature, but their combined activities played no mean part in the venture.

Some of the main ones can be summarized in the fact that (a) the Vatican had her own banks, (b) she had been exempted by Fascism from crushing taxation, and (c) she had at her service an intelligence machinery second to none. The Vatican directly and indirectly controlled several well-established banking concerns, such as the Bank of the Holy Spirit, founded in Rome in 1608, and the Bank of Rome, founded in 1808, in addition to which she had a finger in the internal machineries of various other banking and financial interests which, while seemingly very remote from the Vatican, nevertheless cooperated very closely with it.

Mussolini had agreed to exempt most of the Vatican's investments from taxation, thus indirectly adding more millions to those already received.

The intelligence network of the Vatican, represented by the higher hierarchy, as well as by Catholics placed in key positions in the financial and industrial world, supplied the Vatican's investors with highly confidential information not available to anybody else, thus making the Vatican privy to profitable speculations before the general public, and, indeed, prior even to some official financial centers in Italy and abroad.

Last, but not least, the Catholic Church had the support of the Fascist dictatorship. The latter saw to it that she should identify herself, not only ideologically (e.g. by opposing Bolshevism at home and abroad) but equally financially with the regime, so that the millions which the Vatican was investing in the Fascist economy should become the best guarantors of her support for Fascism, irrespective of minor disputes about local matters.

The Papal-Fascist policy was a resounding success. For the next ten years, from the signing of the Lateran Treaty in 1929 to the outbreak of the Second World War, the millions had been so skillfully invested that they yielded vast profits in liquid money and evaluation of real estate investment and the general upward reassessment of industrial concerns and shares.

The increasing prosperity of industry resulted from the mountingly belligerent policy of the Vatican's partner, Fascist Italy. For Mussolini, meanwhile, had begun to move upon a path of aggression. A few years after the Lateran Treaty, secure in his knowledge of the support of the Vatican, he embarked on his first large-scale foreign aggression. He attacked, invaded and occupied Ethiopia (1936).

The Catholic Church blessed the venture. Priests and bishops sprinkled departing troops, war planes, tanks and guns with holy water . It was a sight to shock the most cynical of unbelievers. In addition to such brazen support, the Church helped Fascist Italy secretly with money and loans, transacted through devious channels, thanks to the close links which existed between the Italian banks and industrial concerns and the government.

It must be remembered that most Italian industry had been geared to this war for some years, and that the Vatican had invested a good share of its Lateran Treaty millions in Fascist war industries. This it had done, not so much to help Fascism as to help itself, in so far as it judged this a good investment, since war industries, when serving a government in need of armaments and of ever more sophisticated weapons, had always been the best yielders of profits. The Vatican, constantly on the look-out for good gains, had heavily subscribed to them, and as an investor whose main concern was profit, it acted as any lay corporation would. Besides which, there was the allure of immense profits to come with the annexation of Ethiopia. Apart from the religious aspect, the Vatican had been greatly impressed by the vista of great financial prospects and of profitable investments in land, real estate and commercial ventures in a new, vast Fascist Empire in Africa. Mussolini had been generous with promises about this so long as he got the papacy's support.

While the Abyssinian aggression was still very much in progress, the Vatican embarked upon a policy of financial and land investment with consummate expertise. In addition, profiting from Mussolini's war adventure, it invested in sounder, even if slower, profit-yielding speculations. This it did by cleverly exploiting the rise in land values caused by the rapid growth and expansion of Rome itself. Within a few years, the Vatican became landlord of ever more profitable real estate within and outside Rome. It began to own large blocks of flats, offices and valuable stretches of development land on the outskirts of the city. The latter yielded a hundred per cent and sometimes a thousand per cent profits with the inevitable construction boom that followed. In this manner, thanks to its financial expertise, foresight and calculations, thanks to Fascist protection and to its vast ecclesiastical and lay machinery, within the brief span of a decade the Vatican built up a large fortune within that very Italy which only fifty years before had deprived it of the Papal States.

While engaged upon the building of a financial imperium in Italy, the Vatican was by no means idly outside it. Indeed, its activities were no less varied and energetic abroad. In nominally Protestant countries like Holland and Germany, where it had quietly amassed vast funds, it continued its policy of acquisition, avoiding, whenever possible, any spectacular move, since silence and unobtrusiveness were the best methods for pursuing a policy of economic penetration in a potentially inimical community.

Wherever its riches were secure, in nations like Catholic Poland, for instance, where its possessions had multiplied since the country's re-birth after the First World War, the Vatican seldom interfered with ecclesiastical pressure in the domestic affairs of the country. The same was true of Hungary, Czechoslovakia, Austria, Belgium and other European countries where the economic affairs of the Church had a certain stability and therefore a potentially bright future. Thanks to this, the properties in those countries continued to increase in value, while its financial transactions, mainly carried out by the national hierarchies, enjoyed the favor of sundry governments.

Where, however, such stability was lacking and the riches of the Church were threatened, there the Vatican intervened by means of religious, political and diplomatic pressure to defend its interests. These were not only of a religious nature, since more often than not they had a solid, earthly character — land, real estate, stocks and shares. Thus, when a semi-anarchical, Communist-inspired, political abortion called the Popular Front took the reins of France in the middle thirties, the Vatican, which had so definitely committed itself with Fascist Italy and Nazi Germany, got scared. The Popular Front, with its semi-Bolshevik program, seemed likely to be the herald of a Communist France. A Communist France would have behaved — so far as the Vatican's interests were concerned — worse than the French Revolution or the Atheistic French Republic of the beginning of the century.

The Vatican, therefore, came out strongly against the Popular Front Government. Catholic right-wing organizations, modeled on Fascism, came to the fore — e.g. *Les Croix de Feu*. There was talk of an impending civil war, and that was not mere scare-mongering. Civil war had already broken out behind the Pyrenees in neighboring Spain, where a similar government had abysmally failed. Economic crises, political chaos and assassinations had become the order of the day; Communism and anarchy loomed real, menacing and imminent.

In the eyes of the Vatican the continuation of such instability endangered not only the spiritual interest of the Church but also her earthly riches; a large portion of these had already gone, for in 1931 the Spanish Republic did exactly what the French and Russians had already done during their revolutions — dispossessed the Church of all her property. One of the Republic's first actions, in fact, had been to despoil the Jesuits of everything they owned.

Their possessions had not been limited to small parcels that would enable the poor of Christ to plant soybeans; nor were they designed solely to provide for destitute widows and orphans. The Church was the largest, richest landlord in the whole of Spain — even larger than the decadent aristocracy with which she had been so intimately linked that often it was difficult to distinguish one from the other. The Republic impartially dispossessed both of their goods, with the result that it found itself with no less than thirteen million acres of land, which it parceled out in small holdings to about a million peasants.

The property of the Catholic Church in Spain at this period (circa 1933) was, according to John Gunther, worth no less than 500 million dollars, most of this being controlled by the Jesuits. When the Spanish Republic confiscated there her

FOUNDATIONS OF 20TH-CENTURY FINANCIAL EMPIRE

"vast holdings," it was officially confirmed that they were worth 6,000 million pesetas, and before the inflation which followed this meant a worth of more than a billion dollars. This colossal sum, it must be remembered, was what remained after the Church's property had already been substantially reduced by wicked legislators during the previous century, when Spain went through one or two bouts of anti-clericalism. In the old days it had been estimated that the Church owned or controlled between 80 and 90 percent of all the accumulated wealth of the Iberian peninsula.[1] By the start of the First World War this had been cut down to 60 percent.

No wonder, then, that in 1936, when Mussolini went to war in Africa and the Popular Front in France was threatening religion and church property, the Vatican sided with a little-known general who in that same year revolted against the Spanish Government in Madrid. His name: General Franco.

The Spanish Civil War had begun. Whether the Spanish Republic deserved to die, whether it was the forerunner of anarchism and eventually of Bolshevism, whether Franco was right or wrong to rebel against Republican weakness, ineptitude, and demagogery, it is for history to judge. One incontrovertible fact, however, is clear; the Catholic Church supported the rebellion to the hilt — she actually sponsored it. Indeed, she was one of the most important agencies in hatching and promoting it.

The motive that prompted her to do this was not only the safeguarding of her spiritual monopoly, but also and above all the *retention of her immense temporal wealth* — a veritable stranglehold on the economic and financial life of the nation.

"Its cardinal sin is that it is rich in a land of poverty," commented a Catholic paper, referring to the Catholic Church in Spain during the Spanish Civil War.

Following almost four years of bloody civil slaughter (1936-1939) and the holocaust of nearly a million dead, finally the Nationalist forces won. The Catholic Church chanted Te Deums all over the Iberian Peninsula. Her one-billion dollar property was no longer threatened. It belonged to her still. The Lord be praised!

CHAPTER 18

THE TOTAL WEALTH OF THE CHURCH BEFORE AND DURING THE SECOND WORLD WAR

The Spanish Civil War had no sooner ended than the Second World War broke out (September, 1939). The former, though ferocious and beset by dangerous international intervention by the Russian communists, the Italian Fascists, the Nazis, the International Brigade, the Popular Front and others, had by and large been fought and won within the Spanish borders. The Roman Church had saved her immense wealth there. But what now that Hitler was challenging the whole of Europe? Where did she stand as regards her political and economic power outside the Iberian peninsula?

The papacy, although apprehensive, seemed to have little fear. Hitler, notwithstanding periodical minor quarrels with the German Catholic hierarchy, had never threatened to deprive the Church of her wealth. On the contrary, he had ensured Catholic property and stability within the Nazi Reich by a solemn treaty — the concordat signed between Hitler and the pope in June 1933, only a few months after Hitler became Chancellor of Germany in January. This happy state of affairs was due to the fundamental fact that the Catholic Church and Nazism had agreed to support each other. While Hitler guaranteed the Vatican her property and sundry special privileges, the Roman Catholicism ordered her clergy to take an oath of fealty to Nazism. Prayers were said publicly for Nazi Germany. The bishops made all Catholic priests swear that they would never oppose or harm the Nazi dictatorship. It was the same kind of formal marriage as that contracted with Fascist Italy only four years before.

Considered in the light of the above, therefore, no matter how bad Hitler was going to be, basically he would be useful —

in so far as he was the opposite of Stalin, the embodiment of Bolshevism, who sought to annihilate the Church and seize all her property. Hitler set out to destroy not only Stalin, but also Russian and European Bolshevism. Hence, war or no war, he became the most effective defender of the Church, and therefore of all her billions.

Such reasoning, seen from the Vatican's self-interest, seemed sound; and that is why its main promoter, Cardinal Pacelli, later Pope Pius XII, pursued a policy of direct and indirect support for the two most vigorous anti-Communist extreme right-wing movements of the period, Italian Fascism and German Nazism, from the very beginning. The Vatican went so far as to pave the way for Hitler, indeed to compel dissident German Catholics to toe the Vatican-Hitlerian line. The four milestones of such policy were established (1) when the leader of the German Catholic party, Franz von Papen, was named Vice-Chancellor of Nazi Germany, second only to Hitler, in January 1933; (2) When the Deputies of the Catholic party in Parliament voted for the granting of absolute power to Hitler (March 23rd, 1933); (3) When the Vatican gave orders to the German Centre party (Catholic party) to dissolve itself, so as to remove political opposition to Hilter — which it immediately did on July 5th, 1933; And last, but not least, (4) when the Vatican and Hitler signed a concordat in the summer of 1933. According to Article 20 of this concordat, "...On Sundays special prayers...will be offered...for the welfare of the Reich (Nazi Germany)." Even more serious was Article 16: "Before bishops take possession of their diocese, they are to take an oath of fealty to the Reich Representative..." All the details of this policy were first made public by the present author in his work *The Vatican in World Politics*.

Seen retrospectively, the Vatican-Hitlerian collaboration looks like a colossal misjudgment on the part of the papacy. Yet, at that period, the menace of Communism in the domestic and international field was real, pressing and imminent. Communism was endangering not only religion but also the wealth of established religion; including all the wealth of the Catholic Church. At the outbreak of the Second World War, therefore, the Church had no hesitation as to where it stood. Of course, as a faith which had adherents on both sides the

Catholic Church had to play the *official* role of neutrality. She could not antagonize hundreds of millions of Catholics in France, Belgium, Holland, Poland, England and, above all, the U.S.A. But, while playing the role of the Universal Father, Pope Pius XII was supporting the Hitlerian crusade, up to the hilt, as did the various Catholic countries outside the Allied field.

The Hitlerian war, seen from Rome, was essentially an anti-Bolshevik Crusade. When, therefore, in June 1941, Hitler crossed the Russian frontiers, there was open rejoicing at the Vatican. Prayers, novenas and the Cult of Fatima, based on the Virgin's promise that "the Holy Father will consecrate Russia to me," were all revived and magnified.

To help the Virgin's promise come true, no less than to make it possible for Pius XII to consecrate Russia to her, Catholic countries sent contingents to the Russian Front. Catholic Spain sent her Blue Division alongside the Nazi armies, and volunteers flocked thither from practically all Catholic countries. While this was taking place, Franco set out to revive his half-destroyed land. This he did by restoring the fortunes of the Vatican in war-torn Spain. Thus, on January 27th, 1940, he signed a decree formally restoring "the vast property holdings of the Society of Jesus, which had been confiscated by the Rupublic in 1932." At the same time he also restored all lands which either the 1931 Republic or the loyalists had taken over from the Church.

To the Vatican this was a great victory; its billions had returned to its coffers. The Nationalist Government started to rebuild. So did the Church. She did this by buying more property, by investing in real estate, blocks of flats, even buying shares in factories, and by searching frantically for millions of pesetas which had been lost during the Civil War.

During the civil war hundreds of millions of pesetas and of dollars' worth of bonds and stocks had either been confiscated or, having been hidden in safe places, had been forgotten, lost or stolen.

The Spanish hierarchy used every available means at their disposal to retrieve the riches of this world, with zeal usually unmatched when dealing with the treasures of the next. They mobilized experts, at home and abroad. They went so far as to use that most undignified lay commercial vehicle: newspaper advertising. And so it came to pass that the business-minded prelates, early in 1940, began to place advertisements in sundry newspapers, giving numbers and other details of the missing shares, and their efforts were crowned with success.

The triumph, however, was a mixed one. For Roman Catholics now, to their surprise, came to know with exactitude how their church, seemingly so concerned only with the riches of heaven and with moral principles, had been and was still no less concerned with the riches she had held in banks, telephone companies, steamship companies, and other such unspiritual concerns long before the Civil War had even begun, and this after her numberless disclaimers, during the conflict, that she had any temporal interests at all.

On January 7th, 1940, for instance, the newspaper A.B.C. came out with an item listing stocks in the Compania Telefonica Nacional de Espana, and on January 24th another item listed stocks in the Compania Transatlantica. The interesting feature of this was not only that the Spanish Church had invested in such lay concerns, but that she had financial interests in international ones. For whereas the second was connected with the Spanish Transatlantic Steamship Company, the first was part and parcel of the American International Telephone and Telegraph Company — which, incidentally, built the first skyscraper in Spain.

The I.T. & T. did not say that it was the Vatican that owned the stock, not even that it belonged to the hierarchy. The Vatican is too skillful a master in the games of this world to allow that. As in Italy, the U.S. and other countries, most of her property, shares and bonds are camouflaged behind the names of individual Catholic laymen or even purely financial or banking or industrial concerns. In this case, however, the certificates declared that besides laymen there were also clearly hierarchs on the financial bandwagon, like the Metropolitan of Valencia, for instance, who owned several hundred shares of Telephone stock. The Casa Diocesane of the Archbishop of Lerida owned fourteen shares of preferred stock, while the rector of the college of San Jose of Valencia, together with the Jesuits, the college of Maria the Immaculate and sundry other Catholic congregations owned the remainder.

Some of the holders of stocks in the steamship line were the Archbishop of Madrid-Acala (fifty shares numbered 91-101-150), the Vicar General of the Congregation of Hermanos Descalzas de la Redcera Orden de la B.V.M. del Carmen of Tarragona. The Church owned more or less one-third of the total wealth of Spain, movable and immovable. To cite only a few of the concerns in which she had total or partial financial interests, here are a few at random, quoted in *L'Espagne au XXe Siecle*; "The North Railroad, the Transatlantic Steamship Co., the orange groves of Andalusia, the mines of the Basque provinces and in the Rif, and dozens of factories in Catalan, are under the Church's open or occult direction."

To believe, however, that the Church was recovering, amassing and multiplying her millions only in Spain before and during the war would be a mistake. For she was being equally active in other countries, for instance Belgium, Holland, Poland and France. In the last-named country, for example, the Vatican used to control the Franco-Italian Bank of South America, which had a capital of 40 million francs (pre-Second World War), the Societe du Textiles du Nord, in which Vatican participation amounted to 70 per cent of the capital, and similar profitable investments, to such an extent that the total stock-holding participation of the Vatican at that time was estimated at 200 million francs in the buying value at the time of acquisition (1939-40).

Besides this, the Vatican, while relying on the Nazi armies to protect its wealth from the communists at home and abroad, nevertheless deemed it wise to project its financial interests across the ocean. Thus, long before the outbreak of the Second World War it had already taken the first successful steps to implement such a precautionary and lucrative enterprise. It began to invest, not only in South American countries, but also in Protestant U.S.A. This was known at the time. What came as a surprise after the Second World War was the volume of the Vatican's investment there. The extent of the Vatican's participation in big business came to light before hostilities ended, when certain documents fell into the hands of the Italian Socialist leaders. These proved that the Vatican had invested very heavily throughout North America, and although they could not tell the whole story owing to the Vatican's policy of disguising her holdings behind a screen of Catholic and even non-Catholic lay concerns, yet one valuation arrived at by means of reliable criteria placed the amount of the Vatican's stockholding in the U.S. at between 700 and 800 million Italian lire, at 1939 values — this, it must be noted, without counting her property, which we shall scrutinize in more detail shortly.

At the same time the Vatican invested in the South and Central American Republics. In some of these she controlled colossal wealth, represented by land, real estate, commercial enterprises, banking, building, stocks and bonds It was estimated that before and immediately after the Second World War the Vatican's wealth in Europe, represented by stocks, bonds, shares and the like was more than 3 billion lire, expressed always in the value of the lira in 1939, or 120 billion in the 1969 value of the lira. And since we are dealing with Italian currency, it might be appropriate to add to the sums above the approximate amount of the Vatican's riches in Italy itself, as represented, either directly or indirectly, by her ownership of land and real estate in that country.

A valuation of the houses, buildings and land held by her through religious orders, religious institutes and the like would be 4,000 million lire at 1939 value or 190,000 million at the 1960 exchange.

When, therefore, Hitler lost the war (1945) and Europe lay in ruins, her material, political and financial structures battered and with Stalin's Red battalions occupying a third of the continent, the Vatican, grateful to God that the Russian Bolsheviks had not planted the Red Flag on the dome of St. Peter's, could still look to the future with understandable assurance and, indeed, confidence. For, while relying upon the protection of the Lord, it felt even more confident that such spiritual protection became more formidable when strengthened by the solid billions in liquid cash, lands, real estate and industrial stock, which it had so providentially amassed in the Old and especially in the New World.

CHAPTER 19

THE VATICAN INVESTS MILLIONS IN WAR INDUSTRIES — TRANSFERS MOST OF THEM TO THE U.S.A.

A Vatican bank, Instituto per le Opere di Religione, was set up with one basic objective: "to keep and administer the capital intended for religious congregations." If there was a classic camouflage behind which to carry on activities that had nothing whatsoever to do with those apparently intended, here was one, since at the time of its foundation the Instituto's specific task was simply to transfer church capital and money out of beleaguered Europe. It was founded in 1942 by Pope Pius XII, at the height of the Second World War, when Hitler, after having successfully reached the outskirts of Moscow, got stuck there and, to His Holiness's chagrin, could not budge.

Pius XII, though still confident of a Hitlerian victory, began to have his first secret doubts concerning the final outcome. For the overall picture of hostilities had greatly changed since their inception. The U.S. had been brought onto the battlefield; the mounting impetus of the American initiative and energy had already begun to affect the balance of power. U.S. armaments, men and industrial might were being felt everywhere. Unless a miracle happened, Hitler might lose the war, after all.

In view of the changed circumstances, therefore, the best policy was to help Providence to take precautionary steps concerning the wealth of the Church by transferring it to safer shores, for instance. And where could these mobile riches find safety better than within the distant borders of the U.S.A.? After all, supposing that God had abandoned Hitler. His designs are inscrutable. What then? Stalin and his Bolshevik hordes might sweep through ruined Europe. What — they might even enter Rome! If the allies prevented that, since it was not in their interests to see the Russians in Western Europe, what could they do if the Italian Communists set up a Communist dictatorship in Italy? Nothing.

A Communist Italy or France or Germany would mean one certain thing: the dispossession of all the wealth of the Catholic Church within the country.

It was with this in mind that Pius XII founded the Instituto, a clever move to safeguard the Vatican's financial interests. For the Instituto, while cleverly integrated within the ecclesiastical machinery of the Roman Church, and to all appearances and purposes a purely religious institution, plausible and logical, in reality — at this stage, at any rate — was nothing more than a "flexible instrument for arranging multiple financial activities."[1]

What did all this mean in the middle of the war? It meant, as an authoritative organ explained, that: "this bank allowed the Holy See to undertake transfers across closed frontiers, and it profited richly from the rare privilege of being able to transfer foreign exchange in a partitioned world."[2]

The partitioned world was truly partitioned. By millions of armed men. By closed frontiers. By barbed wire. By bombers. By tanks. By submarines. Nobody could pass, and that applied to generals, politicians, diplomats, heads of state. There was one exception, however: the representatives of the Vatican. For them, there were no such restrictions. As the envoys of a religion and the delegates of a sovereign state — the officially neutral Vatican City — they could come and go at their pleasure, from one belligerent country to another, from one continent to another. From battling Europe to Canada, the U.S., and South America. The carriers of spiritual comfort — but, even more, the carriers of bank-notes, stocks, bonds, gold and silver.

For that is precisely what the Instituto did. It transferred increasingly large sums of money from the Vatican to Canada and the U.S.A. The valuables were drawn, not only from the coffers in Rome, but from all over Italy, from France, even from inside Hitlerite Germany itself. The pope saw to it that certain very trusted individuals within the national hierarchies — *uomini di fiducia*, as they were and are still called at the Vatican — were charged with this very delicate task.

As operation "transfer of money from Europe to the Americas" progressed, more and more interested parties became involved in it. European and American interests jumped on the Vatican bandwagon, particularly since Hitler's military fortunes continued to plunge downward. American individuals and corporations with stocks and shares in Germany asked the Vatican to help them save what they could from the impending debacle. The Vatican helped, directly and indirectly. It began in earnest to exert increasing pressure upon certain politicians and even the military to ensure the "saving" of certain factories, buildings or installations in various parts of Hitlerite Europe. The pressure to spare such industrial, war-geared installations would, in all probability, have been exerted independently of the Vatican, by interested parties within the U.S., yet it is not amiss to remind ourselves of the fact that at this period the Catholic Church was intimately connected with the war set-up, not only because of the basic policy of support for the anti-Communist front represented by Fascist Europe, but also because of the billions of lire she has invested in the sundry factories within that beleaguered continent.

The Church's connection with war industries was not a recent one. It stretched back during the previous decade. The Vatican, in fact, had invested and re-invested in sundry industrial concerns, via very ingenious and very intricate financial devices, most of the millions of lire which it had received from the Fascist Government in 1929-30 with the signing of the Lateran Agreement. At that time its policy was to use part of the capital in certain booming Italian munition plants which Mussolini had set in motion in preparation for the forthcoming invasion of Abyssinia (1935-6).

When Fascist Italy did eventually invade Abyssinia, these plants naturally became the main suppliers of the invading armies. The Vatican authorities kept a discreet silence about their participation in the profitable enterprise. Fascist Italy saw to it that the Vatican should not be embarrassed in the matter — at least in the financial field, since in the political she came openly to the fore by supporting Mussolini's adventure.

VATICAN INVESTS MILLIONS IN WAR INDUSTRIES

While it is true that Pius XI personally was not directly involved in all this, he nevertheless did not reprimand the Italian Church for the Abyssinian invasion. Concerning the financial support, or rather partnership, which she gave Mussolini, the pope was little aware of the Vatican's financial interest in it all, since the finances were not in his hands. A group of specialists had dealt and were dealing with them as they thought fit. The ramifications and intricacies of their investments were certainly beyond the pope's comprehension. The Vatican's millions had been dispersed in profitable ventures, among which were the chemical and war enterprises which now were supplying Mussolini's armies.

The chief engineer of Vatican involvement in war profiteering was a legendary financial wizard, a Sgr. Nogara. This man, who in fact controlled and played with the Vatican's money for decades, multiplied her millions a hundredfold. His rule was to exclude theology and religion from essentially financial matters, and his motto was that of Pope Benedict XV: Business is Business. Pope Benedict, it should be remembered, invested some of the Vatican's money with the Turks.

War industries have always been celebrated for the profits they yield. Nogara's policy of investing with them continued after the Abyssinian venture. He invested in allied industries, chemicals, steel plants and the like. From Fascist Italy he extended into semi-Fascist Yugoslavia, Albania, and above all Nazi Germany.

Thus the Vatican, prior to the Second World War, had many of its millions involved with a vast complex producing war materials. The secretive financial transactions of Nogara saw to it that they became gold-mines for the Vatican. Nogara also linked Vatican finances with certain large U.S. corporations. When eventually the U.S. was drawn into the conflict and these were geared to war production, the Vatican began to make considerable profits on the other side of the Atlantic. Its financial involvement with the vast war industries of Europe and America has never been fully disclosed, and probably never will be. But indirect and direct evidence from unexpected quarters confirmed its reality and also its extent, although unfortunately details are lacking.

A friend of the present author, Dom Luigi Sturzo, had personal information about the Vatican's war involvement from the pope himself, that is, from Pius XI, the very man who had signed the treaty with Mussolini and who, in a moment of elation, had called the Duce "the man sent by Divine Providence." We have already seen why the Vatican had backed right-wing extremism between the two World Wars to contain advancing Communism at home and abroad. This we have dealt with in detail in another work, *The Vatican in World Politics*. Dom Sturzo was no mean figure. He was the founder-leader of the Italian Catholic party, the only political party which could have stopped Mussolini from becoming dictator. Pope Pius XI, following secret political deals with Mussolini, commanded Sturzo to disband his movement. Sturzo did so. He went into exile, mostly spent in London.

Sturzo was however kept well informed about most of the Vatican's important activities. A year or two before the outbreak of the Second World War, Pope Pius XI realized that he had made a political mistake in supporting Fascism. He tried, but in vain, to remedy the results. He resumed contact with Dom Luigi. Among other things, he informed the ex-leader of the Catholic party of his "deep sorrow" that much Vatican money had been involved in the war industries of Italy during the Abyssinian war, but there was nothing he could do about it, since financial matters were in the hands of certain "lay" people, who did what they wanted with them. He also told him that the Italian factories were preparing for a world war.

After the war, Sturzo returned to Italy, and his Catholic party was renamed the Christian Democratic party. Dom Sturzo was determined to expose the Vatican involvement with Fascism. He had seen documents supplied to him not only by anti-Fascist Catholics but also by certain delegates to the Nuremberg trials. When Pius XII heard of this, he forbade Dom Sturzo to "meddle with things past," lest he harm the Church in her endeavors to "reconstruct a new Europe." Once more Sturzo had to obey.

But the most damning proof of the Vatican involvement in the war industries came from an even more unusual source — this time from Yugoslavia, from a friend of the present author, General Bora Mirkovich. When in 1941 Yugoslavia

VATICAN INVESTS MILLIONS IN WAR INDUSTRIES

signed a pact with Hitler, General Mirkovich, on March 27, 1941, unseated the government, abrogated the pact, and brought Yugoslavia in on the side of the Allies. The importance of the move was tremendous, and directly affected the course of the Second World War. That this was so was proved at the Nuremberg trials. "It became crystal clear that...the decision of 27 March 1941 to choose certain destruction of their homes and country by Hitler, rather than the dishonor of being his accomplices, *had a decisive effect upon history*."

Hitler's war-plan was totally upset. "Hitler reacted immediately. He at once summoned a meeting of his gernerals and the commanders of his satellites. In his secret report of this meeting, held on that same day, he underlined that 'the beginning of the Barbarossa operation will have to be postponed for up to four weeks.'" (Barbarossa was the code name for the attack against Russia.) The four weeks' delay forced upon Hitler by General Mirkovich was decisive for the whole war, according to Karl Ritter, German Foreign Office Liaison Officer with the Nazi High Command. "This delay," he stated, "cost the Germans the winter battle before Moscow, and it *was there that the war was lost*." (Quoted by Anthony Eden, British Foreign Minister, later Lord Avon, in his *Memoirs*.) Winston Churchill that same morning told the British people: "I have great news. Early this morning the Yugoslav nation found its soul."

The writer emphasizes all this to show how General Mirkovich contributed to history and was not one to talk about important matters lightly or without proof. What he revealed to the writer should therefore be taken at its face value and not dismissed with a shrug, since the events just related have had a direct bearing upon our present subject — the Vatican's financial participation in the vast sphere of war industry.

General Mirkovich never mentioned any specific figure or even individual names, but nevertheless the impact of the revelation concerning the Vatican's financial involvement in the war made a tremendous impression upon him, to such an extent that he took a decision which, had it been successfully carried out, would have resulted in a tremendous calamity for world culture. He claimed to have come across financial and diplomatic documents which revealed the extent to which certain Italian financial interests had been involved in supplying war materials to Yugoslovia, controlling interests in Yugoslav armament manufacture and, above all, closely linked with the Nazi war machinery, and that these were closely associated with concerns directly manipulated by the Vatican wizard Nogara. It seemed — always according to General Mirkovich — that the Vatican became so involved with the three partners (Yugoslavia, Italy and Germany) that it could be regarded a silent associate of this unholy trio.

The General's bitterness was the greater since practically all the contraband weapons and armory which the Catholic Croats, the Ustashi, had assembled and which shortly afterwards they used ruthlessly against Yugoslavia itself, had been supplied from such quarters, so that Ustashi had been directly financed, not only by Mussolini, but also by Pope Pius XII.

General Mirkovich had planned to collect all the relevant documents, but the urgency of Hitler's attacks upon Yugoslavia diverted his attention from the matter of the Vatican's involvement. Be that as it may, he was so incensed that he decided there and then to send several squadrons of the Yugoslav Air Force to bomb the Vatican. One squadron was assembled and made ready one night for the raid, but just before orders were given, there was a sudden worsening of the weather and the squadron had to remain grounded. General Mirkovich's bombing expedition had to be postponed, and he decided to try a couple of days later. The postponement saved Vatican City from obliteration, for shortly afterwards the Yugoslav Air Force was crippled by Nazi bombers, which swept over and destroyed most of the Yugoslav craft on the ground. It was thus one of the paradoxes of the Second World War that the Catholic Church owed the salvation of its headquarters to none other than Adolf Hitler.

The destruction of Vatican City, with all its immense treasures of religion, art and history, would have been unforgivable, a loss beyond reckoning for Western civilization. Nevertheless, we have related the episode to show that a man of the caliber and honesty of General Mirkovich, confronted by the financial involvement of the Vatican in the profitable business of war, could be made to lose his better judgment.

As hinted above, the extent of such involvement at this period will in all probability never be disclosed, although, no doubt, screened by the financial convolutions of certain huge industrial giants, it might one day be unearthed and brought to light. While the testimony of the two distinguished and responsible personages we have cited has little support in terms of facts and figures, it may stand as relevant to our enquiry.

The result of the war policy of the Catholic Church or, rather, of the skillful moves she undertook when Nazi fortunes began to decline — was that when finally Hitler shot himself in a Berlin shelled by the Red army, Pius XII, in the total collapse of Hitlerian Catholic Europe, had at least the satisfaction of having salvaged something by the transfer of millions of dollars to the U.S.

The flow of Catholic investments did not stop with the cessation of hostilities, but continued unabated for some years afterwards. For while it was true that the Red Army had been stopped from sweeping over defeated Europe, that the U.S. had become Europe's protector, and that the Vatican had successfully initiated a political-ideological partnership with her, it was nonetheless also true that the Communists of France and, above all, of Italy were seriously threatening to take over the government in Paris and Rome.

That spelled danger for the Vatican, so it continued its transfer policy throughout the years immediately after the war.

The danger became real and immediate during the first decade. Pope Pius XII deemed it necessary to intervene, and he ordered the Italian electorate to vote for the Catholic party. Anyone voting for the Communists or even for the Socialists would be excommunicated.

While stemming the Red menace, the Vatican began to look around post-war Europe with an eye to investing its millions wherever these millions could best be made to yield good dividends; and as Europe began to boom, and sundry "economic miracles" succeeded one another, the Vatican's financial expertise was set in motion. Her skill and intuition in choosing the right investments proved highly successful once more. She redoubled her efforts to consolidate her funds with prosperous industrial and commercial shares, stocks and bonds, with mounting boldness, in private, governmental, small and large concerns, not only in Italy, but also in France, Germany, Switzerland and even in England.

The Vatican unashamedly invested its money in Riviera casinos, such as the San Remo, in beverages as alien to holy water as the water Perrier in France, in the Societa Generale Immobiliare, already mentioned, and in building concerns. Sgr Vittorio Valletta, head of the automobile giant, Fiat of Turin, and Sgr Presenti, head of the Italcementi cement group, were directors of such concerns. L'Immobiliare assets in real estate in 1969-70 were valued at between 18 and 19 million pounds sterling. This company also controlled numerous industrial, touristic and other concerns, including three-quarters of Rome's Hilton Hotel. Sogene, a large branch of the Immobiliare owned other companies in which the Vatican was a large shareholder and which had a board of directors which included representatives of the Bastoggi Financial concern, Italpi, and the big insurance company, Assicurazioni Generali, Ceramica Pozzi, Italgaz, Acqua Marcia, the Pantanella milling and pasta concerns and many similar enterprises. It should be remembered that the Vatican did not pay any taxes in Italy, as in so many other countries, so that for decades it held a continuous and unfair advantage over its commercial, industrial and financial rivals, as much out to make profits as was the Catholic Church.

The grossly anachronistic treatment of the Church's financial tax-exempt manipulations *vis-a-vis* her financial rivals was too blatant not to provoke a general reaction to her privileged status, expecially in view of the fact that, while profiting from the services rendered by the state to her, and paid for by the ordinary taxpayer — she gave nothing whatsoever in return, not even any kind of *ex gratia* offering out of the enhanced profits which resulted from her immunity from taxation. In Italy this anomaly was increasingly resented, but the efforts of various movements to make the Vatican pay taxes were consistently defeated by the dominant Catholic party. Finally in 1968 a climax was reached when the Vatican, after endless legal devices, found itself cornered and agreed to submit to a partial form of taxation "on its stock earnings." The payment due proved to be no less than a thousand billion lire per year.[3]

This sum revealed the enormous financial assets which she controlled in Italy alone, making her, not only a paramount political force but also an economic factor of the utmost importance in the life of the nation. Nino Lo Bello the economic-financial correspondent of the *New York Herald Tribune*, has summarized in detail the paramountcy of the Vatican investments and economic hold in a book well worth studying.[4] The economic weight of the Vatican's wealth and hold on Italian finance, industry, and commerce had now become one of the main factors in the prosperity of the Italian peninsula.

The authoritative *Economist* of London at this period did not hesitate to say as much: "The Vatican could theoretically throw the Italian economy into confusion if it decided to unload all its shares suddenly and dump them on the market."[5]

How large was the Catholic Church's Italian portfolio twenty-five years after the Second World War? The answer to the question is a difficult one, since the Vatican is the only state which has consistently refused to disclose its real budget or to let "outsiders" know the value of its assets. But unofficial estimates by Italian governments at various times, based on the scanty information they were able to come by, seemed to coincide with the nebulous hints dropped by the Vatican.

According to these estimates, the Holy See owned between 15 and 20 per cent of the total stocks quoted on the Italian Stock Exchange. In December 1964 the total value of all these shares was 5,500 billion lire, which put the capital invested by the Vatican, as early as 1964, in Italian stocks alone, at about 500 million dollars. By 1972 this had risen to above 700 million. Yet the Vatican's investments in Italy represented, according to reliable Vatican sources, only beween one-tenth and one-twelfth of the whole of its world investments.

This gives the total astronomical figure of 5,000 million dollars — at a conservative estimate!

CHAPTER 20

WHY THE CATHOLIC CHURCH IS THE RICHEST CHURCH IN AMERICA

The U.S. is nominally a Protestant country. It prides itself on its separation of church and state. It harbors over three hundred prosperous Protestant denominations.

Yet the Catholic Church is the U.S.'s largest single religious unit. She is the most closely knit, with the exception, perhaps, of the Jewish fraternity. She is the most powerful, ethically, socially and politically; and she is the richest church of all, not only in the U.S., but in the whole of the northern hemisphere — and indeed, in all the Americas, North, Central and South.

Her spectacular status in the north cannot be comprehended at one single glance. Although the largest single religion, yet she is still a minority, with some fifty million adherents out of a population of approximately two hundred million.

The explanation, of course, could be found in the elementary formula: Divisibility creates weakness, unity strength. But even while accepting the veracity of this, the Catholic phenomenon is still not so easy to understand.

Here we are concerned with the wealth amassed by the Catholic Church in the U.S. The process and the results need clarification, not only when dealing with the instrumentality of gathering and multiplying riches. The basic method of collecting data about bonds, stocks, and shares, while applicable to a steel corporation or even to Coca Cola, is not appropriate to the Catholic Church. Besides being a corporation — or, rather, a multi-corporation in the ordinary lay significance of that word — she is simultaneously a religious system, and the accumulation of her wealth derives solely from her being so.

WHY CATHOLIC CHURCH IS RICHEST CHURCH OF U.S.A.

Religion is still the greatest imponderable of society. The United States, the most materially prosperous land in the world, is deeply affected by this religious imponderable even more than Europe was in the past, or still is in the present.

Such an intangible factor is basically identifiable with her religious credences. The latter notwithstanding their ideological, denominational and ecclesiastical diversities and even contradictions, have one common denominator. They spend a most un-edifying amount of energy upon the accumulation of material wealth in the guise of opulent, costly and numerous edifices, skillfull acquistion and remunerative exploitation of urban areas, or by the collection and investment of dollars and cents throughout the nation.

These predominantly financial and business operations are promoted, carried out and indeed are energized by the intangible and yet concrete reality of the sundry beliefs, operating via and within the framework of organized religion. Unless this basic factor is taken into account, the phenomenon of the fantastic wealth of the churches of America cannot be fully understood.

It might be argued with justification that the phenomenon is not peculiar to the United States of America. It is not. Yet in Europe it took centuries if not millennia for organized religion to control sizeable portions of the collective wealth of the sundry European nations.

How is it, then, that in so young a country as the United States, born only yesterday, the churches have reached the stage where they can beat the great industrial, financial and oil corporations on their own ground, and indeed at their own game?

The answer is twofold.

It can be found in the most basic characteristics of the American man: (a) energy, initiative, productivity, lack of inhibition, all cemented by the deepest possible concern for material riches and the most idealistic generosity — two features which seem to have become the hallmark of contemporary *Homo Americanus* — and (b) atavistic emotionalism and religious naivete. All this has resulted in making *Homo Americanus* a most generous benefactor to his church, and also making him ready to identify himself, his personal and communal success, with that of his church. Hence, if he becomes rich, why should not his church partake of such riches?

Institutions are the reflection of the type of society which creates and tolerates them. The churches are no exception; hence the churches partake of the materialistic idealism of American society, and they are most successful in exploiting with ruthless enthusiasm the elementary emotionalism of the American believer. When to this there is added a large tincture of patriotism, racialism and clanishness (the chief ingredients of Protestantism), and yet further a mysticism, a sense of uniqueness, and the belief that she is the only true church — which are additional ingredients of Catholicism, then the religious naivete of the American believer is exploited to the full, even more thoroughly than an oil well is sucked dry by any successful oil company.

This is borne out by the concrete, substantial and fantastic yields of the U.S. churches. Their business, it seems, is beating Big Business at its own game.

Consider the following: In 1962, the U.S. Treasury Department showed that church goers of America reported on their income tax returns that they had given 2.9 billion dollars to the churches. By 1966, the Protestant Churches were themselves reporting 3 billion dollars income annually, as shown in the *Yearbook of American Churches*. This figure does not include contributions to either the Roman Catholic or Jewish communities, neither of which officially report to the American public. By 1967, annual giving was estimated by the news services in America, from unofficially governmental sources, as being about 6 billion dollars a year, or 16 million dollars a day.[1] Since then the figures have climbed even higher. In which other country has the value of the churches' possessions grown to such incredible figures within so short a period?

The master in the field, as in so many others, is the Catholic Church. We have already related how back in 1942, Pope Pius XII created the Instituto, with the precise objective of sending money abroad. Much of this was placed in the U.S. Why did he choose the U.S.A.? Not so much because it was geographically safe from the Bolshevik armies or the European red rabbles of the post-war world. Central and South America were equally well placed. Pius sent the Vatican's millions to the U.S. be-

WHY CATHOLIC CHURCH IS RICHEST CHURCH OF U.S.A.

cause the Catholic Church there was already an economic and political power in her own right, and because enough of her members, lay and ecclesiastic, had infiltrated themselves within the framework of the U.S. to identify the interests of the Church with that of the country, and vice versa.

Apart from the mutual communion of ideological and political interests between the Catholic Church and the U.S., which we have treated at length in another book, *Catholic Power Today*, one of the main reasons why the Vatican chose the U.S. as her depository and banker was that the Church there was already a billionaire and that as such she commanded sufficient authority in the monetary field to ensure that her interests were properly safeguarded.

Money is power, and since power can be translated into money, the combination of the two can create a climate for furtherance of the first or of the second or simultaneously of both. U.S. Catholicism was in that happy position, so that after the Second World War we saw the spectacle, not only of the Vatican siding with the U.S., one of the victors, in the creation of a Vatican/Washington Axis during the ideological cold war which followed, despite her consistent support for Hitler during the war, but also in the consolidation of a Vatican/Washington economic front — indeed, a financial partnership.

The Vatican sent millions to the U.S., and the U.S. "lent" millions to the Vatican. The transactions at times followed orthodox lines. At others, they did not. Most were camouflaged, as is the Vatican's custom, behind the screen of individuals, banks and corporations, which served as dummies to save the Church from potential embarrassment. At times deals were carried out above the head of the American administration, and therefore above the heads of the American people, by means of private and secret arrangements between high government officials and the Catholic hierarchy.

We shall content ourselves with quoting one example: that concerning the Strange Case of the Vatican Gold. The first news of this celebrated gold sale "leaked" through a story in the *United Nations World Magazine* of December 1952. The article asserted that the Vatican had purchased many millions in gold ingots from the great United States gold supply in the last few years. In Europe rumor had it that the Vatican was given preferential treatment in these transactions — namely, that the pope was allowed to buy the precious metal at 34 dollars per ounce, one dollar below the pegged rate of 35 dollars per ounce. *The United Nations World Magazine* article further declared that the Vatican was "heavy" with stock in leading American industries.

Several curious Americans thereupon approached the U.S. Treasury Department, as well as the Vatican representative in Washington Msgr. Amleto Cicognani, for confirmation. Over the signature of A. N. Orarly, the U. S. Government officially said that it had sold 26.8 million dollars in gold ingots to the Vatican in a series of transactions. Bishop McShea, for the papal representative, admitted the purchase of gold by the Vatican to the degree of "say, 17 or 18 million dollars" and denied any favoritism in price. He added that a large number of papal ingots were held in the Federal Reserve vaults in New York. The bishop also revealed that the Vatican had over a given period "sold back about $5 million, making a total net sale of $21.8 million." (His figures were more accurate than those of the Treasury Department).

But Bishop McShea denied that the Vatican had invested heavily in American industry and that these investments yielded heavily during the sales boom in the war years.[2] After further enquiries, denials, counter-denials and odd silences, finally in a letter in the April 1953 issue of the *United Nations World Magazine* there came a declaration from the very same Secretary of the Treasury, declaring that there was no truth in the suggestion that the gold had been sold at a dollar below the pegged rate.[3]

The case was illuminating because it confirmed — as if there was any need of confirmation — that the Vatican was buying, at one dollar per ounce below current market price, *and selling for profit*, millions of dollars' worth of gold in the U.S., and also that it was its practice to do business with the U.S. Government, to its own advantage. Further the news of the deal in question had never been made public. It also appeared that sections of the U.S. government machine were influenced and controlled by certain American citizens — that is, by Catholics acting as agents of the Vatican, for example, Bishop

WHY CATHOLIC CHURCH IS RICHEST CHURCH OF U.S.A.

McShea, an American citizen who openly admitted, when asked how he was so well informed on the gold sale, that *he had represented the Vatican at the time of the papal purchase.*[4]

The Vatican's gold purchase just mentioned, was one of many carried out in secret; but the hold of the Vatican upon the financial life of the U.S. is not confined to sporadic gold purchases. It is effective within a far wider and more comprehensive field, although great efforts are made to see that it remains as secret as possible. The Vatican's spokesman, Bishop McShea, denied, for instance, that the Vatican had invested in American industry, yet it was well known that the Vatican had done so, and very heavily, at that!

The Holy See, in fact, besides being an important shareholder in what now is known as the Bank of America, had invested additional millions with sundry corporations — to quote only two; the American Anaconda Copper Company and the Sinclair Oil Company. And this to the tune of about 35 million pounds or $100 million. About twenty years ago it was found that in the New York State banking records the Catholic Church showed investments in stocks and bonds with hundreds of corporations. Among others, these included Baltimore & Ohio R. R., Rock Island, Eire, Seabord, Missouri Pacific, Pere Marquette; Goodyear Tire & Rubber, Firestone, Fisk, U. S. American Smelting; Commonwealth Edison, Brooklyn Edison, N. Y. Edison, Pacific Gas & Electric, West Penn Power, American Commonwealth Power, Texas Electric; Atlantic City Convention Hall, Louisiana Hotel Co., Squire Building, Lane Bryant, Fox Playhouses, Fox Theater (St. Louis), Denver Joint Stock Land Bank, Savoy Plaza Hotel, National Dairy, Thermoid, Washington Silk, Pillsbury Flour.[5]

Since then the Catholic Church has managed to penetrate even more deeply within the financial and industrial framework of American society. This she has done to such an extent that at present she is one of the major factors, practically within most of the big U.S. corporations, trusts, banks and industrial giants of America. Because of her successful infiltration and astounding financial power, the Catholic Church, therefore, is *de facto* one of the most influential "presences" in the economic activities of the U.S. and, as a result, of the economic well-being of the western hemisphere.

CHAPTER 21

MEMBER OF THE BILLIONAIRE CLUB OF THE U.S.A.

Roman Catholic Church in the U.S. is an economic giant, not so much because she has penetrated within the economic sinews of the giant corporatons, trusts and banks of America, but because she has accumulated lands and real estate, and controls institutions whose real, solid, and material value in terms of money made of her an economic colossus in her own right, indeed, perhaps the greatest colossus of all.

If the hyperbolic dictum, "What is good for General Motors is good for the U.S.," should be taken with judicious flexibility, the dictum, "What is good for the Catholic Church is good for the U.S. and vice-versa," although never openly stressed at present is nevertheless one of the most concrete realities of the economic and political life of the country. This is not so much because of the financial speculations of the Vatican or because of its sporadic buying and selling of gold ingots on the fluctuating international market, but because the Catholic Church in America has become the largest institutionalized amasser of wealth in the country. For an institution which came on the North American continent as poor as the proverbial church mouse, this is not only a grand success story, it is the greatest economic miracle of an age inured to spectacular miracles of all kinds.

Miracles are worked by the saints, or by God Himself — it depends on the degree of your faith, or very often on the amount of silver you put in the collection plate. The Catholic Church worked the American miracle by a masterly combination of the two. U.S. Protestantism has the theological naivete of do-good rural adolescents, Catholicism the single-track-minded dedication of religious somnambulists. While the former — that is, the Protestant churches — remain a fairly considerable economic power in the land, the latter, thanks to the massiveness of her wealth, the purposefulness of its use, the numerical integration of her adherents and her single-mindedness, has become the wealthiest religious system in the world, surpassing ever the position of Catholicism in the Middle Ages.

For whereas in the Middle Ages it took her centuries to become rich, in the U.S. she has become a billionaire church with the speed, the energy and the clamor the boy who, from selling newspapers at a street corner, becomes the head of a big corportion when still in his twenties.

How was it done? It was done by the urge to keep the Faith intact. By the urge to proselytize. By the urge to become respectable, powerful, and superior. By the belief that, being the only true church, it is her mission, duty and obligation to convert the U.S. into a fief of Eternal Rome. These and other factors have all contributed from the very beginning to unite the Catholic minorities in racial, ethnic and religious groups which, no matter how diverse, nevertheless have one common link: their Catholicity. With the result that, instead of dispersing their energies, they have united by cementing all their economic and religious forces together.

The sum of all these diversified urges, despite the sense of economic and social inferiority which the Catholics experienced within a community of "heretics," plus the basic fact that the majority of Catholic emigrants were literally the most depressed, illiterate, superstitious and ignorant sections of the emigrants which Europe sent to North America, tended to give to the immature Catholic community a feeling of unity. This sense of imagined and real affinity gave the separate European emigrating section comfort, protection, self-assurance. The last quality, once the Catholic emigrants had shot their roots and began to throw out their first branches, turned overtly into aggressiveness. The process is still in evidence now, although it has not yet passed the second generation, and this could not be otherwise, since by 1972 half of the adult Catholic population of the U.S. were immigrants or children of immigrants.

While it is true that other racial and ethnic groups followed the same process, they lacked the unifying strength which only Roman Catholic Church can give as a kind of spiritual cement to the most disparate and conflicting interests. Such cement is composed of two main binding ingredients peculiar to itself: (a) the protectiveness of a church which is truly universal, and (b) the granitic belief that only the Catholic Church is the true church. These ingredients are the most fundamental inner motive force of Catholicism in general and of Catholicism in the U.S. in particular.

When fifty million people hold these views and are manipulated by a hierarchy which is itself directed from Rome, we find a vast, efficient, effervescent, enthusiastic, dynamic Catholic system which stubbornly refuses to be integrated in the non-Catholic community in which it strives because it is determined to integrate these non-Catholic entities within its own community.

This missionary-inspired system is potentially capable of indefinite expansion. Its basic strategy is not only to keep the Catholics Catholic, but to make Catholics of Non-Catholics, by existing, by expanding, and by conquering.

This must be remembered if we wish to understand one of the most important facets of U.S. Catholicism — the phenomenal growth of its wealth, since this is the inner drive which has knit the Catholic community into such a powerful religious, political, and economic unit within the U.S. This ever-expanding unit has become a self-centered system within the national system, at the local, state, and federal level — not only in the purely religious field; not only within the cultural field, but equally in the financial sphere. Hence the almost frenzied urge of the Catholic Church in the U.S. to control her own cultural system. This she does by founding her own schools, superior institutes and universities. Hence her aggressiveness in the purchasing of real estate, buildings, properties of all kinds. These activities have made of the Catholic Church an important and ever-expanding owner of increasingly valuable pieces of property, and since the bulk of U.S. Catholicism is urban, and since she had to erect her schools in urban centers, her property there has gone up in value, with the result that in terms of dollar power she became a super-millionaire almost without even realizing it.

MEMBER OF BILLIONAIRE CLUB OF U.S.A.

The logical promotion of the strategy which led her to control her own educational system did not end there. It spread of necessity into the medical field. The Catholic Church has her own specific moral and ethical laws, which must not be by-passed or adulterated by a non-Catholic society. Hence the necessity of running her own health service, her own clinics, hospitals and the like. Hence the need to buy land and erect buildings for the purpose. Hence her finding herself, in due course, a multi-millionaire also in the world of medical care. But then, since we live in an age of mass media, the Vatican had also to control, or at least have a say in these as well, and so her exertions were directed in that field with great success. And, since a colossal educational and medical system needs money, it became necessary to find funds somewhere, besides the contributions of the faithful themselves.

And so commercial associations were readily established with the world of business. Shares were bought in prosperous units, land speculations proved remarkably profitable, commercial enterprises were owned directly and indirectly by the Catholic Church, with the result that soon she found herself a multi-millionaire in this field as well.

The numerous dioceses and parishes, the local bishops and cardinals, also joined in these schemes of ownership and all kinds of projects and enterprises raised funds which were invested and made to yield profits, which amounted to millions. In this sector also, then, the Catholic Church in America found herself a multi-millionaire.

Yet while accumulating hundreds of millions of dollars in this way, and while benefiting from the administration of local, state and federal non-Catholic governments, the Catholic Church, unlike all the other multi-millionaire enterprises of the U.S. (apart from the Protestant Churches) did not pay one cent in taxation, so that, while her competitors in the business and financial fields had to pay taxes the Catholic Church was exempt from paying anything at all. This gave her an enormous advantage over her commercial competitors, so that her millions would have multiplied in her coffers even if she had remained inactive. But she did not remain inactive; she plunged with immense enthusiasm into the exclusive pool of the multi-millionaire enterprises, determined to make her millions grow by hook or by crook. Without the burden of taxation, the task became ever easier, particularly when one remembers that tax was being paid by non-Catholics to support her tax-free enterprises throughout the U.S. The result was that in no time she crashed into an even more exclusive club, that of the billionaires, where only the towering giants of U.S. industry and finance are admitted. Having made herself a member, since she had all the qualifications, she then proceeded to make the other members of the club members of herself. That is, she promoted a campaign to make the billionaire club join the Church.

This she did via three basic methods: (a) by constant subtle manipulation of the religious allegiance of individual Catholic members of the giant corporations, e.g. Henry Ford,[1] (b) by business penetration in her own right as a partner within the business framework of the giant corporations through the buying of shares and the like in the business circles of the billionaire fraternity, and (c) by identifying the overall interests of the giant corporations with her own, particularly in fields seemingly alien to business but fundamentally closely interrelated with economic prosperity — namely, the political and ideological ones.

The total result of this triple connection with the giants of the U.S. — i.e. finance, industry and trusts — is a mutual magnitudinous identification of interests. That is, while the extremely wealthy Catholic Church identifies herself with the profits and potential expansion of the giant corporations, they in their turn identify themselves with the religious, social and political power of the Catholic Church in American society.

One trivial although typical aspect of such mutual help is demonstrated by the fact that any giant corporation of the U.S. can deduct 5 per cent of *taxable income* for contributions to churches.[2] Many churches, but above all the Catholic Church, have fully exploited this little-known clause, with the result that the greater part of the giant corporations of the U.S. have given the 5 per cent to the Catholic Church. If one looks at the profits of, say, General Motors, IBM, Standard Oil and so on, one can see what vast sums have been received from the corporations; and as thanks for favors received, the Catholic

MEMBER OF BILLIONAIRE CLUB OF U.S.A.

Church invests as many millions as she can with these same corporations.

This mutual amalgamation of interests is promoted, not only within the geographical borders of the U.S., but outside as well, since both partners, their business and financial feet firmly planted on U.S. soil, are simultaneously international entities through the mere nature of their activities. To a giant U.S. oil or motor corporation, the sky is the limit — or, rather, the geographical borders of the earth. Their activities are as internationally inspired, internationally active and internationally influential in their own fields as are those of the Catholic Church in hers. Their common internationalism, therefore, owing to the identification of their business interests, is highly beneficial to both lay and religious partners, so that the Catholic Church is ready to identify herself with big business abroad as well.

Hence the fabulous expansionistic energy of the American billionaire corporations is for a business-minded Catholic Church a golden means of multiplying her riches also in the international field, in the wake of her financial and industrial associates, while at the same time the fabulous religious, social and political potentialities and influence of the Catholic Church in the world at large are a golden asset to the corporations, of the utmost benefit to their own successful commercial expansionism. In this manner the Catholic Church can exert her influence as a business giant outside the U.S. Such influence, however, would be greatly reduced were she not big business in her own right. Hence her admission to the exclusive billionaire club of the U.S.A.

The Catholic Church in America, therefore, operates like a giant corporation — not only as a potential maker or breaker of politicians at all levels, but equally as a financial giant consorting with her peers in the running of the economic life of the country.

CHAPTER 22

CARDINALS INTO STOCKBROKERS

The U.S. hierarchy, the leadership of the Catholic Church in the U.S., is a new phenomenon in the annals of Catholicism. It knows little about theology. This, however, is counterbalanced by its unique knowledge of rates of interest, and by its astounding capacity to foster the Dime Explosion. Its members are the supreme chartered accountants and bookkeepers of the Catholic Church in the twentieth century, and the ecclesiastical counterpart of the fabulously successful operators of the giant corporations. They are the operators of the giant corporation of the Catholic Church in America. Their reputation is amply justified. In terms of business acumen and successful dollar operations, they can truly stand on a par with the chairmen of any of the top oil, steel or giant motor trusts of America.

This matter-of-fact, business-like approach pervades the whole structure of the ecclesiastical machinery of the American Catholic Church, from top to bottom, with the average parish priest being no less eager to do business than the most celebrated cardinal. No corporation can count on so huge, dedicated and enthusiastic a staff. The hundreds of thousands of cardinals, archbishops, bishops, priests, monks, nuns, teachers and subsidiary workers are all motivated by one single objective: the advancement of the Church, not only in the religious and political fields, but also in the material, e.g. the constant accumulation of wealth.

The cumulative result of this enormous collectivized energy is that the Church has truly attained the redoubtable status of a giant corporation, and indeed surpasses all the giant corporations of the U.S., individually and collectively. The boast of the prelate who prided himself upon this reality was more than justified. "We are already a lot bigger than

CARDINALS INTO STOCKBROKERS

Ford Motors, Shell Oil, and Bethlehem Steel *put together*," he said[1] — a terse summing up of one of the most striking facts of life in contemporary USA.

One of the main reasons why the American hierarchy has no equal anywhere is that it has always excelled in resoundingly successful business and financial transactions, consonant with the interests of the Church. More often than not, these are perilously balanced on the borderline between ecclesiastic and purely lay business matters, a state of affairs which has given rise to widespread concern about the glaringly privileged position of a church whose energy is brassily spent upon the enthusiastic promotion of her very tangible worldly interests, in the name of intangible spiritual wares. Her representatives, high or low, seem to be tainted with the same brush. Thus, whereas in other lands — for instance, in Africa — her clerics' main goal is the number of black converts; or in Europe that of the Jesuits is the influencing of mass media, in the U.S. in addition to the latter, the hierarchy's paramount objective is to possess the best bank balance possible; a praiseworthy aim, no doubt, so long as money does not become the only measure of their success.

The phenomenon of the prelate who is a fabulous success story in the ecclesiastical as well as in the financial fields tends to be the rule rather than the exception. One of he most celebrated cases was certainly Cardinal Spellman, the unofficial Primate of the U.S. Church under Pope Pius XII, Pope John XXIII and Pope Paul VI.

Spellman exerted a preponderant influence, not only in U.S. political and military circles, but also inside the Vatican itself. We have dealt with these activities in other books.[2] Besides acting as chief diplomatic adviser to the Vatican on endless diplomatic missions, he was equally valuable to Rome in the financial field. Thanks to his personal contacts with the top finance corporations and high government officials, Cardinal Spellman could give highly confidential tips to the Vatican and to the U.S. Church concerning impending financial, industrial and other similar operations in the offing, and since these came long before the general public knew anything about them, the Church in the U.S. and the Vatican benefited to the tune of countless millions of dollars. While it was true that this state of affairs was attributed mostly to the close personal friendship between Pius XII and Spellman, it was nevertheless a significant pointer to the paramountcy which the American prelate had in Vatican eyes.

A telling episode, as related by an American friend of the author, already mentioned, Nino Lo Bello, European correspondent of the *New York Herald-Tribune* and a specialist in economic affairs, is enlightening. Referring to the little known fact that Vatican Radio broadcasts daily messages *in code* to priests, nuncios and cardinals, he quoted the experience of an NBC correspondent who, after visiting the Vatican Radio Station, and being told of this daily transmission to the United States, asked in jest: "Is that when Cardinal Spellman gets his orders from the Vatican?" The staff member who was acting as his guide replied with a grin, "No, Sir, it's just the other way round."[3] The remark was neither exaggeration nor a mere facetious retort. It was a comment on a reality — in financial matters, as well as in political and diplomatic issues, as we have seen elsewhere.[4]

The following joke reflects the general high opinion of the cardinal's business ability. Cardinal Spellman, upon giving up the ghost (he died in 1967), observed the rows of the blessed, went among them, chose a chair and sat down. The Blessed Peter frowned disapprovingly. "Sorry, your Eminence," he said, "your place is over there." And he indicated the rows of stockbrokers!

St. Peter was right, Cardinal Spellman being a master at big business on behalf of the Church. One typical example will prove it. One of his most profitable coups, was the purchase in 1952, for only $400,000 of 250 acres of land, which was part of the Reid country estate, Ohhir Hall, Purchase, New York. The cardinal installed on it, at a cost of $15 million, the Manhattanville College, which used to be in upper Manhattan. Thereupon he sold the site of the old college to the city. By this simple operation Spellman recouped $8,800,000 — a financial master-stroke.

Up to 1964, Spellman had built 130 new Catholic schools, thirty-seven churches and five big hospitals. He spent $90 million a year on construction. In 1960, a survey of the financial magazine *Fortune* estimated that his Catholic charities were worth $50 million a *year*, and his schools another $22 million. Spellman used to bring the Pope $1 million in Peter's Pence annually. This was collected, usually in all New York churches, in January of each year. Again according to the authoritative *Fortune*, in 1960 the revenues and collections of Spellman's archdiocese totalled to about *$150 million a year.* No wonder that in the Vatican itself, Spellman had been nicknamed Cardinal Moneybag.

Pius XII upon the guidance of Cardinal Spellman was not exceptional. A friend of the author, who served three popes in the closest possible daily contact, testified that, at any rate up to the time he was sacked by Pope John XXIII, the U.S.'s ascendancy over Vatican finances had become practically the only criterion by which the Church as a whole — always as regards business matters — was "inspired."[5] It is even more true today; and while individual American ecclesiastics have had a good deal of influence, it is the U.S. hierarchy as a whole that has attained to such enviable status within the Vatican. This it has done, because of its business acumen, its relentless drive, and, above all, its seemingly unending success. An expanding promotion of multiple business, of building programs, of financial transactions, and, by and large, of splendid administration, has been the main key to her privileged position of influence within the Church in general and over the financial operations of the Vatican in particular.

The life and career of another U.S. prelate, Cardinal Cushing, are typical. The success of Cushing was, perhaps, unduly magnified by a sycophant Catholic and lay press. Nevertheless, his was certainly a larger-than-life ecclesiastical success story. Although not many prelates could emulate Cushing's legendary money-spinning attributes, yet less resounding successes of the same type, when multiplied by the hundred or even thousand, will make a truly impressive impact on the society in which they occur, and, even more so, in the vaults of their banks. The establishment — in our case, the Catholic Church — which can produce such extraordinary financial and ecclesiastical hybrids, is certainly something to look at with admiration and respect, even in Rome.

Cushing was a confidant of the Kennedy clan and a personal intimate of the assassinated President Kennedy. In 1921, after spending the first eleven months as a parish priest, he was made chief local fund raiser for the Society for the Propagation of the Faith. In 1944 he was nominated temporary administrator of the archdiocese, because of his success in his previous job — that is, in making money. From 1944 to 1969 his archdiocese expanded to embrace two million Catholics, the third largest after Chicago and New York. In it he installed more than sixty religious orders and gave so much money to the Jesuits that every Jesuit in New England Province was under the obligation of saying three masses for Cushing's soul.

During his rule, Cushing was responsible for at least 250 to 270 million dollars' worth of buildings, including four modern Catholic hospitals, ninety new parishes, and about 130 high and elementary Catholic schools. He organized his own banking system, besides setting up an insurance scheme for archdiocesan real estate, by means of which he saved his parishes at least twelve million dollars.

The cardinal's reputation as a money-raiser became such a by-word that letters arrived at his residence addressed "Come on Wealth" Avenue. He specialized in small contributions of half dollars, dimes and nickels — what he called "the mighty mites," with a simultaneous milking of millionaires. In 1963, at the instigation of one of his Catholic political proteges, Senator Robert Kennedy, he raised a million dollars within a few days. He was also a fabulous money-raiser for the Vatican itself. The sums he sent to the Vatican's coffers have never been disclosed, but they ran into millions of dollars.[6] Multiply this energetic money collecting by two or three hundred (there were 235 bishops in 1970) and we have the world's most irresistible ecclesiastical commmando brigade, set upon amassing immense wealth for its Church.

Their methods are not limited to the raising of funds from the members of their congregations, but are constantly directed at taking money from non-Catholics as well, very often by devious means, regardless of whether or not these are consonant with fairness or even common sense. Some of the means employed are perfectly legal and legitimate; others are not. Many are on the border-line of illegitimacy. Not a few could be classed altogether in the field of brassy dishonesty. Perhaps that is the price to be paid, since the numberless individuals and organizations — religious, ecclesiastical and lay — which operate for the Church cannot be fully supervised. Add to this the fact that the volume of business is practically limitless, and it becomes well nigh impossible, even for a church, to check all the operations conducted in her name.

Perhaps that is the penalty of success; but it could be a deliberate policy of profiting by the practical immunity of a church whose influential tentacles can reach the most sensitive nooks and crannies of American society. Be that as it may, the fact remains that the Catholic ecclesiastic and economic octopus operates in almost every field and at every level of the American economic structure.

Its activities range from networks of schools to hospitals, from sport to publishing and liquor manufacturing, from advertising to steel and chemicals, from the buying of land and the acquisition of blocks of shares, up and down the financial echelons, to the clever milking of the acquiescent giant corporations, the whole capped by an immunity from taxation which is increasingly resented, though this privilege is shared by the Protestant Churches. In common with other churches, the Catholic Church enjoys tax exemption on her real estate. Also, it must be remembered, on both her passive and her active business income.

The meaning of this becomes clear if we take a sample at random of, say, diocesan wealth. Although diocesan wealth is seldom disclosed, nevertheless it is possible to assess it, in its totality. In a statement published in connection with a bond prospectus, for instance, the Boston archdiocese[7] listed its assets at $635,891,004, which is 9.9 times its liabilities. This leaves a net worth of $571,704,953.[8]

It is not difficult to discover the truly astonishing wealth of the Church, once we add the riches of the twenty-eight archdioceses and 122 dioceses of the U.S., some of which are even wealthier than that of Boston.

Some idea of the real estate and other forms of wealth controlled by the Catholic Church may be gathered by a remark of a member of the New York Catholic Conference, namely "that his church probably ranks second only to the United States Government in total annual purchase."[9]

But another statement, made by a nationally syndicated Catholic priest, perhaps is even more telling. "The Catholic Church," he said, "must be the biggest corporation in the United States. We have a branch office in every neighborhood. Our assets and real estate holdings must exceed those of Standard Oil, AT&T, and U.S. Steel combined. And our roster of dues-paying members must be second only to the tax rolls of the United States Government."[10]

The Vatican, independently of each successive pope, has been increasingly orientated towards the U.S. and in particular the financial and economic wizardry of the American Church has dazzled its administration. Indeed, the U.S. hierarchy, or rather its method, has partially taken over the inner machinery of the Vatican itself — not by open assault, but by the most irresistible mechanism at their disposal: *success*!

No wonder that Pope Pius XII's Under-Secretary of State, Msgr. Dell'Acqua, upon surveying certain recent administrative and financial "spectaculars" of the Church in the U.S., could not refrain from uttering a word seldom heard at the Vatican: "amazing!" Indeed, after having glanced at her total wealth, he was heard to use another adjective which has never been used there in living memory: "Incredible!"

He was right.

CHAPTER 23

CATHOLIC URBAN TAKE-OVER IN THE U.S.A.

It is related that three clerics once dined together: a Protestant clergyman, a Catholic priest, and a Rabbi.

"Tell me, Mr. Smith," asked Father O'Brien. "What do you do with your plate collection?"

"I divide it into three equal parts," replied Mr. Smith. "One I give to the poor, one to the church, and one I keep myself. What about you?"

"I divide it into two equal parts," replied Father O'Brien. "One I give to the church, the other I keep myself."

"I toss the whole collection upwards," commented the Rabbi, "and say a prayer: 'O Lord, take what You need, and leave the rest to me.'"

A hackneyed little joke, but in our context the characters assume a special significance in so far that of recent years they have changed their order of priority.

The rabbi now becomes the one to ask the vital question, with the implied triple division and distribution of the plate collection. Mr. Smith remains in second place. It is Father O'Brien who has taken the place of the rabbi, for the little prayer, "O Lord, take what You need and leave the rest to me," has been adopted as the slogan of the Catholic Church in the U.S.A.

Now, whether the Almighty is pleased with his share of the collection has never been thoroughly certified. The U.S. hierarchy is emphatic about it. He has consistently given His share to them. With interest. This He has multiplied, not the standard tenfold or even the fabulous hundredfold, but a thousandfold. And without taxation.

For the doubting Thomases, another proof is that His representative on earth, the pope, has never objected to the mounting flood of dollars from U.S. The Vatican's financial machinery has been quietly geared to the American success formula, and in fact the Holy Father is one of the main beneficiaries of the U.S. church spectacular. When, during one of his visits to New York, Pope Paul VI celebrated mass at the famed Yankee Stadium, many among the millions of TV viewers were surprised.

"What?" replied a U.S. prelate, to the naive remarks of some European press correspondents who were also amazed. "Don't they know that the stadium's ours, too?"[1]

That almost casual "too" was more than significant; it was portentous in its implications, since to that prelate it had become as natural as the air he breathed to assume that, besides all the multitudinous ecclesiastical and semi-ecclesiastical concerns, the famous stadium, celebrated for its sporting events, should also be the property of Mother Church. Her transactions have no limitations. Taboos, whether of a religious or of a moral nature, are by-passed with the utmost ease whenever there is a good profit to be made. The most notorious battalions to specialize in this seem to be the U.S. Jesuits. Whether their traditional reputation abroad is justified or not, we don't know. In the U.S., however, it is certainly sustained by their highly dubious but successful exercises in getting hold of real estate and lands.

The clergy at large have specialized in individual and collective "ingratiation" with prominent personalities in key civil, economic, administrative, political, urban, local and state key positions. Many of these "bribees" and "bribers" are lay Catholics, and thanks to this, the U.S. hierarchy and their lay agents are given the opportunity to control every acre of land they can, paying as little as possible — in some cases nothing at all.[2]

We shall confine ourselves to quoting a few concrete examples, since these demonstrate better than anything else the pattern of the deals, speculations, real estate control and land acquisitions which have become the standard practice of large powerful sections of the U.S. hierarchy, clergy, and various religious and lay Catholic concerns. We shall mention cases reported by a careful and documented survey of the matter.[3]

CATHOLIC URBAN TAKE-OVER IN U.S.A.

"The Roman Catholic flair for acquiring public land was nowhere more convincingly demonstrated than in New York City, where a tremendously valuable site at Lincoln Square fell to the Jesuit Fordham University. The school paid only a fraction of the fair value of the land, then obtained more Federal aid to develop the campus. Manhattan College, an institution of the Christian Brothers, famous for their wines and brandy, obtained a large factory and assistance in remodelling it for college purposes from Governor Rockefeller's Dormitory Authority. The Department of H.E.W. came through handsomely for the Roman Church on Long Island where a part of the surplus was awarded free of charge to Cardinal Spellman for parish schools. In Queens the borough officials acquired North Hills golf course for a "park," then turned over twenty-seven acres of it to Cardinal Spellman for the Brooklyn Diocese."

Jesuit operations in all their deadly effectiveness were observed in Chicago where the Department of H.E.W. donated, without charge, a sixty-acre, four-and-a-half-million-dollar tract at the site of the Hines Veterans' Administration Hospital to the Jesuit Loyola University. Originally Loyola had sought the land through a direct, legislative give-away via bills introduced in Congress by Senator Paul Douglas, Senator Everett McKinley Dirksen, and Representative E. R. Finnegan. When public reaction became hostile the bills were withdrawn and a quieter method of administrative give-away was arranged. Father James F. Maguire, president of Loyola, approached Veterans' Administrator John S. Gleason, Jr., a Roman Catholic, at that time serving on Fr. Maguire's Advisory Board. Mr. Gleason promised to get the Hines site for Loyola without charge. Mr. Gleason then undertook to get a government declaration that the Hines site was excess to V.A. needs. Fred B. Rhodes, Jr., V.A. general counsel, and a Baptist who believed in church-state separation, balked at the give-away and refused to approve it. He was then ousted and replaced by a devout Catholic. As soon as the newcomer went into the general counsel's office an opinion favorable to the give-away came out.

Another devout Catholic was head of G.S.A. which had to pass on the proposal next. G.S.A. quickly declared that the Hines Veterans' site was surplus to government needs.

At this period there was no Catholic at the head of H.E.W. Secretary Abraham Ribicoff, however, proved to be just as good. Fr. Maguire and Mr. Gleason went straight to the top and got Secretary Ribicoff's commitment. Strong Catholic support for Mr. Ribicoff in his Connecticut campaign as U.S. Senator was no accident as subsequent events were to prove. Ribicoff in due course became Senator Ribicoff. He reached the Senate not only with the Jewish vote, but mostly with Catholic political patronage, interlinked with that of Senator Edward Kennedy. This was demonstrated on sundry occasions. The two Senators very often supported their respective policies, even when in so doing they looked absurd. A typical instance was in 1971, during the civil war in Northern Ireland. The Irish War is a purely religious problem, since basically it is a conflict between Catholics and Protestants. The Irish Republic, 95 per cent Catholic, want total unification of Ireland. This is opposed by Northern Ireland or Ulster, two-thirds of which is fanatically Protestant. The problem is discussed at length by the present writer in his book *Religious Terror In Ireland*.[4]

In October 1971 Senator Kennedy openly intervened in Irish affairs, by asking that the British Army, then "in occupation of Northern Ireland to protect the Protestants," be withdrawn. He even introduced a resolution before the U.S. Senate. This he did jointly with Senator Abraham Ribicoff. A strange bedfellowship, considering that while Kennedy could be excused, because of his Irish origin, and his Catholic religion, Senator Ribicoff had no interest whatsoever in the religious disputes of Ireland, owing chiefly to the fact of his being of the Jewish persuasion.

The political alliance of the Catholic and Jewish Senators, however, was another telling demonstration of the reality which economic vested interests exert in the political life of the nation, when it comes to supporting the financial affairs of sundry religious establishments.

But resuming the thread of our original tale. The rest was mere routine. H.E.W. officials went through the half-hearted motions of reviewing the "bids" for the land and the award to Loyola was soon announced. Loyola, which had already accumulated millions for the erection of its buildings, got the site free. Only the taxpayers were out. As a sop to the indignant public, the state of Illinois was given about thirty acres of the V.A. land for a mental hospital.

The bold Jesuit grab of the Hines site followed an even more brazen acquisition by the Church. In 1959 a thirty-acre tract in a Chicago redevelopment program which had been scheduled for low-cost housing was sold instead by authorities to the Archbishop of Chicago — for a seminary to train men for the Catholic priesthood.

In St. Louis, Mo., the large Mill Creek renewal program was conceived and executed for the benefit of St. Louis University, a Jesuit institution. Hundreds were ousted from homes and businesses in order to provide a new campus for this school.

St. Louis University, and the twenty-seven other Jesuit colleges in the United States, are all organized in exactly the same way: all the trustees of these institutions are Jesuit priests and the whole operation is under rigid Catholic control. The property is owned ultimately by the pope. In the Mill Creek project the school did repay a small part of the cost of the land as is customary in renewal projects. The taxpayers footed the rest of the bill. In order to stimulate sagging enrollment at the enlarged St. Louis University, Cardinal Ritter issued an order to all Catholic students requiring them to attend a Catholic college unless they obtained written permission from him to do otherwise.

In Philadelphia, an old plunder ground, the Roman Church announced that it had obtained from taxpayers not only land for a new parochial school, but also $300,771 in federal funds to clear the land and develop it. The Church repaid $60,350 of this amount. The lucky school was St. Joseph's College High School, another Jesuit institution. Earlier, St. Joseph's parish church had benefited to the tune of $100,200 in an urban renewal program, plus an additional $46,200 in a special Congressional act. Funds were expended to clear land and to enhance the Church.

In Milwaukee, the Jesuit Marquette University has been awarded thirty-five acres acquired by public condemnation, paid for by Federal and municipal governments and handed over to the them, apparently without any charge. The Milwaukee Jesuits added a new fillip to the give-away technique — they were not only taking land away from the public, they were also taking it away from the Lutherans, by planning to take over a multi-million dollar Lutheran hospital even before it was built. The hospital, a Lutheran memorial, was to be built by terms of the will of wealthy Lutheran Kurtis R. Froedtert. The trustees planned to complete it and turn it over to Jesuit Marquette.

In Pittsburg, the Holy Ghost Fathers who operate Duquesne University announced plans for a twenty-one-acre expansion program that would cost $9.2 million in public funds. The project followed a long period of fraternizing between the director of the redevelopment authority, and the president of Duquesne. Nothing was said about competitive bidders for the land or about reimbursing the government.

Boston, Massachusetts, is one of the better-known preserves of the Roman Catholic Church. Church and state have at times become virtually indistinguishable as the latter had outdone itself for the former. The Legislature authorized the commissioners of Middlesex County to convey to Cardinal Cushing forty acres of public land for the erection of a church building and a school. Apparently the land was a gift, though all financial details were a closely guarded secret. Inquirers were laughingly told that it was none of their business. In Boston and environs it has become almost routine to convey public school properties to the Catholic cardinal for a dollar apiece.

Other sections of Massachusetts have caught the vision. In Fall River, 37.66 acres of city-owned land were "sold" to Roman Catholic diocesan Bishop Connolly, who duly paid a dollar for the land. The bishop said he intended to use it for a boys' school and a monastery.

In the District of Columbia, Societa Generale Immobiliare of Rome, a Vatican financial subsidiary, as we have already seen, was permitted to buy a substantial area to erect a $75-million project. It was supposed to be a luxury housing unit, but non-profit organizations could also be housed there according to zoning regulations. It is true that the going price was paid for the land, but the Vatican at once received preferential treatment in an easement of building restrictions which was going to enable the building to rise to 130 feet.

In New Jersey the Roman Catholic university of Seton Hall has been taken to the heart of certain officials who vie with one another in giving away the public's assets. Biggest grab by the school was $40-million Jersey City medical center along with various public grants to operate and enlarge it.

The give-away of public hospitals to the Roman Catholic Church has almost become common practice. Here are a few: Silver Spring, Maryland; Baudette, Minnesota; Irvine, Kentucky; Ketchikan, Alaska; West Allis, Wisconsin; Opelousas, Louisiana; New Castle, Wyoming; South St. Paul, Minnesota; Jeannette, Pennsylvania; Iberia, Louisiana.

Another substantial source of grants of public land has been Congressional act. In the 87th Congress, for example, thirty-nine acres of land belonging to the Chippewa Indians at Fond du Lac reservation was donated to the Roman Catholic Church of St. Mary and St. Joseph by H.R. 10459. This same tribe of Chippewa Indians had "to convey 4.78 acres of tribal land to the Little Flower Mission of the St. Cloud diocese by S. 2895".[3]

The impetus of the Catholic Church's acquisition of valuable lands has been growing faster than ever. Since, if we be permitted to paraphrase the old saying, the appetite grows with the eating, the Catholic Church's greed for land seems to grow daily the more land she acquires.

The examples we have just quoted are typical in so far that they occur throughout the United States. We see it in New Jersey, in Rhode Island, in Massachusetts, in New York. We see one of the most valuable sites in Manhattan turned over at a give-away price to the Roman Catholic Church to own and hold tax free in perpetuity for its operations. The give-away of public properties to the Church is on, and the spigot of public subsidies to church operations has begun to flow. Across the generations the cumulative process moves with increasing speed towards its tragic finale. Such a finale has always spelled inevitable tragedy; and this has been seen again and again in Europe. It is approaching now in the U.S. at an ever-accelerated speed.

The American Catholic Church is undoubtedly careering towards spiritual ruination. Economic expansion spells economic stranglehold, and this creates social and political problems. Political problems are dangerous when they are closely intermingled with controversial imponderables on the local, state and federal level, since whenever a church, or rather her material vested interests, are inextricably involved in the network of conflicting business, that church is inevitably drawn into a jungle where morality is adulterated, by-passed, and more often than not disregarded altogether. So that material possessions and financial puissance, when overwhelming, far from becoming beneficial will draw the church into the morass of secular conflict, and true religion has always been made to suffer when drawn into it. Will the U.S. hierarchy refrain from increasing concern with economic take-overs, powerful acquisitions, land and building control throughout the North American continent? Judging by their current activities, the answer seems to be a resounding "No!"

CHAPTER 24

THE WEALTHIEST GIANT THEOCRACY OF THE AMERICAS

The Catholic Church in the U.S. is "a nation within a nation." This is no mere figure of speech. It is a solid and irrefutable fact of American life.

When U.S. Catholics talk about American freedom, American democracy and the like, they always mean American Catholic freedom and American Catholic democracy, since their ultimate objective is a Catholic U.S. Constitution as the final stage to a totally Catholic America.

Theirs is not mere abstract wishful thinking. The process is in operation now and is gaining momentum. The Vatican is building her empire within the U.S. with such success that she no longer fears serious opposition to her continued expansion, indeed, to her inevitable takeover. She is active at all levels of U.S. society, horizontally as well as vertically. The result is that practically all U.S. structures are intertwined, directly or indirectly, with Catholic structures. The consequences of such intimacy are like those of an oak tree embraced by a vigorously healthy ivy.

The spreading ramifications in our case are the numberless institutions which have penetrated the U.S. fabric. These go from Catholic Mother of the Year, Roman Catholic Legion of Decency, Roman Catholic Book and Record Clubs, to Roman Catholic Postal Employees' Association, Roman Catholic Radio and Television Guilds, Roman Catholic Press Association, Roman Catholic insurance companies, Roman Catholic war veterans and an infinite variety in between. All such Roman Catholic organizations are supported by remarkable financial assets, which, when taken as a whole, must amount to millions of dollars.

The most impressive of such Roman Catholic units are those in the educational and medical fields. Here the Catholic Church has become truly, not a nation within a nation, but a religious-financial empire within the U.S. Federation. Her educational machine is operating from kindergartens to graduate universities via all the intermediary stages; her medical machine from the humblest clinics to the most up-to-date efficient hospitals. The financial assets of these educational and medical structures reach the billion figure, and these billions are not solely the result of Catholic energy. A substantial part of them has been, directly or indirectly, "relegated" to the Catholic Church by the average Protestant taxpayer.

This is done via an open and devious by-passing of the U.S. Constitution, by the hidden Catholic pressure group within the U.S. Government, federal and local, by the legal, semi-legal and dubious politico-financial manipulations of sly Catholic dealers relentlessly operating in the legislative, financial and real estate fields on behalf of the Catholic Church.

Thus, for instance, in 1965 in Mississippi a $7,000,000 government-sponsored program for the retraining of the unemployed was run by an agency organized by a Roman Catholic Diocese; the seven million dollars were financed by the government. Under the Johnson administration (1963-9) hundreds of federal programs provided vast amounts of U.S. government money to church-related agencies, most of them Catholic. Millions of dollars passed through ecclesiastical coffers.

In 1954 the Hillburton Act authorized grants to meet from one-third to two-thirds of the cost of the building of general hospitals. In 1964 this act was broadened to grant money to chronic rehabilitation treatment centers and the like. From 1947 to 1964 no less than 7,372 such pojects were approved. The U.S. churches collected a fortune with similar bills. Thanks to the one just mentioned, for instance, the Catholic Church got $305 million, the lion's share, as compared to $168 million granted to all the Protestant and Jewish churches put together.

To quote only a few telling figures, in 1947 and 1948. The Catholic Church received an average of $14 million a year of taxpayers' money, thanks to such bills. This means that she collected *$1.2 million a month*, or about *$40,000 each day* from the average U.S. citizen, the majority of whom, it must be remembered, are Protestants. From 196l to 1966 the annual amounts have more than doubled to $30.5 million each year, or about *$83,500 every day*. The Catholic Hospital Association had reported that Catholic hospitals in 1968-70 had a current value of over $1.5 billion. The U.S. taxpayer contributed no less than 305 million of this.[1]

The property owned by the Catholic Church via her educational program is no less staggering. She controls more than 2,500 Catholic high schools, 300 Catholic colleges and universities, seminaries and the like. Most of their buildings are valuable real estate assets. To buy, finance and run these the Church has received and continues to receive an increasing volume of money from the government, which is supposed to be wholly separated from organized religion.
Senator, Wayne Morse of Oregon, to quote only one typical case, introduced in the Senate a special amendment asking for seventy-five million dollars *a year* for the construction of private and parochial schools, the majority of which are Catholic.

The truth of the matter is that millions of U.S. Protestants and even agnostics are contributing millions of dollars annually for the buying and maintenance of the Catholic Church's property, under a variety of federal programs. Subsidizations, called "research grants," are obtained by doubtful legal and political devices by the Catholic Church throughout the U.S.

One institution of Catholic Higher Education, Marymount College in Boca Raton, Florida, is typical. Although in 1968 it had a student body of only 350 and was founded in 1963, it managed to get from the govenment two million dollars in housing grants to build dormitories, a $55,000 anti-poverty grant to study migrant children, and a similar $10,000 educational grant.[2]

The parochial schools are growing faster than the public shools, which again means that the Catholic Church is getting ever larger grants, and subsidies from a predominantly Protestant country.

This was brought to the fore by the fact that in 1968, for instance, a *ten percent* tax surcharge was put on the U.S.

citizen, although the churches were receiving *sixteen million dollars a day* in federal tax money alone. The Catholic Church of the U.S., however, clamored for more. Her bishops' demands would have cost the U.S. taxpayer more than *twenty-two million dollars a day*. This meant a compulsory donation of $280 federal tax money, $70 per person in America.[3]

To gain some idea of the wealth of the Catholic Church in the educational and medical fields alone, it has been set forth by a most level-headed trade journal, that the annual dollar value of the construction of Catholic schools, colleges, hospitals and churches (in that order) is at the rate of *$1.75 billion a year.*

The Vatican's financial commitments and profit-seeking enterprises are as varied as those of any of the most energetic and advanced global business concerns. As already seen, its financial ramifications branch off from the Societa Generale Immobiliare in Italy, with gross assets of 170 million dollars (in 1967) and controlling over fifty Italian companies, to its offshoots in Washington, Paris and New York City; also in Canada, where there is a company known as Ediltecno, and a Latin American affiliate, Ediltecno de Mexico, based in Mexico City.

The Vatican controls or partly controls vast buildings and speculative enterprises, ranging from those in the Foggy Bottom section of the U.S. capital, approximating seventy million dollars, to the Montreal Redbrook Estate, the buildings in the fashionable Paseo de Las Palmas and in Mexico City, or, back in Europe, estates in the chic Avenue des Champs Elysees in Paris. In Rome itself the Vatican not so long ago owned over 102 million square feet of property "within the city's limits." Nino Lo Bello, a newsman for the *New York Herald-Tribune*, specialized in economic affairs, a liberal Catholic, had to admit, after years of research in to the Vatican's economic might, that "so widespread and complex are the Vatican's money making enterprises that it is almost impossible to get a clear picture of all of them."[4] He was right, particularly in view of the fact that he discovered to his astonishment how the Montecatini-Edison, "one of the largest corporations in Italy and indeed in the world, which deals in mining and metallurgical products, fertilizers, synthetic resins, textile fibers and pharmaceuticals, as well as electric power...was...bound to the Vatican with hoops of steel."

The picture is no different — in fact, it becomes even more significantly blurred — when we enter into the purely financial field. Here the Vatican's investments are even more widespread. Most of its millions are deposited in non-Italian banks. "Some are in America and many are in Switzerland, where the Vatican maintains its funds in numbered accounts. Nobody knows how much money it has in Swiss vaults ... The Vatican also uses its Swiss accounts to maintain its anonymity when gaining control of foreign corporations."[5] A practice which has given the Vatican vast unknown profits this last decade.

The result of this last practice, perfectly legal of course, is that the Vatican, unlike most big concerns of Europe and America, which are restricted by their governments, is wholly free to speculate and to transfer vast funds here, there and everywhere, whenever a profitable opportunity arises — and opportunities are very seldom missed. Consequently the most financially potent concerns have been either "penetrated" or are being run by long-range remote control through Vatican investments and policies.

This means that the value of the Catholic Church's property is increasing annually. Her wealth is widespread and reaches most of the channels of the economic life of the nation. It is often totally unrelated to religion, as such. Yet it is tax exempt on religious grounds. Catholic action groups fall into such category. These are affiliated with her, and are wealthy in their own right. They carry on business, possess portfolios and produce profits. Typical of such groups are the Opus Dei and the Christophers, to mention only two.

There exist well over 250 affiliated Catholic associations all buttressed by substantial financial funds. Most of these quasi-religious concerns operate commercially. Furthermore, the Catholic Church, like the Protestants, conducts insurance business via church-related companies. One of these is the Catholic Association of Forresters "chartered by law to serve Catholics only". Recently it stated that it paid over $62 million in benefits. Another is the Knights of Columbus which has well over $1.5 billion of insurance "for Catholics only."

Another commercial cultural aspect is the publishing field. In 1972, there were ninety-eight publishing houses for books, and over 517 Catholic periodicals with circulation exceeding thirty million. Added to this, the Church makes profit from "unrelated business" such as the ownership of denominational cemeteries. Then there are the so-called feeders — agencies. At least two of Chicago's largest garbage dumps for instance were owned by the Catholic Archdiocese of Chicago. The Archdiocese of New York on the other hand sold its one-half interest in sales royalties of Listerine for $25 million. Another feeder was the University Hill Foundation, of the Roman Catholic Loyola of Los Angeles. This was operating twenty-four separate businesses; such as a foundry, a hotel, a printing press, dairies, oil burners and the like.[6]

The De Rance Inc. of Milwaukee was a feeder foundation for the Roman Catholic religious orders. Among other assets De Rance had a 47 per cent interest in Miller Beer. The preceding year, Miller had sales totalling $145 million. It is the eighth largest producer of beer in the U.S.[7]

That the Catholic Church should be involved in the wholesale of alcohol is not exceptional. Several of her religious orders are doing just that. The Christian Brothers, for instance, advertise the largest-selling brandy in the U.S. The Carthusian Order of monks produces and sells Chartreuse, which is a kind of "super-liqueur." American monks and nuns are busily engaged upon making profits. The Trappist monks of St. Joseph's Abbey, Mass., for instance, manufacture twenty-seven flavors of jelly on their 2,300-acre farm. The monks of Our Lady of Gethsemane Abbey, Dardstown, Ky., run a prosperous business in cheese, cakes, hams, bacon and sausage. The Abbey of St. Benedict Aspen, Colorado, have 500 head of cattle, herded by cowboy monks, in their 3,800-acre ranch. The Cistercian monks have a dairy and beef business near Dubuque, Iowa. They have 2,000 acres, and large herds of dairy and beef cattle. They operate also a sawmill, a stone quarry and other business. The Daughters of St. Paul have a profitable printing business. The Marist Fathers have a recording business in Hawaii. Religious Orders owned or still own, directly or vicariously, department stores in St. Louis, Missouri, Camden, New Jersey and in Philadelphia,

Pennsylvania. In Hartford, Connecticut, they bought the Bond and Vendome Hotel; in Columbus, Ohio, the Montgomery Ward building; in Newport, Rhode Island, the Strand Theater; in New Haven, Connecticut, the New Haven Railway Headquarters Building, and the Sheraton Hotel; in Detroit, Michigan, the Crucible Steel Company's warehouse; in Chicago, Illinois, the Brunswick-Balke-Collander Buildings; in Bridgeport, Connecticut, the $1.9-million steel tube mill of the Bridgeport Brass Company.[8]

The wealth of one of these orders, the Marianists, is illuminating. On one occasion, having decided to float a bond issue, they sent out a prospectus indicating that the Society had assets of more than $515 million, from which it derived a net income *tax free* of $669,000 a year.

There are hundreds of similar religious orders, running prosperous businesses and yet paying not a cent of tax, on the ground that they are religious institutions.

Some of them, although only partially religious, or rather more lay than religious, are financial giants in their own right. One of these is the Knights of Columbus. The Knights have assets exceeding $200 million. Their portfolio includes $55.5 million in securities; several million in Canadian government bonds; $4.8 million in railroad issues; $18 million in utility stocks and bonds; $12 million in industrial securities; and U.S. government bonds. It owns such properties as the Yankee Stadium in New York City, the former New Haven Railway headquarters building, Crucible Steel Co.'s Detroit warehouse; Brunswick-Balke Collander Co.'s building in Chicago; the site of a new $5 million Sheraton hotel in New Haven; department stores in St. Louis (property value - $4.5 million), Camden, N.J. ($2.5 million), and Philadelphia ($2 million); a new $1.8-million steel tube mill of the Bridgeport Brass Co.; and others.[9] They run a vast insurance business. In 1966 they reported assets of $281,228,300. Now these have exceeded the $300 million.

The most important order, however, as a true religious order, in terms of importance and of influence, is that of the Jesuits. The Society is paramount in the educational and in the financial fields. It operates twenty-eight Catholic Universities. Some of these, like the Fordham in New York

City and the St. Louis University, get enormous subsidies from the government, notwithstanding the fact that the order is engaged directly or vicariously in very profitable businesses. Their financial transactions and links criss-cross the American fabric. In San Francisco, for instance, decades ago, they financed a Sicilian, Di Giorgio, in the expansion of his fruit company. Today the order has control of the structure. Di Giorgio Fruit Company operates in California, Florida and Central America and runs its own steamship fleet.[10]

Even more telling is the fact that fifty years ago, they furnished A. P. Giannini, an Italian promoter, with half of the starting capital for the Bank of America. Today, the Jesuits still own 51 per cent of the stock.

According to a reliable source, "The Jesuits are one of the largest stockbrokers in the American steel company, Republic and National. They are also among the most important owners of the four greatest aircraft manufacturing companies in the U.S., Boeing, Lockheed, Douglas and Curtis-Wright. Furthermore, they have a controlling interest in the Phillips Oil Company and in the Creole Petroleum Co. which has a great many oil concessions in Venezuela."[11] The Jesuits also own large interests in TV and radio. The order is perhaps the wealthiest of all the religious concerns in the U.S., with an unofficial income of between $250 and $280 million a year. Again, the order does not pay one cent of tax.

It must be remembered that there are hundreds of such orders. Contrary to general belief, they are as numerous as in Europe. In the U.S. in fact, there are 125 orders of monks and 414 orders of nuns, a total of 539 operating all over the states. Unlike their European counterparts, they are financially minded. A few random examples of the assets of some of the women's orders should prove the correctness of the statement. The assets of the Grey Nuns of Charity are $3,500,000. Those of the Sisters of the Immaculate Heart of California total $7,500,000; the Sisters of St. Joseph of Newark, $17,899,384; the Little Sisters of the Poor, $25,000,000; the Sisters of Mercy, $39,754,132; the Sisters of Charity, $66,533,833; the Sisters of Charity of Providence, $90,187,000; the Sisters of the Sorrowful Mother, $93,636,516; the Sisters of the Holy

Cross, $110,892,759. Martin Larson and Stanley Lowell, in their book, *Praise The Lord For Tax Exemption*, give a list of twenty-three women's orders and their assets. The total is an astronomical one, $705,968,300, an average of $30,695,513 for each order. "Extrapolating on this basis," they conclude, "the assets of the 414 women's orders would be a grand total of $12.7 billion." One of these, the Little Sisters of the Poor, with three provinces in the U.S., and a hospital in almost every diocese, have wealth totalling at least one billion dollars.

Then there are the religious orders for men. On the basis of a $90 million average, the same writers have reçkoned that the 125 men's orders would show a total wealth of $11.2 billion. In this manner, the grand total for the religious orders of the Catholic Church of the U.S. would be $23 billion. As a matter of fact, the present writer believes this to be grossly minimized because many assets which are on the borderline of legal ownership have not been taken into account.

We have quoted the assets of the Religious orders since these are supposed to be "poor," although their "poverty" amounts to about $24 billion. What are the total assets of the Catholic Church were one to scrutinize property, investments, industrial shares, and the like? An idea can be given, if one quotes the value of the Catholic churches and rectories alone. Back in 1936 their value was $891,435,725. Forty years later, it had multiplied beyond recognition. As of 1968, the wealth of the Catholic Church, wealth limited to purely religious function it must be stated, exceeded $54 billion.

This is only the portion of the Roman Catholic financial iceberg which is visible above the water, since its commercial operations in the U.S. are so vast and so well concealed from the public that it is almost impossible to ferret them out. Recently, for instance, a Washington, D.C. luxury housing project valued at $75 million was announced by Societa General Immobilaire of Rome, which as we have seen, is a subsidiary of the Vatican, but not a single newspaper mentioned the fact.[12]

If, to them, one adds the properties owned by the thousands of Catholic parishes throughout the U.S., the result is truly staggering, though the amounts have never been disclosed. Yet a summary but fairly accurate figure can be reached by consulting declarations at the tax office. Even so, such declarations should never be taken at their face value since the assessment of such property is usually far below the actual or market value.

One typical case should suffice to prove this. In Buffalo, N.Y., tax assessors rated the tax-exempt Roman Catholic church, school, college and hospital land and building at $51 million; but the hierarchy's own privately released figures gave the total church assets there, mainly real estate and buildings, as $236 million.

The Research Department of American United, in a study of District of Columbia tax office figures, learned that although the Roman Catholic Church claims but 19 per cent of the population of the nation's capital, it owns 38 per cent of the dollar value of all religious tax-exempt property and 50 per cent of the physical land area so exempted. The Church's elementary and high schools in the District of Columbia cover 68.1 acres with assessed value of $6,430,000. Colleges and Universities cover 265.5 acres with an assessed value of $24,557,000. The total acreage in these categories (333.6) bears interesting comparison with the Vatican's 108.7 acres.

The total assessed value of all Roman Catholic tax-exempt property in the District was $87,557,000 in the above categories. This did not include investment properties held by church agencies, or by the Vatican itself. Then, in addition, there is the District's "foreign government" tax exempt list which includes the Washington headquarters of the pope's Apostolic Delegate, a plush establishment on Massachusetts Avenue covering two acres and bearing a tag of $550,000. A further interesting disclosure was the fact that the Roman Catholic Church in Washington, D.C. invests less of its money — only 18 per cent — in charitable programs than it does in any other category.

The May, 1961, *Church And State* estimated, on the basis of the Buffalo diocese, that the total of directly owned tax-exempt property of the Roman Catholic Church in the U.S. is about $11 billion. An estimate is based on simple arithmetic. A financial credit rating for the Buffalo diocese has put the Church's assets in this one diocese at $236,000,000. Its average gross income is $24,500,000. Taking the Buffalo membership of 860,000 in ratio with the claimed total American membership of 40,000,000, a total national wealth close to $11,000,000,000 is indicated. This, however, is an understatement.

Those reliable investigators, Larson and Lowell, have tentatively given a conservative estimate of the Catholic wealth in the U.S. In a careful tabulation of their assets, they have come to a grand total of colossal proportions. Between these, they have singled out — annual voluntary contributions, $5,000,000,000; active business income, $1,200,000,000; stocks, bonds, real estate, $13,000,000,000; commercial business property, $12,000,000,000; religiously used real estate, $54,277,600,000. With sundry other assets which they mention, the grand total is $80,177,600,000.[13] The present writer, however, reckons that they have underestimated the total value since a vast amount of financial commercial and religious activities cannot be assessed within any conventional framework owing to their intangibility and therefore, escape detection. Such elusive and yet concrete wealth should be taken into account, and it surely would not be underestimating its true value were we to add another $20,000,000,000 to the 80 billion mentioned above.

We shall mention two or three cases to prove the validity of the concreteness of these invisible billions. The Catholic Church, for instance, systematically solicits wills. Catholic organizations are in the habit of contacting lawyers with a reminder that a good Catholic should put his church in his will for at least 10 per cent of the corpus. The harvest is never fully disclosed. But it is reckoned to run into hundreds of millions per year. Although bingo is legal in only eleven states — the Catholic Church makes profit in all fifty. M. Larson and S. Lowell have reckoned that since many parishes net $50,000 a year from bingo "if this should be the average, the total would be about a billion dollars." This is their factual assessment after scrutinizing concrete figures of profits netted by Catholic parishes. Another invisible asset is tax exemption. The two investigators quoted above have reckoned that Catholic miscellaneous properties used for religious purposes and exempt from taxation are now worth well in excess of $60 billion.[14]

But the most astounding feature of all such wealth is that the Church receives additional wealth, as a "free gift" from the Government itself, e.g., out of $125 million of public tax funds going to church-related hospitals only a while ago, the Catholic Church received the lion's share: no less than $112 million.

The anomaly of the situation is made even more absurd, as we have already mentioned, by the fact that the Catholic Church, while receiving so many millions from the taxes paid by the ordinary U.S. citizen, *does not pay any tax* herself on her colossal properties or income. The latter is between 12 and 13 billion dollars ($12,785,000,000 in 1970). In fact, out of a grand total of all the churches of the U.S., including the Jewish, of $141,813,400,000, well over 50 per cent is owned by one alone, the Catholic Church (Jewish wealth $7,547,800,000; Protestant wealth $54,088,000,000; Catholic wealth $80,177,600,000).[15] No taxes have ever been collected, and no accounting ever been asked, upon such immense wealth.

As we have already said, all religious organizations are exempt from taxes, federal, state and local. They pay no real estate tax, no iheritance tax, no income tax, no sales tax, no gift tax, no employment tax, no social security tax. All income, even from a business which is church owned, is exempt. Thus the hundreds of businesses owned and operated by the various religious orders of monks and nuns, or by the sundry dioceses and archdioceses all over the U.S. or even by affiliated companies or feeders, do not pay the 52 per cent corporation tax which any other businesses are forced to pay by the device of holding title as a church or a church convention, or a church association. Furthermore, they are exempt from making any report, from disclosing their budgets, their profits, or any other financial transaction, no matter what their economic activities may be.

They are exempt from tax on interest dividends, real estate, royalties, rentals and capital gains.[16] By June, 1965, the Catholic Church had accumulated a minimum of $80 billion in real estate of the total 325 billion dollars' worth of privately owned real estate in the U.S. And that is 25 per cent of all privately owned land. Of this, 56 per cent is held in trust for the Vatican.[17] By 1972, the combined assets of the U.S.'s five largest industrial corporations totalled about $46.9 billion. Those of the Catholic Church between $80 and $100 billion.

In virtue of this, the Catholic Church, therefore, has become the mightiest corporation of the U.S., a colossus before which the wealth of even the most powerful American concerns shrink into insignificance.

Thus, within a single generation, she has contrived to transform herself into the wealthiest giant theocracy of the western hemisphere, if not of the entire world.

CHAPTER 25

THE RICHEST AND THE POOREST, THE CHURCH IN AMERICA AND THE CHURCH IN RUSSIA

Once during a solemn ceremony at St. Peter's Basilica in Rome, Pope Paul VI took off his tiara and placed it on the altar. "This tiara is a gift to the millions of poor people throughout the world," he explained.

The perplexed cardinals approved. The gesture would help to silence the growing criticism about the Church wealth.

The tiara, however, far from reaching the poor of the world, somehow ended up as a private possession of the ablest ecclesiastical financial wizard of America, Cardinal Spellman. Later, because of protests, the tiara was put on permanent display at the National Shrine of the Immaculate Conception in Washington, D.C. where it has been ever since.

Cardinal Spellman's act of acquisition, prompted perhaps by a simple romantic impulse, and therefore with no other ulterior motive, nevertheless was interpreted as the epitome of the American Church, whose principal objective seems to be the relentless pursuance of wealth.

Although the last preceding chapters should have sufficed to justify this belief, at a risk of repetition, a bird's-eye view of her immense financial massiveness should make any thinking man ponder, with even greater earnestness, about the impending perils of such a state of affairs.

Not only because her policy is the brassiest stultification of Christ's dictum — "my kingdom is not of this world" — but also because her reputation, as the greediest church in the world, could become the indirect promoter of her potential downfall, in a near or distant future.

That this is not mere rhetorical speculation, is proved by the fact that the Catholic Church in America is careening at breakneck speed towards the accumulation of more and more wealth with such light-hearted unconcern as to be almost worthy of admiration, if it were not so tragic.

All her energies seem to be spent almost exclusively upon the acquisition, control and multiplication of real estate, business concerns, banking operations, and undisclosed financial conglomerations of all kinds, some of which we have already examined in detail, but of which would make a thousand Mammons livid with envy.

Was such acquisitional lust confined to her clergy, that would be bad enough. But her most pious sections, namely her supposedly contemplative religious orders, have caught the contagion as acutely as her heirarchy.

The fact is the more regrettable, if we remember that many of such orders have "dedicated themselves to God in perfect charity." Indeed, some have started and are still officially "mendicant orders," "living off alms," and bound by "vows" and "practice poverty." "Poverty" is the word. And yet many, if not all of them, are so earth-bound with wealth as to make them almost the visible negatives of the very Christianity which they claim to represent.

Their names and the list of their financial holdings, property and general operational activities, seen in the previous chapters, makes most of them prosperous, rich, and in many cases, embarrassingly wealthy.

The two extremes appear to be the Jesuits and their opposites, the Pallotines. The pugnacious Jesuits, about 8,000 in the U.S. alone, out of 35,000 in the Order, by 1983-4 had increased their income to between 300 to 350 million dollars, and were the controllers, even if tangently, of the largest bank in the world, the Bank of America.

The "poorest," that is, the Pallotine Fathers, claiming only a few hundred priests in five provinces in the U.S., had enough energy to out-do any other poor mendicant order. Between November, 1972, and November, 1975, to give a striking example, they "begged" by sending out 270 million pieces of fund-raising mail. The postage alone cost over 5 million dollars.[1]

Fund-raising experts estimated that the Order's 106 million letters in 1974 made between 10 and 15 million dollars in "donations." Although one of the smallest religious orders, the Pallotines, "living off alms," built an impressive financial empire. An audit for 1974-75 showed that the Order used only 74 per cent of more than 20 million dollars collected for "missions."[2]

Multiply these by the hundreds and corporate wealth of these religious "mendicant" orders, about 500 of them, reach astronomical dimensions. This, it should be noted, without even adding the hundreds of subsidiary cultural, business and similar concerns, directly or indirectly financially related to them.

Catholic dioceses, although not claiming any special vow of poverty or otherwise, individually or collectively, are not far behind their "poor brethren" as examined in preceding chapters. One of the most typical examples being that of the Hartford Archdiocese which used to own more land than the very state of Connecticut itself. With a market value of 350 million dollars in 1969-70, and even if tangently, due to inflationary erosion, to about 450 million in 1983-84.

The wonder is that the Church is not even richer than it actually is, considering the obsession of the U.S. hierarchy with acquiring, producing and multiplying wealth.

The archtype of such American hierarch was money-bag, Cardinal Spellman, obsessed by a "building mania," a typical affliction common to most American clergy as we have already indicated. When Spellman was posted to New York, he was burdened with a debt of 28 million dollars.

In no time, with a yearly outlay of over 50 million dollars, the New York Archdiocese turned Spellman into the biggest builder, second only to the City itself, the richest Archdiocese not only of America, but also of the entire Catholic world, and the most generous contributor to St. Peter's Pence, as already seen.

Between 1939 and 1967, he had invested about 150 million dollars and had accounted for nearly a half billion dollars worth of new construction.

Another cardinal worthy of Spellman was Cardinal Francis

McIntyre of Los Angeles, a dog-collared stockbroker. He outsmarted Spellman, himself.

No less typical was Cardinal Cushing who said that he could outsmart his two colleagues at their own game; that is, accumulation of property, which he did. Cardinal Cushing boasted that during his 26 years in office, he had raised 350 million dollars. "This breaks down to 37,000 dollars a day," he used to declare, "or roughly 25 dollars a minute." His fund-raising record was unmatched, as were his light-speed results.

In 1962, Robert F. Kennedy, then Attorney General, asked him if he could find one million dollars within the next 24 hours. The cardinal promised he would phone him back. That evening, by 6 o'clock, Cushing told Kennedy that the million would be handed over the same day.

When he needed money, Cushing used cunning persuasion and bullying. He incited his flock to compete with other dioceses. Once he told them that whereas Chicago had raised 43 million, New York 39 million, Brooklyn 38 million, Boston should outmatch the lot and raise at least 50 million. Which it did.

The additional wealth received annually by the Catholic Church cannot be ascertained because of its secretive nature. Yet it has been estimated, in conservative quarters, that it ranges between 700 million and one and a half billion dollars each year. All tax free.

The Church furthermore, is also the recipient of a recondite, but continuous flow of gifts — cash and real estate — from generous well-to-do Catholics, some from the richest families of the U.S.A.

Then there are Catholic charities, sponsored by philanthropic persons or corporations, that give large donations, openly or often anonymously, to the Church.

The total figures of such contributions, annuities, land, buildings and cash have been estimated to reach another one to one and a half billion a year.

But without enumerating individuals or single details of her wealth, as represented by her multifarious split-financial persona, as we have already done in the preceding chapters, a mere glance at some of her characteristics and features should help to evaluate the massiveness of her financial might.

The Catholic Church in Washington, D.C., for instance, owns or used to own until recently, 60 percent of all tax-exempt land, apart from that held by the Federal Agencies. The real estate of the Catholic Church in Washington, D.C. is, or was until a while ago, three times the size of Vatican City.

In 1983, the Catholic Church owned more property than any private organization in the whole of the United States. They rank *second* only to the U.S. Government in total annual purchase of real estate.

The Catholic Church is the richest of all religious denominations of America. The Catholic Church of America has more land holdings than the Vatican in the rest of the world. Contributions of U.S. Catholic parishes reaches over 2 billion dollars a year. The Catholic Church of America is one of the greatest fiscal powers in the whole world. Her combined assets in the U.S. and Canada have been assessed at well over 120 billion dollars with a cumulative income of about 14-15 billion dollars a year.[3]

An expert on church wealth and income in the U.S. has found that as far back as 1973-74, the Church and her subsidiaries had an income in excess of 9 billion dollars. It owned tax-exempt real estate worth about 75 billion and it had assets over 170 billion.[4]

It has been estimated that by 1983-84, figures would have increased by at least 10-20 percent, making the Catholic Church a serious competitor to the largest industrial giant conglomerates of the entire U.S. Not even the Vatican can compare with such financial ponderousness.

And that is not all. Potentially, she has at her disposal the goodwill of between 55 to 60 million Catholics whose characteristic, besides their religious loyalty, is unprecedented generosity to their church. Their motto, as one enthusiastic bishop fund-collector put it, was "Pray, pay and obey," the most concise summing up of the uniqueness of the immense wealth of the Catholic Church of the U.S. of today.

Another church operating with the same obsession, the Greek Orthodox Church of Imperial Russia, once as financially omnipotent as U.S. Catholicism is now, was made to tumble under the immense weight of all the riches which she had accumulated through the centuries.

Her financial puissance vanished with the social order which had permitted her to flourish as she had, when Caesar-popism — that is, the identification of Orthodoxy with Czarism and their joint mammonish ownership of land and real estate — was made to crash into the dust.

The Russian Church's long identification with the wealth and the power of the system which supported her, by provoking the ire of angry men, brought upon herself lasting ruination.

So that, not only were many of her splendid churches and cathedrals destroyed, closed down, or turned into cold museums, her clergy imprisoned, persecuted and exiled, but even God himself, was "banished" from the very people whom the Orthodox Church was charged to lead in humility and evangelical poverty.

Today, U.S. Catholicism, by allying herself with dollar-popism, that is, by identifying herself with the financial might of the dollar, appears to be following on the footsteps of the Russian Orthodox Church herself, when dulled by her own immense wealth and the Caesar-popism of Imperial Russia, she became the ultimate cause of her own downfall.[5]

History has always had the characteristic of repeating itself. The systematic despoliation of the Church in past centuries, from the Reformation down to the French and Mexican Revolutions as seen in previous chapters, is a sad reminder that attempting to serve both God and Mammon is bound to meet with sure disaster.

When churches are turned into stock-exchanges and their clergy are consulting the bulletins of Wall Street instead of the gospels, as they do in the U.S., then they are surely preparing for a repetition of what happened to Russian Orthodoxy since the Bolshevik Revolution: either reduced to hollow shells, converted into historical curios, cultural showplaces, or into anti-religious centers.[6] Indeed, several of them are now atheistic museums such as the magnificent former St. Isaac's Cathedral in the very heart of Leningrad.[7]

Another no less splendid church of that city, was made to go even further. The present author's astonishment knew no bounds, when one day, having casually walked into the former ecclesiastical renaissance-style edifice, he came face to face with an enormous portrait of Lenin, placed where once there had stood the main altar, in an otherwise totally bare, whitewashed church. The motto of Liberation Theology of Latin America, "Ubi Lenin ibi Jerusalem," — where Lenin is, there is Jerusalem — came to his mind, no longer as a rhetorical slogan, but as the stark reality. The reality of a godless society which, having overthrown a Church obsessed so long with Mammon, now had substituted her with a Bolshevik prophet, proclaiming him the only true Savior of the Russian people.[8]

And yet, notwithstanding the sadness of the sight of so many former churches, the mute symbols of the utter collapse of organized religion in Russia, a flicker of light shone unexpectedly amidst that depressing desolation.

One day, while visiting the National Cemetery of Leningrad, the present author, upon hearing the pealing of church bells, headed towards a large edifice nearby, which he entered.

It was an ancient church, with a lofty cupola, its walls covered by frescoes of stiff Byzantine saints, virgins, and angels. Several bearded priests were officiating. The worshippers, holding small lit candles, which they stuck at intervals upon an iron grill and who, now and then, kissed an ancient icon, were reverent and silent and praying.

The KGB companion at his elbow then explained, "The edifice," she said, "is a cultural monument, the original cathedral founded by Peter the Great." "Of course," then she added, indicating the worshippers, "we have still small pockets of superstition. But they are fast disappearing — time and education will see to that."

She had sounded unconvincing. And looked embarrassed.

Weeks later and thousands of miles away, the present author spotted the single golden cupola of a typical traditional small Russian church near the harbor of Sochi in the Black Sea.[9] The following day, a Sunday, he and an Irishman from Dublin who wanted to hear mass, communism or no communism, met there at 7 in the morning. It was packed. Women, their heads covered with scarves, prayed devoutly, now and then kissing the marble floor or making the sign of the cross in unison with the officiating clergy. An invisible choir in the organ loft was chanting liturgical chants, as a bearded priest read the gospels and three others distributed communion. The devotion was impressive. The singing of the choir, even more so.

The Irishman began to weep unashamedly. "I have never felt so near God in all my life," he whispered.

It was a moving sight. For notwithstanding the haunting music, the splendid Orthodox liturgy and the profound piety, there was an all pervading feeling of immense, terrible resignation.

A feeling that they, the worshippers, were merely tolerated by a society which had rejected their belief, and where they no longer had any power, status, or influence.

God had been banished, and with Him, their church. The state had replaced both with atheism, Christ with Lenin, wealth with poverty.

The splendors and riches had all gone, as had the third of the lands of all Russia, which once she had owned.

Now, despoiled of honor, wealth and privilege, she owned nothing, got nothing, expected nothing. She was forced to live in utter evangelical poverty by an atheist state.

Then as the chanting surged and the congregation crossed themselves, an ancient ascetically frail priest appeared, holding a wooden plate. The Irishman gave a few kopecks. The present author did the same. Then remembering the utter poverty of a once proud church, now a beggar, he put a handful of rubles. The ancient priest stared and then bowed his head in utter stillness. The reflection of regret and of the penance of the Old Russian Orthodox Church, now humbled and powerless, at last had learned her lesson.[10]

Later on in Moscow, the present writer, one night, after walking alone to the center of the city, found himself in Red Square. A full moon hung right above the forbidding walls of the Kremlin. The massive black Mausoleum of Lenin looked solitary and sinister.

The gold-gilded turrets and onion-shaped cupolas of St. Basil, opposite, once a magnificent Cathedral, shone fairy-like against the deep violet, nocturnal midnight sky.

Pinnacled upon the tallest tower of the Kremlin, there shone blood-red, a colossal star, whose gigantic size dwarfed to insignificance the crosses capping the golden cupolas of St. Basil.[11]

A terrible symbol. And even more terrible, a terrible reality.

Reliving the events which had turned St. Basil Cathedral into an empty shell and had put that massive Red Star above the Cross, remembering the relentless obsession of the Catholic Church of America, with her feverish accumulation of wealth, prestige and political power, although, or perhaps because of the eery silence in the deserted square, the present author, thinking about her future, trembled for her.

For truly, the richest Church of the Western world had not yet learned the lesson, so bitterly learned by her sister in the East.

Mammon had become her God. While Christ the poor, by now to her was nothing but a myth.

CHAPTER 26

ORIGIN OF THE CURRENT COLOSSAL WEALTH OF THE CATHOLIC CHURCH

The current spectacular accumulation of wealth by the Catholic Church is a comparatively recent phenomenon. As we have already seen, it really was initiated within what she considered one of the most infamous crimes committed against the See of Peter — her deprivation of the Papal States by the Italians in 1870. These included Rome itself and comprised almost one-third of the Italian peninsula.

It was then that she began the accumulation of riches according to the success formula of the modern industrial and financial world, in preference to the anachronistic methods by which the papacy held the sovereign possession of territories which were becoming more and more untenable in a society rushing towards the complexities of the twentieth century.

The first foundation stones of the current accumulation of Vatican wealth, however, were not laid when Pope Pius XI signed the Lateran Pact with the Fascist dictator, Mussolini, in 1929 when the Vatican formally renounced the Papal States and accepted as compensation a vast sum of money, as already mentioned. Her plans were laid by a previous pope, Benedict XV (1914-22), during and after the First World War (1914-18). It was he who originated today's Vatican policy that church and papal investments should not be limited by political or religious considerations but instead should be handled purely on the basis of sound, good, concrete and profitable business.

The new formula was put into operation during his pontificate. The Vatican at that time had not the liquid resources which it received a decade later from Facist Italy, but it had sufficient millions to invest in the world markets. Benedict XV, to prove that he meant business when he promulgated the new policy, promptly invested most of the Vatican's money. Where? Shades of the crusading pontiffs! In Turkish Empire Securities! It was the beginning of a road which was to bring the Catholic Church into the ranks of the top billionaire corporations of the twentieth century.

By 1929, the time of the Lateran Treaty, the Vatican's State treasure had become an official fund, so that when Mussolini in that same year turned over 1,750 million lire (the equivalent, at that time, of 100 million dollars) to the Vatican as a final settlement of the Roman question, Pope Pius XI, no less a good businessman than Benedict, invested most of this vast sum in America immediately after the market collapse. The move was a profitable one, for, following the great depression of the thirties, the Church reaped colossal profits when the U.S. economy recovered.

But, while investing largely in the U.S., the Vatican was sufficiently astute to invest a good portion of the Lateran compensation in Italy itself. The results, by any standards, have been staggering. It is estimated that at present the Holy See owns between 10 and 15 per cent of all the stocks and shares registered on the Italian Stock Exchange.

The value of the wealth of the Catholic Church in Italy attained truly astronomical figures. At the close of 1964, for instance, the total of her investment was said to be 5,500 million lire. This would make the total capital invested by her in Italian securities *alone* 550 million lire, or 323.5 million pounds sterling, or over 810 million dollars at the 1972 rates of exchange. But even this staggering sum falls short of the truth, according to the matter-of-fact British periodical, "The Economist."

For the Vatican's wealth in the Italian peninsula is not confined to stocks and shares, but has ramified, as we have already seen, into vast real estate ownership and direct and indirect involvement in industrial and commercial enterprises, some of which are on a world-wide scale. The Vatican, in fact, has succeeded in increasing its initial capital within Italy in such a spectacular way that as "The Economist" put it, "it could theoretically throw the Italian economy into confusion if it decided to unload all its shares suddenly and dump them on the market."[1]

ORIGIN OF CURRENT COLOSSAL WEALTH OF CHURCH

This was confirmed a few years later by the Italian Finance Minister when in February, 1968, he declared that the Vatican owned shares worth approximately 100 billion lire. They brought a dividend of three to four billion lire a year. The sum did not include bank deposits, state bonds, or the assets of the sundry Vatican Banks, interlinked with international concerns abroad. An American writer, friend of the author, in a remarkable and reliable book, wrote that "the productive capital of the Vatican can be reckoned at between 50 and 55 billion Swiss francs, that is at 7,000-8,000 billion lire."[2]

The Vatican paper, "Osservatore Romano," wrote that these were lying figures. "The productive capital of the Holy See," it replied, "is far from reaching one hundredth of this sum." Yet if those figures are divided by one hundred, minus 70 billion lire, we can still get the remarkable sum of 46 million pounds, or 110 million dollars at the 1972 rate of exchange.

Perhaps that's what the pope meant when he said that "the Church presents herself as she is...as the Church of the Poor!"[3]

His statement was challenged by many Catholics. Some went so far as to demonstrate against the "scandalous wealth of the Church." Catholic priests protested in the U.S., France, and even Italy. In October, 1971, Catholic priests demonstrated in St. Peter's Square, in the presence of the pope. They carried a banner with the words, "Church, do not give crumbs to the poor. Go, sell what you have, and give them that."[4] Soon afterwards, Archbishop Teopisto Alberto of Caceres in the Philippines, spoke during the Third World Synod of Bishops held in Rome, with the pope presiding, and asked "whether the Church's wealth was always used to serve the poor."[5]

Protests from within the Church multiplied, to the embarrassment of many sincere but bewildered Catholics. The truth of the matter was that the wealth of the Church, besides becoming an increasing moral embarrassment, had become also a financial dilemma. The Church found herself top-heavy with wealth, not only because of the laborious collection of money derived from thousands of religious, ecclesiastic and lay organizations, but equally because of the skill of top financial brains which, since the Second Wold War had invested the Vatican's billions in most parts of the world with dexterity second to none. Their skill, with the help the global intelligence at their disposal, had truly turned the Vatican millions into billions. Not only in Italian lire, but also in sound American dollars and Swiss francs. The gold bullion deposited at Fort Knox in the U.S. could vouch for that.

The accumulation of such colossal riches made the haphazard methods of the past obsolete, indeed, dangerous. The pope was compelled to set up a special body, the Prefecture for Economic Affairs.

The Prefecture, directed mostly by American, French, German and other brains, had to operate mainly outside Italy, since the largest bulk of the invisible and yet concrete Vatican investments were spread over a wide international, if not global, field. The celebrated Jewish house of the Rothschilds — who, incidentally, had been lending money to the Vatican since 1831 — came once more to the fore with the buying, selling and amalgamating of millions of shares and other investments on behalf of the Vatican. The beginning of this liaison between the Rothschilds and the Vatican was in 1969-70, when the Vatican sold the controlling share of the giant Immobiliare to the Parisbas Transcompany of Luxemburg, which was controlled by the mighty Banque de Paris et de Pays Bas. This, it must be remembered, belonged to, or rather was controlled by, the French branch of the Rothschilds. Afterwards, the Vatican sold hundreds of millions worth of shares and other investments with Hambros Bank and the Continental Bank of Illinois, at that time presided over by David Kennedy, the U.S. Treasury Minister. It is interesting to remember that the President of the French Republic, Mr. Pompidou, for many years worked for the private bank of the Rothschilds.

Money, by trespassing from the national to the international fields, can create a variety of problems which can and did bring the Vatican to the limelight of international fraud. Scandal of magnitudinous proportions eventually erupted in the eighties to the astonishment of millions of Catholics and the chagrin of many who genuinely thought the Vatican was engaged only on charitable operations.

Vatican financial operations, at times, because of their diversity, can trespass into semi-illegality because of their indetectability. When light is cast upon them, the Vatican has to rid itself of profitable concerns. For instance, when it had to sell the Serono Institute because of the "pill."[6]

By and large, however, its investments are well looked after by financial experts whose experience is second to none. The Vatican's traditional financial dealers are a mostly non-Catholic fraternity of Protestants, agnostics, non-Christians, Jews and even atheists.

Its traditional financial transactions have been handled for years by the great banking concerns of J. P. Morgan in New York (mostly for American investments), Hambros of London for British investments, and the Swiss Credit Bank of Zurich for European investments — without mentioning the Vatican's own concerns such as Banco di Roma, Banco Commerciale, Banco Santo Spirito, and other less known but equally skillful entities handling and multiplying the Catholic billions throughout the globe. The last-mentioned bank, for instance, a few years back, reputedly invested 175 million pounds in France and no less than 250 million pounds of Vatican money in Italy.

Now, it must never be forgotten that all the above form only the "liquid" financial assets of the Holy See. We have entirely excluded the solid properties, real estate, lands, industrial and commercial concerns owned and controlled by the Catholic Church in Italy, Spain, Germany, Great Britain, and North, Central and South America. To estimate the actual current values of the Church's tremendous possessions and real estate properties is an impossibility. Those owned by the Catholic Church in the U.S. alone should be a reliable guide. Add to them the real estates it owns in Africa, Asia, Australia, and so on, and the total amount is, to say the least, staggering. Even this, however, is not all. It must be remembered that the Vatican — or rather, the Catholic Church — owns thousands upon thousands of churches, cathedrals, monasteries, nunneries and sundry edifices practically throughout the Western world. What is the value of the land upon which all these buildings stand, in current money? What is the value of the actual buildings themselves? If one should give modest prices for the humble parish churches and parish halls, what prices would an estate agent give, for instance, for St. Patrick's Cathedral in New York, Notre Dame in Paris, and St. Peter's in Rome, to mention only a few? Then one should not forget the vast properties owned by the sundry hierarchies in Catholic, Protestant and even non-Christian lands everywhere.

We glanced very briefly at the details of such property in the U.S. Its value there runs into billions of dollars, and it is increasing daily. The same process has occurred and is currently occurring in many other countries, including England and the rest of Europe.

The claim that such property is not owned by the Catholic Church is as insubstantial as the claim that the Catholic Church must have property on earth the better to deal with the issues of the spirit in heaven. It is like saying that a Communist dictatorship does not own anything because all property is owned by the people — the substance of the matter of course, being that it is the Communist state which owns everything, while the people in reality own nothing. When the Catholic Church sells a piece of land or buys one, the bishop as a rule signs the deed, which means that his See becomes the owner or receives the money. Whether the transaction is localized to the diocese or deputized from the national hierarchy or from the Vatican, is basically irrelevant since ultimately it concerns the property of the Catholic Church.

In some countries, not only does the Church evade taxation, but the state itself collects taxation on her behalf. This absurdity has been one of the most extraordinary peculiarities of Germany, where the Vatican and the Protestant Churches are better treated than any of the giant industrial concerns responsible for Germany's economic prosperity. The German state, in fact, "compels" German citizens to pay a church taxation. This is called the Kirchensteuer (Church Tax). It was first inspired by the Weimar Constitution of 1919, was confirmed by the pact between Hitler and the Vatican in their concordat of 1933. The Kirchensteuer was made constitutional in 1949, after the Second World War.

The Catholic Government — that is, the Christian Democrats — not only enforced the church taxation upon an unwilling populace, it put the state machinery at the disposal of the Church. Thus the Government collected the tax, enforced its payment, and then handed over the money thus collected to the Church.

Before the Second World War, the German citizens used to pay an average of two to three marks a year. By 1972, the figure rose to between fifty-five and sixty marks. In rich districts like Dusseldorf, for instance, the citizen was compelled to pay between 110 and 120 marks. It has been reckoned that the two main churches, Catholic and Protestant, in 1965 received 3.2 billion marks, of which 2.8 billion came directly from the Kirchensteuer, to cite only one example.[7] That figure had almost doubled by 1982. The Protestants extracted almost two billion by 1982. This church tax represented a heavy burden upon the taxpayer, already heavily burdened by other taxation — that is, between 10 and 14 per cent of his income tax. In addition to this, the Church got an additional 250 million marks a year, so that the two churches compelled the German taxpayer to supply them with about 90 per cent of their total revenues.

The Protestant Church of Germany thus became one of the wealthiest churches of Europe, surpassed only by the Protestant churches of the U.S., where they were almost on a par with the Catholic Church with its wealth running into hundreds of billions of dollars.

In Germany, therefore, the Vatican, besides enjoying outstanding financial benefits from its skillful penetration of the giant industrial concerns as it did in Italy and in the United States, had its coffers replenished with additional millions from the Kirchensteuer, to the tune of some 350 million dollars a year, the scheme being the result of the political Catholicism which dominated the life of post-war Germany for so long.

We have already mentioned that the Vatican had financial interests in England as well, with industrial concerns, some of which were actually subsidiaries of the giant British Courtaulds.[8]

The SNIA-Viscosa Corporation, for instance, in which the Vatican had invested hundreds of millions, had as its agents the Hambros Bank. Many of Hambros' financial affairs were in their turn controlled by other subsidiaries, among which was the Westminster Hambros Trust, owned jointly by Hambros and the Westminster Bank.

During the eighties, the Hambros and the Westminster Banks became involved with the IOR, even if tangently, when a scandal involving about 1.4 million dollars, brought down Italy's major Catholic Bank in 1982, as we shall see presently.

Similar concerns in which the Vatican's millions were invested and re-invested existed practically all over Europe. We have already glanced at the industrial, commercial and financial concerns with global ramifications. The Vatican, as we have already reiterated, has large investments with the Rothschilds of Britain, France and America, with the Hambros Bank, with the Credit Suisse in London and Zurich. In the United States, it has large investments with the Morgan Bank, the Chase Manhattan Bank, the First National Bank of New York, the Bankers Trust Company, and others. The Vatican, as we have already seen, has billions of shares in the most powerful international corporations such as Gulf Oil, Shell, General Motors, Bethlehem Steel, General Electric, International Business Machines, TWA, etc. At a conservative estimate, these amount to more than 500 million dollars in the U.S. alone.

The Catholic Church, therefore, once all her assets have been put together, is the most formidable stockbroker in the world. The "Wall Street Journal" said that the Vatican's financial deals in the U.S. alone were so big that very often it sold or bought gold in lots of a million or more dollars at one time.[9]

The Vatican's treasure of solid gold has been estimted by the "United Nations World Magazine" to amount to several billion dollars. A large bulk of this is stored in gold ingots with the U.S. Federal Reserve Bank, while banks in England and Switzerland hold the rest. But this is just a small portion of the wealth of the Catholic Church, which in the U.S. alone, as we have already seen, is greater than that of the five wealthiest giant corporations of the country.[10] When to that is added all the real estate, property, stocks and shares abroad, then the staggering accumulation of the wealth of the Vatican becomes so formidable as to defy any rational assessment.

ORIGIN OF CURRENT COLOSSAL WEALTH OF CHURCH

The enormous financial reserves of the Vatican in the seventies and the eighties can be gauged by the fact that its financial reserves equalled the official holdings of France, both in gold and foreign securities. The Vatican could be a match, not only for France but equally for Britain herself. The United Kingdom's dollar reserves, in fact, were estimated at 1,000 million dollars,[11] a sum equivalent to only one-fifth of the Vatican's marketable stock, which, according to level-headed and reputable financiers, totalled the world over more than 2,000 million pounds sterling or between 5,000 and 6,000 million dollars. Reliable sources at this period indicated that the Vatican at the same time had a gold reserve of 11 billion, three times the gold reserve of Great Britain.[12] This is a very conservative estimate. Furthermore, it must be remembered that it covers only the Vatican's holdings on stock exchanges and other negotiable values. In short, this astronomical sum is limited to the Vatican's "liquid capital reserves."

Taken in this way, therefore, the Vatican at a most conservative estimate is "the world's largest shareholder, with a portfolio of quoted securites totalling the equivalent of 5,600 million dollars"[13] and 6,000 million dollars by 1970-71. The volume of the Vatican's world-wide stocks and shares in the eighties was put at "5 billion to 10 billion dollars."[14]

Thanks to this, therefore, the Vatican was, and still is, the most redoubtable wealth accumulator and property owner in existence. No one knows for certain how much the Catholic Church was, or is, worth in terms of dollars and other currencies, not even the pope himself.

That is the true situation borne out by a Vatican official who, when asked to make a guess at the Vatican's wealth today replied, very tellingly, "Only God knows."

The tersest summing up of the matter!

CHAPTER 27

THE BEST THING TO HAVE HAPPENED SINCE JESUS CHRIST

The economic magnitude of the Vatican wealth in the seventies was bound to create problems peculiar to the world of big business with the result that the Vatican, in common with other financial giants, became increasingly concerned about the future of its investments. The more so, since the mercurial ups and downs of political instability and the economic fluctuations of world economy were becoming alarmingly frequent.

In Italy the portents were even more ominous. The Italian Government, pressurized by left wing groups, was demanding that the Vatican be forced to pay its millions of arrears taxation, promising future tough legislation on tax evasions.

Abroad, Europe's prosperity had begun to look unhealthy. The Vatican, sensing the shape of things to come, began to seriously rethink its vast financial empire. Its reformulation was soon encapsulated into: gradual but steady transference of capital, liquid and otherwise, to safer lands, chiefly to the U.S.A.

When, in 1971, therefore, Pope Paul VI told the world that "the Church must be poor...and should also be seen to be poor," his words were heard with silent cynicism by the professional money managers, busy with Vatican deals.

What had prompted Paul VI's comment was that for some time now, the Vatican's expenses had been greater than its income. Also, that Peter's Pence had sunk to a mere 3 million per year. Strictly speaking, the pope had been correct. Insofar that he had referred exclusively to the Vatican's administrative budget and not to the Church's vast annual income.

The complaint of the Vatican deficit, since then, became a kind of ritual smoke-screen. It helped the Church to project an image of parsimonious existence, which was wholly unrelated to the factual state of her financial affairs.

The operation is always successful with the public, confused by the diverse faces of an organization which acts within a veil of financial convolutions, religious-diplomatic equivocations and departmental euphemisms.

Each time the Vatican declares it has suffered a deficit, therefore, the declaration is accepted at its face value, so that it is seen as an impoverished concern which, having had more expenses than income, is bound to collapse for lack of funds. It is a move which has always yielded world sympathy and a flow of cash to match, sometimes, from outside, but very often from inside the Vatican itself since the money, far from being scarce, is overflowing from the coffers of the very Church it represents.

Pope Paul VI was certainly not the first to ask for financial help. His predecessor, the popular Pope John XXIII, set the example following the second Vatican Council which he had summoned in the sixties.

The Council produced a bill of about 4 million dollars. Pope John, at first declined paying it on the grounds that the Vatican had not the money. Then hard pressed by the harder facts of life, he sold 4 million in gold to the U.S.A.

The total cost of the Vatican Council, however, was far heavier — more than 20 million dollars, with an additional 10 million for "extras."

Again the Vatican complained loudly that it could not afford to pay. It appealed to the faithful, who donated more generously to Peter's Pence, and "special" offerings. Then pressed by hard-faced creditors, he found the money from the Church herself.

Twenty years later, Pope Wojtyla played the same "lack of funds" trick. In November, 1979, he summoned the entire College of Cardinals to Rome — the first time of its kind in 400 years — to discuss the piteous state of the Vatican's "deficit" which amounted to 8 million pounds sterling.

After the meeting, Cardinal Carpio, the Vatican's top financier, announced to the incredulous world that "we, the Church, are reduced to charity." The assembled cardinals were baffled. "We have seen the accounts," said one, "but we can't make out whether the Church is booming or on the verge of bankruptcy."[1]

The "deficit" had trebled by 1982-83. By 1984 it would have doubled, it was said. Then it was predicted that it would treble by 1984-85. Indeed, an official went so far as to declare that the Vatican would become "bankrupt" within five years.

Faced by such a gloomy future, Pope John Paul II summoned the Sacred College of Cardinals a second time (November, 1982) to study the situation. The true motive, however, was more serious. It was the financial scandal of the IOR, that is the Vatican Bank, in which it had become deeply involved in a fraud, running into hundreds of millions of dollars as we shall see presently. At the end he said, simply, that the Church had to, and should, live only on the proceeds of the charity of good Catholics.

The absurdity of the whole thing was that at the same time one of his cardinals had raised over 85 million dollars from one diocese alone, that of Cologne, to send to Latin America. Also, that a few years before, the Vatican lost between 40 and 80 million dollars in financial operations. And even more absurd, that the Vatican was, as ever, one of the wealthiest entities in the world.

The truth of the matter, of course, was that Pope Wojtyla, like Pope Paul VI and his predecessors, claimed poverty, knowing very well that they were the legal representatives of immense wealth, invested in the liquid assets, bonds, shares, real estate and holdings of the Catholic Church.

But reverting to the complaint of Pope Paul VI. At a conservative estimate, in the seventies, the total income of the Church, according to an authoritative assessment of a U.S. financial correspondent of the *Institutional Investor*, a U.S. magazine highly regarded by American professional money managers[2], was more than substantial.

The impossibility of assessing the exact figures was due mainly to the fact that the man who should have known, Cardinal Vagnozzi, head of the Vatican Prefecture for Economic Affairs, for all his cooperation, avoided direct answers to direct questions.

After four laborious interviews, however, the magazine concluded that the income, as far as it was possible to see from what the cardinal had revealed, was about 140 million dollars.

When it was pointed out that the general assessment of the Vatican's total wealth was about 5 billion, the cardinal protested, calling the figure "absolutely wild." When pressed, however, he admitted that yes, 500 million was closer to the truth.

So much for Pope Paul VI complaining that the Vatican that year had suffered losses of about 11 million when, in fact, its stocks, holdings, shares and financial ramifications and multiplications of dividends in Italy and abroad, were flourishing more than ever.

Witness also the fact that at that very period it had just sold off, as already seen in the previous chapter, two-thirds of its 15% interest in the Immobilaire, the company that built Washington's famed Watergate. This, in addition to having stocks in General Motors, General Electric, Shell, Bethlehem Steel, Gulf Oil, IBM and other similar mighty financial concerns.

Following his well publicized pleas of poverty and the ambiguous information of Cardinal Vagnozzi, Pope Paul VI began to take the first silent steps aimed at reorganizing the Church's financial structure. The main objective of the operation: the sound reinvestment of the Vatican's funds, and above all, its massive transfer of its visible and invisible assets abroad.

To that effect, he chose three financial experts. Cardinal Vagnozzi, a former Apostolic delegate to Washington, and an open admirer of the American way of doing things — especially in financial matters — and who could never give enough praise to the American hierarchy for the way they managed to run and increase the wealth of their dioceses — Vagnozzi's heroes being cardinals Spellman, Cushing and McIntyre — whom we have already encountered.

Archbishop Caprio became the head of a team of financial and real estate experts specializing in international operations with one Paul Marcinkus from Chicago, the latter to direct the Institute for Religious Affairs, another name for the Vatican Bank.

The Institute for Religious Works, or IOR for short, besides being what its name implied, was also an entity which provided a full range of banking services that embraced not only the whole of Europe, but also certain branches of the banking system of the U.S., as we shall have occasion to see presently.

Pope Paul's plans to transfer the Vatican's funds outside Italy was first given sudden urgency with the international financial crisis provoked by President Nixon's moves to shore up the dollar (August, 1971).

The Vatican, to minimize its losses, was forced to change most of its millions of dollars into German marks and Swiss francs. This it did, before Nixon's decision had been announced, thus reducing its potential losses by millions. The warning, given in secret from the U.S., saved the Vatican millions. The passing of secret information from the U.S. to the Vatican, prior to official financial U.S. moves, was not the first time nor the last, since the Vatican has always had an eager group of American bankers, the financial experts, eager, indeed, ready to pass such information to Rome. These are not only Catholics, but a band as varied as there can be, amongst many, to cite only two, Morgan Guaranty Trust and Hambros Bank. By 1983, the volunteers have multiplied by the dozens. Notwithstanding the secret warning, the Vatican's reserves that year, in U.S. currency, had been reputedly cut to a mere million.

The experience caused the Vatican to take action in earnest and go ahead with the original vague plans to move its funds to safer grounds. The mounting pressure in Italy for the Vatican to pay its taxes, including its arrears, did the rest. This, notwithstanding the fact that the Vatican, after pleading poverty, promised that it might pay "in installments" because it was "too poor."

When 1970 came, and then 1980, the Vatican had not paid one single penny. By 1983, after having paid a nominal small sum, it claimed again preferential treatment, thus justifying its nick-name of the "biggest tax evader of the country."

Paul VI's rethinking was not an original idea. The Vatican had done its rethinking, in financial terms, long before. In fact, it began when Mussolini signed the Lateran Treaty in 1929, and Italy gave the Vatican about 100 million dollars as compensation for the Vatican territorial losses as already indicated.

Pius XI, then reigning pope, asked a banker, B. Nogara, an Italian Jew, for his advice as to what to do about the money. Nogara suggested that the money should be invested, however without any theological consideration or restrictive moral scruples since money has its own laws that are outside religion. He wisely said that one third of the 100 million dollars be turned into solid gold and placed in the U.S. (in Fort Knox, where they have been to this day) and the rest turned into shares and real estate.

By the time that Nogara died, in 1958, the Vatican, thanks to Nogara's policy, had become involved with a vast network of thousands of holdings, companies, real estate, chemicals, constructions, electronics, plastics, cements, the owner of many large insurance companies, industrial concerns and the controller of banks throughout Italy.

The Nogara Midas touch, in fact, was so successful that thanks to his principle that the Vatican must not be restricted in its financial dealings by theological consideration, his original investment, by 1982-83, had made the Vatican one of the heaviest investors, to the tune of more than 1,200 million on the New York Stock Market, to quote only one typical example. So much so, that the Vatican financial might by 1983 was realistically estimated at more than 12,000 million dollars.

No wonder that Pius XI's papal successors are credited with having called the appearance of Nogara at the Vatican as "the best thing to have happened to the Church since our Lord Jesus Christ."

Pope Paul VI, while not an expert on financial affairs, nevertheless was anxious to see that the Vatican money problems be handled with expertise by the right people. With that in view, he scanned the horizon to discover someone who, like the fabulous Nogara, could not only safeguard the Vatican's wealth, but equally, if possible, increase it.

When exiled in Milan, northern Italy, by Pope Pius XI because of his left wing leanings, Archbishop Montini,[3] as he then was, met a little known Sicilian "financial expert" who appeared to make money from practically nothing. The man proved his worth by helping Mgsr. Montini to solve an urgent local financial problem with uncanny efficiency and promptitude.

In addition, the man seemed to have specialized in the recondite operational criss-crossing of national and international financial concerns, with its concurrent transfer of capital from Italy to other countries, the very qualification which the Vatican needed most at that critical period.

When Mgsr. Montini eventually became Pope Paul VI, and the harassing problems of the transference of the Vatican assets outside Italy, plus the pressing demands of the Italian Government for the payment of tax arrears, confronted his pontificate, he remembered the Sicilian financier, the Howard Hughes of Italy, as he was later to call him.

The Sicilian expert, one Sindona by name, welcomed the papal invitation. Thereupon, with the pope's blessing and the millions of the Catholic Church at his disposal, he plunged headlong into coordinating, transferring and multiplying the Vatican financial fortunes.

The Vatican had found a worthy successor to the miracle man, Nogara, at last.

CHAPTER 28

THE POPE'S VERY OWN FINANCIAL LITTLE FOX

In the seventies, as the Vatican's financial problems multiplied, a man like Sindona seemed to have been sent by Divine Providence. Sindona accepted the task with unbounded enthusiasm. He always felt at home whenever dealing with high finances and complicated national and international deals.

When Pope Paul VI, therefore, asked him to help solve the Vatican's current financial impasse, Sindona had no doubts about his ability to do so. The pope thought likewise. He had already had positive proof of Sindona's magic touch, back in 1962, when as Archbishop of Milan, he had found himself in trouble in connection with the building of an old-folks home.

Sindona had volunteered to help with finding the money. He would use his banking connections, he promised, and presto, he presented the delighted Mgsr. Montini with two and a half million dollars. It was a miracle, or more accurately, the work of a financial wizard. Archbishop Montini was impressed, and the two men became friends.

The archbishop's confidence was justified. For although Sindona at this time was hardly known in high ecclesiastical circles in Rome, Mgsr. Montini had rightly reckoned that Sindona's skill could and would free the Vatican of its increasing monetary worries. The man's achievements, after all, were there for all to assess.

Within less than two decades, Sindona had formed and controlled no less than 22 international companies, all interlocking within such a complicated financial maze that nobody appeared to comprehend it with the exception of its manipulator, Sindona himself.

The prestigious magazine, "Fortune," was so impressed that it focused its keen financial eyes upon his operations. It came to the conclusion that Sindona was worth a startling 450 million dollars, the richest man in Italy and one of the richest in Europe. The achievement, more than exceptional, was almost unique, since the man had started from nothing.

Sindona's grandfather had been a chicory seller back in Sicily; his father, a poor farm worker. Sindona had his first studies with the Jesuits, then at Messina's University where he became one of its youngest lawyers. He began at once to act for emigrants with interests in America.

While busy with them, he sought the friendship of the most energetic Archbishop of Sicily because he had a record number of church buildings to his credit. At the same time, he tried his hand at international taxation. In a very short time, he became the legal tax expert in Italian-American issues and a favorite consultant with Italian-American investors.

Then he met a man, a small banker who controlled a minor financial concern, called the Banca Privata Finanziaria. The man owned also a steel foundry. The banker told Sindona that he wanted to get rid of the foundry. Sindona obliged, bought the foundry himself, and then he promptly sold it, at a good profit, to the U.S. American Crucible Company. Shortly afterwards, cash in hand, Sindona also got hold of the bank itself. He used the latter as the first stepping stone to realize his dream: the takeover of international concerns via international operations.

One of his earliest achievements was that of getting hold of 10 per cent of the shares of Libby's Food Company in Italy, which he promptly sold to Nestles. The move netted him several million dollars.

Success breeds success, and now Sindona, more confident than ever, ventured outside Italy to a notorious tax-exempt haven, Liechtenstein. There he set up a holding company under the former vice-president of the American Crucible Company.

The transference proved so beneficial that Sindona dared to approach well-known private banks: Continental Illinois National Bank and Trust Company of Chicago, and Hambros of

London, with whom he linked his own Banca Privata Finanziaria.

It so happened, and that was certainly no surprise to him, that the former bank had very strong ties with the Vatican's most important financial department, namely with the Institute for Religious Works, (IOR) a channel to anybody wanting to transfer money anonymously in and out of Italy.

Sindona was the ideal man since he had a habit of keeping tight-lipped about anything he did, especially about his main client's discreet financial operations, the Vatican.

Astute observers, however, soon noticed how he always benefited as much as his august client, whenever making a deal. Yet, because of the nature of most of his clandestine operations, it was impossible to substantiate the charge.

Sindona's activities could, and did, stultify friends and foes alike, not excluding the Vatican, where, it was rumored that even the pope was never sure when his chief financial adviser was operating for the Church, for himself, or for both simultaneously.

When, therefore, such rumors reached Cardinal Vagnozzi, Chief of the Prefecture for the Vatican's Economic Affairs and Bishop Marcinkus, the head of IOR, they did not mind. Sindona's operations were advantageous to the Church, they declared. And that's what mattered.

The cardinals' toleration appeared to have been justified. Since Sindona, by now, had become almost indispensable whenever the Church found herself in some embarrassing or difficult situation.

Thus, whereas it was true that Sindona used the Church whenever dealing with some dubious financial operations of his own, it was equally true, that the Vatican used him as a front man, each time it was confronted with painful dilemmas.

Such as when, for instance, it was disclosed, as mentioned previously, that the Vatican owned and controlled a chemical concern that manufactured contraceptives, and even explosives, the Instituto Farmacologico Serona of Rome. Furthermore, that the Instituto's chairman was none other than Prince G. Pacelli, a nephew of Pope Pius XII. And this, at the time when the pope was condemning, almost daily, birth control.[1]

The dilemmas with which occasionally the Vatican was faced were varied and many. For example, it so happened that once the Vatican found itself consorting with some notorious Marxist bedfellows. These had managed to establish themselves within the board of the Vatican's own controlled Banca Unione.

Amongst others, the rabid revolutionary family of the Feltrinelli publishers, whose founder not long afterwards blew himself up when attempting to plant dynamite against a high-voltage electric pylon outside Milan, while, so it was said, trying to carry out a daring act of sabotage against the establishment.

The bedfellowship had made the Vatican increasingly uneasy. The problem was put to Sindona. Sindona bought the bank and ousted the offending bedfellow at once. It had been as easy as that.

Sindona, however, had caught two birds with one stone. Since, by freeing his Vatican's client from an impossible political nightmare, he had simultaneously made a very good deal for himself.

Once under his control, the Banca Unione, until then a semi-dormant provincial bank, was suddenly revitalized. Sindona offered its investors double interest rates. The result was predictable. The Banca Unione's deposits rose from 70 to 165 million dollars practically overnight.

Sindona continued to operate with the aid of the Vatican. Like when, for instance, the head of the IOR, Bishop Marcinkus, suggested to him that he should buy the Vatican's interest in La Centrale Finanziaria Generale and resell it to the Banco Ambrosiano of Milan, the focus of an impending scandal of the eighties.

Or when Marcinkus convinced the pope to compel the Patriarch of Venice to sell his controlling interest in the Banca Cattolica del Veneto, a local Venetian bank, to Sindona who then resold it to the Banco Ambrosiano, where the Vatican had already substantial shares to partially control it.

These, and similar operations, impressed not only the Head of Economic Affairs for the Vatican, but also the pope himself. The latter was so satisfied with Sindona, that in one of his rare moments of enthusiasm he called Sindona his "very own financial little fox."

Sindona's fame spread in Italy and abroad. In the U.S., David Kennedy, who had been president of the Continental Illinois National Bank & Trust Company of Chicago, considered Sindona a financial wizard.

The importance of such a reputation can be judged by the fact that years later, Kennedy became Treasurer Secretary in the first Cabinet of President Nixon. An invaluable political and social asset for Sindona.

It was at this stage that the Vatican, harassed by Italy's threats to force it to pay tax on its holdings in the Italian Stock Market, and furthermore, to pay arrears and future taxation, decided to play it safe by transferring its money outside the country.

Like with the Banca Unione, Sindona was asked to help the Church out of this ever menacing nightmare. Sindona accepted, under one condition. The Vatican had to help him to deal with Italy's biggest real estate and construction unit of the period, the 175 million dollar Societa Generale Immobiliare.

This was the same company which had built the Watergate complex in Washington, D.C. for about 70 million dollars, mostly with Vatican money. The Societa, behind which there were very substantial Vatican shares, had built, via front companies, the Cavalieri Hilton Hotel in Rome, and many other valuable constructions in Italy, the U.S. and elsewhere.

Sindona, true to his practice, bought out the controlling interests which the Vatican had in the Societa and sold 16 per cent to Gulf and Western Industries. Then, he kept 40 per cent controlling interest for himself, giving 5 per cent to his main client, the Vatican.

The manner of disposing of the SGI by the latter is interesting insofar that it throws a light upon the Vatican-Sindona team strategy. Early in 1969-70, the Vatican declared, wishing to discard the image of acting as a business concern, that it had sold its holding in the SGI to "Americans," meaning that it had no longer anything to do with the SGI itself.

The "Americans" turned out to be the Gulf & Western Industries, the owner of Paramount Pictures Corporation, whose amount of shares in the Societa had been so substantial that it practically controlled it. The key men behind the transaction: Charles B. Blundorn, the Gulf & Western Industries' Chairman, and Michele Sindona, the Vatican's financier in chief.

By now, Sindona was acting, not only for the Vatican, but also tangently for the no less powerful concerns, enjoying by now, the confidence of a growing number of American business companies, beginning with the Jesuit controlled Bank of America, the Celanese Corporation and other big U.S. bodies.

To complete the transfer, Sindona acquired the 3.5 per cent of the Societa's shares, which until then, had been owned by the Assicurazioni Generali. The Assicurazioni, it should be noted, was yet another insurance company partially controlled by the Vatican, via heavy acquisition of shares.

Thanks to such brilliant operations, Sindona was elected to the board of directors of the Societa Generale Immobiliare itself. It was a vindication of his financial capabilities. His most secretive sponsor, the Vatican and his U.S. supporters, were delighted.

Sindona became the favorite financier of sundry Catholic commercial quarters in the U.S., from which he drew an unlimited amount of good will, protection and funds.

The Vatican, meanwhile, had become so pleased with him that it put at his disposal a unique team of international experts, composed of 18 top businessmen. Their task — to give Sindona professional advice. The importance of the offer can be judged by the fact that the team had been approved personally by the pope himself. It was composed of individuals drawn from the very top of U.S. financial echelons.

To mention only a few: John Bugas, Vice-President of the Ford Motor Corporation, Vermont C. Royster, Senior Vice-President of the Wall Street Journal, I. A. Farley, former Postmaster General of the U.S., Martin R. Gainsbrugh, Chief Economist of the U.S. National Industrial Conference Board.[2]

Supported by such a formidable all-American think-tank and the blessing of the pope, Sindona plunged headlong into "business."

The Vatican, of course, continued to remain his main sponsor, protector and client. This meant that he was called in, with even more urgency, each time that the IOR, burdened with inconvenient shareholdings or real estate, was anxious to get rid of them without much fuss or embarrassing disclosures.

To get quick results, very often Sindona used his own peculiar method. He bought whatever the Vatican did not want. Whether the operation made Sindona the real buyer or was acting as a front man for the Vatican, did not bother anybody, beginning with the Vatican, as long as Sindona operated in her interest.

The Sindona phenomenon grew without relenting, so much so, that around the seventies, Sindona had become indispensable to the Church whenever she had to deal with major financial operations.

Within a few years, thanks to his energy, the Vatican's portfolio not only grew by leaps and bounds as never before, it became greatly diversified with stocks of the most varied character. These went from Chase Manhattan Bank to Standard Oil, Celanese, Colgate, Unilever, General Foods, Procter & Gamble, Westinghouse and the like.

Simultaneously, the Vatican became involved, even if tangentially, with vast construction projects. For instance, that in which it substantially financed the 3,000 million dollar scheme cooperating with concerns such as the Uris Building Corporation or Tisham Realty & Construction. It provided also financial aid for the buildings of the New York World Trade Center.

The relentless, and often dubious, Sindona operations created widespread suspicions and ultimate animosity. The Bank of Italy, its main spearhead, led the campaign. The Hambros Merchant Bank of London severed their connections, as did many other financial bodies.

Sindona, faced with growing general ostracism, decided to shift his ground of operations and to transfer himself, lock, stock and barrel, to the U.S.

CHAPTER 29

THE CHURCH, NIXON, THE FREEMASONS AND THE JAILED "VATICAN WIZARD"

Before taking the fateful decision to go for good to the U.S.A., Sindona consulted his two most powerful friends in Rome, the Director of the Vatican Bank, and the pope. The men gave him their blessing, plus secretive recommendations, to top American bankers and businessmen, a brilliant mixture of Catholics, Protestants, Jews and agnostics.

It was agreed that Sindona would continue to act as the Vatican's chief financial adviser, but — in secret. Sindona promised. He would do his usual best, as successfully as he had already done in Europe.

Thereupon, having established himself in New York City, he began operations. His first steps had already been taken: the early purchase of three companies: The Oxford Electric, Interphoto and Angus, Inc.

In 1972 he bought 52 per cent interest (1.6 million shares) in Talcott National for 27.3 million dollars, and 21.6 per cent interest in the Franklin New York Corporation, the holding company for Franklin National Bank — a million shares at 40 dollars per share, when it was selling at 32 dollars.

After that, having done further subsidiary profitable coups on the side, he promptly donated one million dollars to the 1972 Nixon campaign funds. Most of the funds, it was believed, came from the Vatican's bank. The rest came from Sindona and from the secret purse of members of the Freemasonic brotherhood of Italy, which had special bonds with prominent lodges of the U.S.

The offer was refused because a recent law had made secret contributions to political parties illegal. There were more practical political considerations to it, however, than mere moral rectitude. At that particular period, these had become of paramount importance, since clandestineness might have backfired against both those who gave and those who had received.

It is worth recording that since then open contributions to political parties in the U.S. have reached monstrous proportions, a state of affairs as worthy of condemnation as clandestine subsidies used to be before they became illegal.

Within one decade, from 1972-1982, for instance, ten Republican Senators reelected in 1982, spent an average of about 1.7 million dollars — more than five times what they spent back in 1976. The Democrats were not far behind, with 1.4 million each.

Sindona's single million, when seen retrospectively therefore, seems child's play if compared to the fact that only ten years later, the House and the Senate candidates spent about 300 million dollars, over 25 per cent more than they had spent only two years before in 1980. Another public interest lobby reckoned that it would double altogether by 1984.[1]

Such figures are only the tip of the iceberg. Since beneath the permissible contributions, secret funds used for political promotion, although still illegal, have continued to pour into the coffers of the political machine feeding political factions at a local and federal level far more efficiently than they did when Sindona and the Vatican Bank tried to feed the Nixon campaign.

The reticence of Nixon's supporters in refusing the Sindona-Vatican offer had been prompted, not only by political consideration, but also by the fear of an impending scandal, which, if permitted to burst in the open, might have affected the pendulum of the election, with the potential dislocation of a disturbed Catholic vote.

Their apprehensions were justified, since, years later, in 1980, an American court charged Sindona with having siphoned 45 million dollars from the Franklin funds into an unauthorized venture, mostly back in Italy.[2]

Sindona's affairs, meanwhile, continued to go from strength to strength. His fame, as a generous and daring financier, grew. The financial community, impressed by his patrons, the Vatican and the Church, no less than by his positive success, began openly to esteem him.

Everything was prospering. Sindona's future seemed assured. After all, he had managed to get the control, almost at one single stroke so to speak, of the 20th largest bank in the U.S. No mean achievement.

Things were going smoothly, when rumors had it that the Bank had lost 39 million dollars, it was said, because of unauthorized trading in foreign currencies. Sindona's various sponsors, the Vatican and the Italian-American Masonic Lodges, the latter only tangently interested in Sindona's marginal activities in the Franklin affair, became alarmed. They agreed to help.

The mysterious IOR, that is the Vatican Bank, raised 30 million dollars and loaned it to the endangered Franklin National Bank in New York. The rescuing operation was carried out in total secrecy.

The efforts proved to be in vain. The crash came earlier than expected and it could not have come at a worse moment. Since, back in Italy, Sindona's own Banca Privata Italiana of Milan, had already been liquidated because, it had been rumored, 300 million dollars could not be accounted for.

As a result of the latter, an arrest warrant had been issued on the grounds that Sindona had taken money from the Milan bank illegally. Furthermore, that he had faked the balance sheet to cover up the operation.

An Italian court convicted Sindona on 25 counts of banking irregularities and sentenced him to 30 months in prison. But even more serious, it asked for his extradition, charging him with fraudulent bank manipulations. The charge, had he been apprehended, could have brought him at least 15 years in jail.

While all this had been going on, the U.S. Securities and Exchange Commission accused Sindona with rules violations and filed a suit in Federal Court.

Sindona was indicted on 66 counts of fraud connected with Franklin National's operations, the largest banking collapse, to date, in American history. Notwithstanding the disaster, he was set free on bail of 1,500,000 dollars, in August, when he promptly vanished. He came back in October.

NIXON, FREEMASONS AND JAILED "VATICAN WIZARD"

During the two and a half months of his disappearance, Sindona, risking arrest, visited Europe. He contacted the Vatican and pleaded for their help at his forthcoming trial in Manhattan's Federal District Court.

The Vatican could not and would not become openly involved in the scandal. Bishop Marcinkus was vague and evasive. Undeterred, Sindona went to Frankfurt, Germany. There he had a secret encounter with the Papal Nuncio, Monsignor Del Mestri, accredited to Bonn, Germany.

The Papal Nuncio promised to help. He would lobby the three top financial bosses of the Vatican, he told him — two friends of his, Cardinal Gerri, Cardinal Carpio, and even the reluctant Bishop Marcinkus. He would try to persuade them to stand by him in the American court.

The three men agreed. Yes, they would vouch for Sindona's good character. To that end, they prepared a video-tape to be used in court. When, however, Federal Judge Marvin Frankel went to Rome to collect it, he was forbidden to do so. The veto had come from none other than Cardinal Casaroli, the Vatican's Secretary of State, second only to the pope.

It was obvious that Pope Wojtyla, was unwilling to risk embarrassing disclosures (Pope Paul VI had died in 1978). He was aware of the deep involvement which the IOR had had in prolonged disruptive adventures in Central America and in Communist Poland in which the CIA and the IOR had been heavy financial investors. Such disclosures would be of a most explosive nature, and could become far more damaging to the Church than any financial losses, no matter how heavy.

Such a political scandal, unlike a financial one, might have endangered the cornerstone of the pope's new alignment — The Vatican Washington Alliance.[3]

The better to justify the Vatican's apparent lack of concern in Sindona's collapse, it was then claimed that the Church had lost very little. Bishop (now Archbishop) Marcinkus, confirmed the claim. The loss had been amply compensated by profits made on previous deals with Sindona, he declared.

Years later (1982) Sindona himself agreed. "Marcinkus has earned at least 200,000 dollars from me," he said, "The Vatican did not lose one single dollar."[4]

Public opinion, however, continued to assess the Church's losses, at about 60 million dollars. Swiss expert disagreed. The Vatican had lost more than 250 million dollars, they commented. Others, including American pundits, assessed the total loss of the Vatican-Sindona partnership at 750,000 million dollars.

Faced with the magnitude of such scandal, Marcinkus then declared to an incredulous world media, who knew how Sindona and he had been golf-pals for years at the Acqua Santa (Holy Water) Golf Club outside Rome, that he, Archbishop Marcinkus, had met Sindona only once.

Yet the true facts, disclosed again as late as 1982, were that during 1973, one year prior to Sindona's collapse, Marcinkus had been closely questioned by U.S. authorities in connection with counterfeit securities frauds believed to have been related to some of Sindona's operations, when the IOR, presided by Marcinkus, according to yet another source, had lost at least 80 million dollars.[5]

Even more serious were rumors that the U.S. at one time had become convinced that the Vatican Bank had been part of a scheme meant to use about 900 million dollars in counterfeit bonds. The rumors were never confirmed and no one was charged with the offending allegations. Yet they persisted, and at one time, they seemed to be so close to becoming positive accusations that the authorities made ready even for official indictments.

The charge, if proved, could have provoked a bombshell of such potency that its reverberations might have created reactions throughout the Catholic world, including the U.S. The more so, since it appeared that the potential offenders were not only the Vatican Bank, but equally a cardinal second only to the pope himself, Cardinal Tisserant, Dean of the Sacred College of Cardinals. Cardinal Tisserant was never accused of any offence, since he died in 1972. Yet the curious fact that he gave strict instructions that his diaries should be taken outside the Vatican immediately after his death, revived the suspicions of his involvement in the counterfeit bonds.[6]

But if the fear of a major scandal had made the Vatican apprehensive. It had also frightened certain political elements in the U.S. The specter of a potential scattered Catholic vote

NIXON, FREEMASONS AND JAILED "VATICAN WIZARD"

scared the U.S. Administration in office. Had the U.S. investigators pursued their trail, the Vatican scandal would have rocked not only the Vatican, but also the Catholic Church in America, with results difficult to envisage in political and party terms.

The investigation was stopped. By whom, it was never divulged. Although, even at that time, it had been whispered that it had been done at the instigation of Nixon, pressured by a potent Catholic entourage and the counsels of an American cardinal and Jesuit friends. One of Nixon's main speech writers during three whole years was a Jesuit father, the Rev. John McLaughlin, who wrote the Nixon speeches at a salary of $32,000 per year.

Whether it was Nixon, or someone else, the fact was that the investigation came mysteriously to an end. Too many interests of a financial and political nature were at stake. And too many people would have been hurt via the destabilization of the Catholic vote, had the investigation been permitted to take its natural course.

But if the potential scandal of the counterfeit bonds was nipped in the bud, others, even if of minor dimensions, were not. The following year, 1974, when the Sindona financial empire finally crashed, the Vatican Bank lost 50 million dollars, via speculations, ascribed to an executive of the Banco di Roma, per la Svizzera. The Banco's executive, who vehemently denied the charge, was later found mysteriously dead across the railway line. Officially presumed suicide, in effect, believed murdered.

Cardinal Vanozzi, Head of the Vatican's Prefecture of Economic Affairs, following speculation as to the Vatican's financial losses, declared that the Vatican's assets around the world at one time were still about 125 million dollars. As for the Vatican's relationship with Sindona, he then added, that had been confined to the minimum: the sale of the Societa Generale Immobiliare.

The true facts were otherwise. In February 1973, when the U.S. Stock Exchange stopped the trading in Vetco Industries, it came to light that 20 per cent of the 27 per cent (454,000 shares worth 16 million dollars) had been bought by the Vatican via a Liechtenstein company in which Sindona had had a "substantial" interest.[7] After paying a fine to the SEC, the Vatican sold all its Vetco shares at a profit.

That was not all. The Vatican had had also 22 per cent equity participation, worth 19-20 million dollars, in Geneva's Finabank — the Banque de Financement, yet another of Sindona's banking operations. (In 1975, the Swiss Government closed the bank, following large losses.) Also Hamburg's Bankhaus Wolff, which controlled the Finabank, was closed following Sindona's Franklin crash. Sindona, meanwhile, following his disappearance act after his bail, was indicted on 66 counts of fraud. Having been taken to trial in 1980, he was found guilty on 65 charges. and given a total of 25 years in prison.

But if the Vatican did nothing to help its former financial adviser, the Freemasons of Italy, and some of the U.S. did. Or at least tried to. A powerful lodge, whose members could be found in the highest echelons in Italy and in America, chief amongst these, the Lodge of Licio Gelli P 2, mobilized aid for their jailed "brother" Michele. Called "Propaganda 2," the Lodge was an off-shoot of the orthodox Italian Freemasonry, whose main objective was to provide a clandestine base for the attainment of political power.

That the inner financial manipulators of the Vatican and Co. should have had "dealings," no matter how tenuous, with the Masons, although a surprise to many Catholics, was not to the Vatican, who had long since accepted their existence in the U.S., because there, Masonry was "different."[8]

The difference, as a noted cynic explained, was the amount of money, and above all, political influence which they exerted in the highest financial and political circles of the U.S. itself, where Sindona and thus the IOR, had been spinning their complicated financial webs. This had reached the most recondite nooks and crannies, not only of Italy, but also American life. The adversary of the leading political party, to whom Sindona and the Vatican had offered their one million dollar fund contribution, was found to be involved, even if tangently, with "Brother" Michele Sindona, himself. And thus, by association, with the Vatican.

That that was no idle speculation was proved by the fact that after the grandmaster Gelli's arrest, amongst his papers,

NIXON, FREEMASONS AND JAILED "VATICAN WIZARD"

there was found an exchange of letters between him and Philip A. Guarino, the Chief of the American Republican National Committee. Their goal: to aid brother Michele, whose case in 1979, had looked somewhat hopeless.

When in 1980, Sindona's case deteriorated even more following another list of additional frauds prepared against him, and the brothers of the Lodge in Italy and in the U.S. had vainly hoped that somebody at the Vatican would help him, they complained bitterly that "nobody has come to Michele's defense." "Yet two weeks ago," wrote chief of the American Republican National Committee, "everything seemed to be going well." — a reference to the efforts of the Papal Nuncio in Germany after he promised to lobby the top cardinals connected with the Vatican Bank, as already seen, when the cardinals said they would testify in favor of Michele. "His Eminence, Cardinal Casaroli, the Secretary of State forbade their Eminences to do so," he ended.

"Nobody has come to his defence," he then concluded bitterly, "Even the Church has truly let him down."[9]

Guarino was right. The Vatican Secretary of State, who knew which way the wind of potential financial scandal was blowing, as we shall see presently, tried to wash his hands of their former partner, the fallen, but still potentially dangerous, Sindona.

The ominous warnings of the oncoming new scandal were already there for all to see. In 1980 and 1981, following additional investigations into the Sindona aftermath, the top senior executive of the IOR, that is of the Vatican Bank, and his successor, were arrested. The following year, July, 1982, Sindona, although serving his 25 years in an American jail, was indicted once again about another case of bankruptcy. Twenty-five other persons, including an officer of the Vatican Bank, were accused of fraudulence, bankruptcy, and of falsification of company figures.

L. Mennini, the highest top official of the Vatican Bank, and second in command only to Archbishop Marcinkus and to Pope John Paul II, was also indicted.

The trial was set for 1983.

Pope Paul VI's very own financial little fox had not only been abandoned by the Vatican which he had served so well, he had been caught by the hounds of the law which, thanks also to the ambivalent protections of the Church and Freemasonry, he had so dexterously outsmarted for so long.

CHAPTER 30

GOD'S BANKER, LODGE P2, AND THE VATICAN

Freemasonry, to the Catholic Church, had always been one of the greatest aberrations of society, worse than atheism or Bolshevism. Catholics were forbidden to sympathize, support or join it in any way or form. Had they done so, they were ipso facto, excommunicated. Papal fulminations had seen to it that the prohibition was maintained. Punishment to any Catholic who disobeyed was precise: exclusion from the communion of the Church here on earth; hell in the next world.

Then one day in 1974, the Vatican dropped a bombshell. It gave official permission for Catholics to join a Masonic lodge, in particular cases, that is. The permission was used in certain quarters in Italy, Switzerland and in the U.S.A. Or rather, it had already been used by Catholics, prior to the official permission, simply because many of them had been dealing with sundry financial affairs of the Vatican Bank.

The Vatican's curious liberalization could never have occurred had it not been for the discovery of the body of a Lugano banking executive across the rails of a Swiss railway, as already mentioned. The man, employed by the Banco di Roma per la Svizzera, had illegally gambled with the bank's funds, it was said, with the loss of millions of Swiss francs. At first, the official version that he had committed suicide, was accepted. Then, however, it was noticed how the Banco di Roma per la Svizzera seemed to have lost the 50 million dollars for someone else; that is, for the Vatican Bank. The IOR, it came out, had a 51 per cent control of the Banco di Roma, itself. Hence, its million losses. And even more interesting, it had had — even if tangently — financial connections with Sindona's Franklin Bank.

When Sindona's empire collapsed in 1974, the IOR, although losing its chief financial wizard, had already replaced him with another no less able adviser. The Sindona successor had been discovered by Sindona himself. He had found him operating as a junior employee in a sedate provincial private bank in 1969, the Banco Ambrosiano, patronized by the Archbishop of Milan, Northern Italy.

The master and his pupil, one Robert Calvi, formed a working alliance, with the result that, as early as 1971, they had already set up a financial entity outside Italy, the Banco Ambrosiano Overseas, in Nassau. Sindona, by then at the top of his financial career, introduced Calvi to Bishop Marcinkus who had been the head of the Vatican Bank since 1969. Both asked Marcinkus to operate with them via the Banco Ambrosiano. The Bishop accepted, and was listed as one of its directors.[1]

Subsequently, as the overseas operations of the Banco Ambrosiano and hence of the IOR expanded, their financial ramifications embraced several other overseas concerns. Within a few years, the IOR had come to control, indeed to own, as the London Financial Times later was to report, seven Panamanian banks.[2]

From 1971, when Calvi began to operate under Sindona's protection and the blessing of Bishop Marcinkus, his career became unstoppable. He was promoted, first to Managing Director, and then to the President of the Banco Ambrosiano. His rapid climb was due, not only to his abilities, but also to Sindona's financial propping him up. As early as 1970, in fact, Sindona had given Calvi, and it was said, also to Marcinkus, no less than 6 million dollars for combined operations.[3]

Whether this was true or not was never proved, although years later, in 1982, Marcinkus and several other high officials of the IOR were accused of dubious financial improprieties in connection with Sindona's operations carried out before 1974.

Sindona's downfall gave Calvi the chance to emerge as a bright, ascending, financial star, not only in the banking firmament of Italy, but also in that of the Catholic world. From then onward, in fact, the Banco Ambrosiano, already patronized by the Archbishop of Milan, started to control subsidiary Catholic financial concerns such as the Banca Cattolica del Veneto, and other minor Catholic subsidiaries.

GOD'S BANKER, LODGE P2, AND THE VATICAN

The Banco Ambrosiano's expansion became even more rapid owing to its characteristic religious orientation. Would-be investors had to prove, to Calvi's satisfaction, that they had been baptized. This they did, by showing their baptismal certificate. Also that they were practicing Catholics. Failing that, they were excluded on the grounds of their non-Catholicity. The President always closed the proceedings of every major financial operation, and each meeting, with the motto, "Praise be to God."

The reputation for piety and financial brilliance soon put the Ambrosiano on the map. Its ever closer relationship with the Vatican did the rest. Calvi's limitless energy began to impress men and institutions alike. The media, who had tended to ignore him, now became enthusiastic. So much so that it dubbed Calvi "God's Banker." They gave him the nickname, not so much because of his ever more close relationship with the IOR and Bishop Marcinkus, but also because his operations seemed to have reached every nook and cranny of the financial field in which the Vatican was active.

Calvi's influence, however, besides deriving from his Vatican connections, came also from another, additional, source of power: from Freemasonry. Or rather, from a peculiar kind of Freemasonry known as P2 Lodge. The P2 Lodge was regarded as a distortion of true Freemasonry, formed, it was said, to provide clandestine stepping stones to political power for its members. Its objective was also the shaping of financial matters in Italy, abroad, and even inside the Vatican itself.

Roberto Calvi and his associates, while quizzing any would-be investors about their Catholicity, by exercising the "acceptance clause," however, at the same time, took part in Masonic ceremonies which, theoretically, were against the Church's regulations. As a P2 Mason, he had to take secret vows of loyalty to the lodge. The ceremony was carried out with the candidates dressed up in black robes and black hoods, like friars. From then on the new members called themselves "fratelli," that is, brothers. Mason, in Italian, derives from "masso," the word for brick — the brick assuming a ritual significance in any Masonic ceremony.

Among the leading figures of P2 Lodge's 933 names, was Licio Gelli, who served as a grand-master of the P2, U.

Ortolani, with vast banking interests in Latin America, Roberto Calvi, and last, but by no means least, his mentor, Michele Sindona. The Lodge, or rather, the "fratelli," controlled the members. It sponsored them in politics, and in finance. In Calvi's case, they aided his meteoric career in the banking world. It was convenient to have a "brother" on the highest financial pinnacle who could help them with their recondite activities in national and international operations.

As a result, the Banco Ambrosiano with its close financial relationship with the Vatican, in due course, became the de facto lay bank of the IOR itself; a kind of secular equivalent, or rather, lay transmitter, whose funds were put at its disposal for finalizing operations which could by-pass monetary control without detection.

The riddle of practicing Catholics having become Freemasons in the P2 Lodge, when seen in such light, therefore, was another additional proof of the inter-relationship of the Vatican's financial involvement with forces operating at different levels within and outside the Church. The stunning public concession of the Vatican permitting Catholics to become members of Freemasonry derived directly from it. Hence, the participation of the Vatican Bank in the activities, even if by remote control, of the P2 Lodge.

When, therefore, Sindona's Banca Privata Italiana collapsed, Calvi, a member of P2 Lodge as was his patron, Sindona, commenced his meteoric rise, propelled simultaneously by the powerful secretive influence of the lodge and of the Vatican. The double protection gave Calvi vigorous connections in both the Roman Catholic and the Masonic worlds. These in their turn, put him in touch with the banking and financial community. The result was the rapid purchase of outlandish banking subsidiaries in Panama, Liechtenstein, Luxembourg and other central American "shell" companies. Their purchase and their equivocal activities aroused the suspicions of more traditional bankers. The general apprehension about Calvi did the rest. The Bank of Italy, which had been following his wheeling and dealing, ordered him to systemize his sundry operations, and to put the lot under one single umbrella, that of the Banco Ambrosiano.

GOD'S BANKER, LODGE P2, AND THE VATICAN

When finally, in 1978, as a result of general incertitude, the Bank of Italy arranged a general audit of Calvi's operations, they noticed that the Ambrosiano's subsidiaries were "running all types of operations outside their control." But even more ominous, that the Ambrosiano's holdings could not be separated from the Vatican's holdings because of the complex interlocking financial ramifications between the two. In addition, they discovered a very intriguing connection with the old Sindona's collapsed empire. From these it appeared that a certain American bishop and a certain Milanese banker had received substantial bribes, when dealing with the Banco Ambrosiano and other Catholic banks, as already mentioned.[4]

Between 1978 and 1979, and then again in 1981, the Ambrosiano and its subsidiaries raised yet another large amount of money, about 1.2 billion dollars. Various banks lent at least 800 million dollars to its "shell" companies, which Calvi had set up in Liechtenstein, Panama and Luxembourg. The "shell" subsidiaries, meanwhile, had used 400 million dollars to buy stock in the Ambrosiano and other Catholic securities. In addition to which, another 400 million dollars appeared to have been siphoned through these same agencies to finance shady Latin American deals, many of which were used to sustain politically committed investments.

In July, 1981, Calvi and some of his friends were charged with illegally exporting 26 million dollars from Italy during 1975-76. Calvi was found guilty, fined a total of 11 million dollars and sentenced to four years in jail.

The headquarters of the Masonic Lodge P2 was raided and names of its members made public. The discovery that many of the "brothers" belonged to the highest strata of the political and financial circles created such a crisis that it toppled the Government of Italy. The affair compelled the P2 Grand Master to go into hiding.

Notwithstanding the P2 debacle, however, Calvi, after his sentence, having been released on bail pending an appeal, reactivated his sundry operations. He set up new financial concerns in Buenos Aires, Managua, Montevideo and Lima. Rumors had it that this was done with the full cooperation of various "brothers" of the P2 Lodge and of the Vatican, as Michele Sindona asserted afterwards from his U.S. jail.[5]

The "operations" directed at postponing the impending disaster, in all probability accelerated the impetus of what was bound to come. Creditors from dozens of banks in Europe and the U.S. pressed for repayment. Calvi asked the IOR to help and told the Vatican Bank to pay the debts incurred by the "shell" companies abroad. The Vatican Bank, however, would not, or could not produce the missing millions. Nevertheless, to prove that it was willing to aid him, Archbishop Marcinkus supplied Calvi, on behalf of the IOR, (the Vatican Bank) with extraordinary documents. These were called "comfort letters." "Comfort letters" were nothing new in themselves, since they had been accepted as a standard practice by the international financial community.

```
ISTITUTO
PER LE
OPERE DI RELIGIONE                CITTÀ DEL VATICANO    20 gennaio 1975

Prot. N.° 634792
Posiz. N° 1120

                              Spett.le BANCO AMBROSIANO S.p.a.
                                         M I L A N O

              Con la presente ci riferiamo al dossier
     titoli esistente al 31 dicembre 1974 concernente la Società
     SUPRAFIN S.p.a. Milano- di pertinenza di questo Istituto
     e Vi preghiamo di voler procedere nella forma più opportuna
     alla gestione e amministrazione del dossier in oggetto
     provvedendo alle convenienti operazioni di investimento e
     di disinvestimento.
              Vi preghiamo di volerci ragguagliare pe-
     riodicamente della situazione del dossier sopramenzionato
     e delle pertinenti operazioni.
                           Distinti saluti
                                        ISTITUTO PER LE OPERE DI RELIGIONE
```

Facsimile of a "letter of comfort" issued by the IOR, on behalf of the Banco Ambrosiano, years before the Ambrosiano-IOR scandal exploded in the summer of 1982. The scandle was brought to light by the "suicide" of the Ambrosiano Director, R. Calvi, under the Blackfriars Bridge, London, England. The above letter was issued as early as January, 1975, less than one year after Sindona's collapse. Similar letters helped to accelerate the inevitable Ambrosiano disaster. When the IOR refused to reissue any more such letters the chain-reaction was triggered which ended with the massive Ambrosiano-IOR disaster.

Because of such acceptance, "comfort letters" were regarded as the guarantors of utmost financial reliability. As reliable as those who wrote them. By issuing such letters, the Vatican had assured the creditors for the credit worthiness of the Ambrosiano's "shell" companies. It implied a moral obligation concerning the debts in question. It meant also that Archbishop Marcinkus took full responsibility for them.

Five days before, Calvi had addressed the IOR with a document of his own. This was called a "liberating letter." The "liberating letter," in effect, negates the "letters of comfort." That is, it relieved the Vatican of any responsibility for the companies involved. The letter was never made known to the Latin American banks of the Ambrosiano, which lent the money to Calvi's "shell" firms.

The arrangement between Calvi and the Vatican Bank, in short, was a deliberate conspiracy to withhold fundamental data from the principal lending banks. Later the Vatican denied having anything to do with the "shell" companies, disclaiming any responsibility for the "lost" one billion dollar loan. This it did, even after the Italian Government insisted that the IOR connections with the Ambrosiano proved otherwise. Reports that the Vatican Bank controlled, and indeed even owned, even if tangently, at least 10 of the "shell" agencies, were vehemently denied as false rumors.

The "comfort letters" of Archbishop Marcinkus and the "liberating letters" of Calvi brought a transient confidence to both the Ambrosiano and the IOR. Outside them, however, the storm was gathering momentum. Since the fact that the "shell" subsidiaries still owed the Ambrosiano about 1.2 billion dollars, an 800 million which they had borrowed, plus the 400 million in interest, was there for all to see. The stark reality would not go away. As the pressure mounted hourly, Calvi approached Marcinkus once more to renew his "letters." Marcinkus refused on the grounds that he could not "compromise" the IOR.

The Bank of Italy, meanwhile, had renewed her request for more information on the Ambrosiano's groups of foreign subsidiaries. On May 31, 1982, it declared it wanted precise data about the 1,400 million dollars of loans. Soon afterwards Archbishop Marcinkus, after consulting with the pope, unexpectedly resigned from the board of the Nassau agency, which held the key to all the other loans. The resignation accelerated the already growing panic amidst the financial community all over Europe. Dozens of reputable banks which had "lent" money, starting with the Midland Bank of England, threatened to call in the very large loans it had made to the Ambrosiano.

Other respectable banks, such as the powerful National Westminster Bank of London, said they would follow suit. Dozens of others promised to do the same. They all wanted to know where the money had gone and pressed for the refunds, which had been overdue for a long time. Their chief target, the Ambrosiano, could not, or would not, give any satisfactory explanation. At this stage, the Vatican Bank was by-passed because of the general belief that it had little or nothing to do with the "shell" companies.

It was obvious that the Ambrosiano had gone bankrupt. Who had been behind it, or what had caused the failure? Could it be that the Vatican, hiding behind the screen of the IOR, as rumors had it, had been involved in the whole business, more than at first had been believed? It was obvious that the key to the whole truth rested with two men: the President and the Vice-President of the Banco Ambrosiano. They could have named the names of the mysterious people who had gotten the millions for the Panamanian "shell" companies.

Roberto Calvi, who at that time was in Rome where he had two "vital appointments" inside and outside the Vatican, became suddenly unavailable, or could not talk, or avoided any further contact because he was afraid for his life. His fear had become accentuated by the worsening situation, the pressure from the Bank of Italy, the refusal of the IOR to help, the obscure menaces of hostile forces by which he was surrounded. These were anything but imagination. They had compelled him to travel with at least a dozen bodyguards wherever he went. Even prior to his going to Rome, he had already had more than one million dollars budgeted for his personal security.

Roberto Rosone, his Vice-President, had had no such fears. But on April 27, however, his legs were shot from under him by a professional gunman. The gunman was promptly shot in his turn, and killed on the same day by persons unknown. The situation had become seemingly desperate. Calvi, after trying once more to contact mysterious individuals of the IOR, suddenly, on June 15, 1982, vanished from Rome.

Two days later, June 17th, back in Milan, the directors of the Banco Ambrosiano voted to strip him of his power. The Bank of Italy appointed a committee to take over the Ambrosiano in an effort to find out the truth about the puzzle of the missing 1,400 million dollars.

Only hours afterwards, June 17, 1982, Graziella Corrocher, the faithful Swiss secretary and longtime confidante of Calvi, had plunged to her death from the fourth floor of the Ambrosiano building in Milan, leaving a "suicide" note. Graziella Corrocher knew as much as Calvi about his secrets. Not only the secrets of the Banco Ambrosiano, but also the secrets of the IOR and of the P2 Masonic Lodge. Indeed, the secrets of all three and perhaps more. Had she talked, or had she been forced to talk, a whole world might have been made to collapse upon the heads of many exalted people in the financial community, inside the Vatican, in Italy and abroad.

It was safer for them all for her to be dead.

CHAPTER 31

THE MAN UNDER BLACKFRIARS BRIDGE, THE MISSING 1.4 BILLION AND THE DEATH OF A CARDINAL

Early in the morning of June 18, 1982, a man was found hanged under Blackfriars Bridge, London, England. In his pockets there were 1,400 dollars, a passport, a visa for Brazil and several bricks. Also a list of names.

The police cut down the body, and having identified the dead man, ended a nine-day manhunt. Or so they thought. The affair had started in Italy, in connection with the man's sudden disappearance from Rome, where he had been due to appear before a court for an appeal against a four-year sentence for illicit export of currency. Less than 24 hours before, his life confidante had committed a dramatic suicide.

His name: Roberto Calvi, God's Banker, former President of the Banco Ambrosiano.

The bricks in his pockets had been clearly intended to give a ritualistic significance to the death of a "brother" who had infringed, or who was about to infringe the rules of his lodge. The choice of the bridge, even more so. Black, the first word of Blackfriars, was the black, hooded, ritual dress of the P2 Lodge used by the members for their official meetings. Friars was what those of the Lodge called themselves. The bricks were the unmistakable symbol of Freemasonry. The list contained names of the P2 Lodge.

The authorities, having swiftly discarded the impression of a classic suicide, suspected murder. On July 28th, an official inquest, however, reached the opposite conclusion. An obtuse British coroner's jury decided that Roberto Calvi had indeed, killed himself.

MISSING $1.4 BILLION AND DEATH OF A CARDINAL

The verdict was challenged at once. Not only by the Calvi family and his close associates, but equally by others in England and in Italy. Some accused the coroner of having known too well what had "really" happened. Others declared that the jury had been unduly influenced by a magistrate whom the "brothers" of Italy had contacted prior to the inquest. The accusations were never substantiated, although the latest facts on the whereabouts of the dead man, before and during his stay in London, pointed to the theory of a well planned "execution."

The absurdity of the jury's conclusion was so self-evident that speculations about it having been an unnatural judicial surrogate were widely accepted as the most likely alternative, except in certain quarters, located mostly in the city of London, the most influential financial center of the world.

A minimal examination of the factors connected with the "suicide" proves at once the absurdity of the judgment of the London jury. Calvi flew into London from Rome, just to hang himself. Under a bridge, sinisterly called Blackfriars. The next night after his arrival, to do so, he left a rented flat, walked four miles along the Thames to a high bridge, although he suffered from vertigo. Once there, he leaned under that same bridge to spot a scaffolding which could not be seen directly from the top (the present author, after the suicide, could not, as others could not). Thereupon, having crossed the bridge to a building site, filled his jacket with bricks, recrossed the same bridge, again climbed down a twenty-foot ladder level with the water, and in the dark, jumped across a three-foot gap upon a slippery wood plank, got hold of a piece of rope conveniently floating in the current, heaved himself to one of the poles of the scaffolding, tied one end to another pole of same, the other end to his neck, added more bricks to his trousers, and then just threw himself off into the void, his feet touching the water of the river.

When assessed in such light, it was obvious that the "suicide" had been nothing other than a well planned murder. As already indicated, the choice of the bridge with its ominous name and symbolical connotations was the clearest indication that it could not have been anything else. Blackfriars Bridge, therefore, as a symbolism, was purposely meant to tell a tale to the "brothers" whom Calvi had, or could have, endangered had he been permitted to break their secrets. In short, the chilling vows, which had bound him to his Lodge, had been carried out to the letter. As a potential traitor, he had been ritually killed, in a special macabre manner, as a reminder to all the other "black friars" that anyone who dared to break them would be made to suffer the same fate.

A few days after the "suicide," June 21st, the Bank of Italy, worried about the dimension of the financial impasse of the Ambrosiano, appointed three commissioners to clarify the true state of its affairs. Also to trace its main links with suspected financial associates. One of these turned out to be the IOR, in other words, the Vatican Bank. And even more interesting, that the IOR had been the Ambrosiano's top partner.

The Bank of Italy informed the Government of their findings. The Italian Government, thereupon, (July 6) formally asked the Vatican — via its Treasury Minister — to accept responsibility for the Ambrosiano's debt. To indicate their goodwill, the Bank and the Government (July 10) encouraged six major Italian banks to help solve the problem of the colossal monetary "hole" in the Ambrosiano. At the same time, it asked the Vatican to investigate the role played by its own IOR. The Vatican, stung by growing speculation about its part in the affair, thereupon appointed three practicing Catholics to investigate the IOR's financial links with the bankrupt Ambrosiano.

Simultaneously with all this, two great British Banks, the Midland and the National Westminster, followed soon by others, called default on loans to Ambrosiano holdings in Luxembourg which had raised 450 million dollars. Following the moves, the Bank of Italy, supported by the Italian Government, told the Vatican to come out in the open and to accept the IOR's responsibility concerning the IOR's repayment of the 1,400 million dollars attached to the mysterious overseas loans of the "shell" companies. As a reply, the Vatican, then, to the surprise of everyone concerned, denied having anything to do with the "shell" companies, that is, the missing 1,400 million dollars.

MISSING $1.4 BILLION AND DEATH OF A CARDINAL

Shortly afterwards, Italy accused Britain of a massive cover-up. Vital information on the Calvi "suicide" had been deliberately withheld, it said, because important people were directly involved. Rumors had it that Masonic financial interests had been at work in London, before, during, and after Calvi's death. Hence, the stopping of further investigations. The case, however, was revived again one year later when a retrial was held in London following the majority suicide verdict which meanwhile had been squashed by a High Court. After sitting two whole weeks through detailed evidence, the second jury returned an open verdict on June 27, 1983. The mystery of who killed "God's Banker" remained a mystery, hidden, as the Lord Chief Justice declared, "...in a concatenation of financial intrigues." (London Times, June 28, 1983)

It was obvious that the deed had been carried out by professional criminals. In fact, it was even hinted that undercover work by British and American men had been involved. The suggestion, although seemingly improbable, however, was not as groundless as it sounded. Since the Italian Government, in its attempt to penetrate the "thick spider's web" spun by the Luxembourg and its affiliated "shell" companies in Latin America, was actively "boycotted" during its investigation. Their officials had even become the target of "veiled threats" as Italy's Treasury Minister admitted officially in Parliament.[1]

Additional investigations, however, having discovered further links between the Ambrosiano and the Vatican Bank, brought more proof to the fact that the Ambrosiano and the IOR had been "factual partners." The Vatican denied the accusation, saying they were without any foundation. Italy's Minister Andreatta, counter-accused by declaring that the Vatican had participated in dozens of transactions directed at diverting huge sums from Calvi's bank. Indeed, he added, most of the missing 1,400 million dollars had ended up in loans to sundry Panamanian and other "shell" companies. The latter were controlled, and even were "owned" by the IOR itself. The whole transaction had been guaranteed by the IOR's "letters of comfort."

To further stress the point, the minister then pointed out that Archbishop Marcinkus, Director of the Vatican Bank, besides having been a business associate of Calvi, had been also on the board of the off-shore subsidiaries in Nassau. The dispute eventually was handed over to Cardinal Casaroli, the Vatican Secretary of State, who appointed three top lay financiers to ascertain the liabilities of the IOR, as already seen.

The major banks involved in the affair, meantime, had met to discuss the Ambrosiano-IOR-Luxembourg relationship and their responsibilities with the missing 1,400 million dollar loans. Result — a cool acknowledgement of a major financial disaster: default of more than 200 million dollars by the major banks of West Germany, Britain, and Switzerland, due chiefly to loans to the Luxembourg subsidiaries. The 250 banks had lent "collectively" more than 400 million dollars.

As the stark facts emerged and the links of the IOR in the whole sorry affair became ever more apparent, the Vatican began to admit, even if reluctantly, "partial responsibility." Then, when it was proved that at least seven of the "shell" companies, most of them linked with Luxembourg, were "controlled" and, indeed, were even *owned* by the IOR, it finally admitted possible liability.[2] Such liability, however, it declared, amounted only to 250 million out of the missing 1,400 million dollars.

Italy then asked Cardinal Casaroli to reveal what the "three wise men" had discovered. To impress upon him the seriousness of her request, she began by indicting the two highest officials of the IOR itself, on charges rising from another bank scandal, the Sindona collapse in 1974.

Not content with that, it hinted that if Archbishop Marcinkus left Vatican City, he would be promptly arrested for complicity. The justification for the arrest was given further validity by the intervention of ex-Vatican financier, Sindona himself, who, from his U.S. jail came out with the statement that Marcinkus had received a 20 million dollar commission when dealing via the dubious operations with sundry banks connected with the Ambrosiano.[3] Following words with deeds, Italy then sent a formal subpoena to Archbishop Marcinkus himself, already a virtual prisoner inside Vatican City. The document was rejected "unopened," on the grounds that it should have been sent via diplomatic channels.

MISSING $1.4 BILLION AND DEATH OF A CARDINAL

Italy then accused the Vatican of having "intentionally hidden" from the Bank of Italy the relevant facts of the Vatican Bank's true relationship with the Ambrosiano. And even worse, of the "shell" companies. Further it informed the Holy See that it had found an additional "hole" of 280 million dollars in the Ambrosiano-IOR accounts. All in all, the Vatican Bank was liable for at least 766 million dollars out of the missing Ambrosiano's 1,400 million.

Unexpectedly, rumors had it that the pope was ready to reach a "secret" compromise. The result, it was said, of the meeting in Rome of about 100 cardinals, where the IOR's problems were discussed. Also, it was suggested, thanks to the offer of financial aid which had come from Opus Dei, a powerful, wealthy, semi-secret organization which Pope Wojtyla had patronized, ever since he became pope, as we shall see presently.

While all this was going on, a group of seven Italian banks, in a brave attempt to rehabilitate the Ambrosiano, resurrected the same with a vigorous financial injection and a new name, the Nuovo Banco Ambrosiano. The rescue operation was not new. Earlier in the year, another group of Lombard Banks, all strictly Catholic, had drafted a document warning the pope about the impending disaster, as we shall see in the next chapter. The Ambrosiano, and thus the IOR, they told the pope, were dealing with Freemasonry. Calvi and Archbishop Marcinkus were associated with the notorious P2 Lodge and its shady operations. These were bound to discredit the Church.[4]

Prior to and after the formation of the New Banco Ambrosiano, meanwhile, the Milan Public Prosecutor had issued a warrant for the arrest of two top Masons, Licio Gelli and F. Carboni. The charge: complicity in fraudulent bankruptcy. While determined to indict Archbishop Marcinkus, Italy had simultaneously warned Switzerland of the impending visit of the two top men of P2 Lodge, whose objective was the immediate withdrawal of funds deposited in dubious numbered bank accounts. The Grand Master of P2 Lodge, Licio Gelli, went to Switzerland as predicted, and tried to withdraw 60 million dollars. He was promptly detained in Geneva by the authorities.

The arrest caused a stir, since the traditional secrecy of a Swiss bank appeared to have been impinged upon. Yet, the equivocal identity of both the depositors and the manner in which the millions were about to be withdrawn by a member of the P2 Lodge, made it compulsory on the Swiss authorities to act. The Ambrosiano-IOR had shaken to its foundations the banking community of Western Europe. That included Switzerland. The seriousness of the matter was that the most respected institutions of the Western world had been all interlocked in the Ambrosiano-IOR "imbroglio" via equivocal activities with international Freemasonry, with the Vatican and with political subversion in Eastern Europe and with South American republics.

Because of such potentially dangerous connections, therefore, the identity of the millions deposited in the Swiss banks had first to be identified, before the withdrawal by any potential claimants. The Grand Master of P2 Lodge had attempted to withdraw 60 million dollars from funds which, it was said, had been put there by various "associates." Amongst these were sundry "shell" companies and, therefore, by association, the IOR, or the Vatican Bank, the Ambrosiano and members of the P2 Lodge.

The wisdom of the Swiss caution was confirmed by yet a second withdrawal attempt. Masonic "brother" Carboni, the friend of the Grand Master, had also gone into sedate Switzerland for a silent withdrawal from a numbered bank account. Carboni was the P2 Lodge "brother" who had helped Calvi's mysterious journey to London via Venice, Austria, and finally, England where he eventually joined him during a vitally brief period of time, immediately before Calvi's "suicide."

After Calvi's death, Carboni flew to Edinburgh, a notorious Freemason center, and from there by private plane to Switzerland, where he tried to withdraw an undisclosed number of millions of dollars. He was quietly arrested near Lugano, 42 days after Calvi's death, not far from the same bank where the executive had committed "suicide" across the railway line, when accused of disastrous financial speculations.

The arrests led to the discovery of an interesting fact: about 100 million dollars of the Ambrosiano had been secretly deposited in several numbered accounts at the Union Bank of Swizterland, in Geneva. Following the arrest of the two Masons, Switzerland froze all their funds pending clarification as to their legality.

The birth of the New Banco Ambrosiano, meanwhile, had not gone as smoothly as at first envisaged. Recondite forces seemed to be at work to hamper its progress. Rumors had it that Italy's insistence about her determination to charge the Vatican Bank with fraud and embezzlement, perhaps had something to do with it. Others than the hand of Freemasonry were also at work. The rumors appeared to have been justified when Guiseppe Della Ca, "fell" mysteriously from the fourth floor of the Ambrosiano's building in Milan and was instantly killed. Guiseppe Della Ca was the Deputy Director of the New Banco Ambrosiano.

The similarity with Calvi's secretary was too striking not to be remembered. The more so since he had obviously been "flung" out of the window, as she had been.

Ruthless forces were clearly working behind the scenes at all levels of ruthlessness.. Those who had suffered immense losses, that is the groups of lending banks, as hopelessly impotent of solving the Ambrosiano-IOR puzzle as the rest, stepped up their pressure on the Vatican. Their formality and deference were replaced by blunt requests and even veiled threats of "damaging revelations" about the IOR's involvement with shady international "dealings."

The result was seen when a council of cardinals from all over the world met in Rome to discuss the matter in November, 1982, and an unprecedented remedy was adopted to produce the money with which to pay the Vatican's debts, as we shall see presently.

But if the mystery of the Nuovo Banco Ambrosiano and of the IOR stayed a mystery, another no less puzzling one remained tantalizingly unsolved: the enduring immunity during all this time of the Vatican Bank's Director, Archbishop Marcinkus. While his immunity from Italy's arrest was accepted as the result of having immured himself inside Vatican City, his immunity from the pope's condemnation, or at least reprimand, was not.

True, when the pope visited Spain in November, 1982, Marcinkus, as a rule an indivisible papal companion-cum-bodyguard, had been conspicuously absent. Also, that he had been by-passed before the Calvi affair, when he had been mentioned as the potential successor of the recently deceased Cardinal Cody of Chicago. His nomination there would have meant not only a promotion, since he would have been nominated cardinal, but also the leadership of the richest diocese of America.

The presence of Marcinkus there, whose reputation in monetary matters, had been criticized because of his relationship with Sindona, would have added fuel to additional speculation of financial improprieties on the part of yet another Catholic hierarch. Since the previous occupant, Cardinal Cody, a personal friend of Pope Wojtyla, when he died in April, 1982, had been under the cloud of a great financial scandal himself, accused of having given one million dollars of church funds to a woman friend.

Wojtyla's papal predecessor, Pope John Paul I, had even planned to demote him because of it. Documents relating to the case were carried in his bedroom the very night when he was found dead, after only 33 days of pontificate.[5]

Marcinkus' prolonged cordiality with Pope Wojtyla prompted more and more people to ask embarrassing questions. Lay Catholics, no less than ecclesiastics, voiced their concerns, at first in private and then in public. Rumors and conjectures, many of them fanciful, created suspicions and even accusations. Allegations of hidden intrigues, of a personal ethnic (Marcinkus and Wojtyla spoke a common Lithuanian-Polish dialect), Masonic, and ideological character, multiplied. Was Marcinkus' immunity, due to his potential capacity to provoke a scandal of disproportionate dimensions for the Vatican, it was asked, or was it because someone, perhaps the pope himself, had something to hide?

MISSING $1.4 BILLION AND DEATH OF A CARDINAL

These and other rumors, most of them without any foundation, multiplied to such an extent that many insisted that something be done to stop them. Marcinkus' prompt removal would have done just that.

As the months went by and nothing happened, cardinals joined the crusade. One of the most prominent, Cardinal Angelo Rossi of Brazil, repeatedly asked the pope to dismiss Marcinkus. Archbishop Rossi was not only an important cardinal. He was equally the head of one of the most prestigious congregations: the Prefect of Propaganda Fide. And to cap it all, he was also one of the five members of the special commission charged with looking into the secret affairs of the IOR-Ambrosiano financial operations.

The most openly persistent hierarch, however, was a no less prominent member of the Church, Cardinal Benelli, currently Archbishop of Florence. Cardinal Benelli was no mean cleric. He had been the right hand man of Pope Paul VI during no less than 15 years, directing the foreign policies of the Vatican practically until the last days of Paul's pontificate. He had been one of the foster-fathers of the Vatican Moscow Alliance. As if this had not been enough to single him out, Benelli had been the most serious rival papal candidate during the last two conclaves. In the first, he was by-passed for political considerations by Pope John Paul I, the 33-days pope. In the second, following John Paul's mysterious death, by Karol Wojtyla, later Pope John Paul II.

Cardinal Benelli, who had commenced his campaign after Calvi's death, expecting the resignation of Marcinkus as the Director of the IOR, seeing how the resignation or dismissal never came, began to ask what was at the bottom of the mystery. Also, why the Vatican was so eager to exempt the archbishop from his obvious responsibility. Once, at a Rio de Janiero airport, when someone pointed out that Marcinkus, as a Director of the IOR since 1969, should remain where he had always been, Cardinal Benelli had a snappy retort. "In the Church," he replied, "no one fills a place forever."

When a newsman reminded him that Marcinkus could not be removed because he was a personal friend of Pope Wojtyla, the cardinal was even blunter. "The fact that Marcinkus is a friend of the pope," he rebutted, "does not mean that he has to remain in the post."

The cardinal became relentlessly determined to have the mystery of the missing millions clarified for "the good name of the Church." "The forces active behind them had to be exposed, whether within or outside the Vatican," he explained. In private, he even hinted at their potential identification. Friends advised caution. They reminded him that certain inexplicable deaths had occurred before, during and after that of Calvi's. Benelli, howver, a forceful personality, insisted that since the IOR's liability had been well established, it was high time that those who had been responsible for it be exposed.

When reminded that Marcinkus had powerful protectors, more powerful perhaps than the cardinal had ever envisaged, Benelli indicated that other no less powerful forces would be at work behind the scenes on his behalf. "In fact, I do not exclude that Marcinkus will be forced to resign his post before the end of the year," he then declared.[6]

A daring prediction. And even more, a perilous challenge. A few weeks later, Cardinal Benelli, the keeper of the Vatican's most recondite secrets, suffered a deadly "heart attack," and died October 26, 1982. He was only 61 years old. Many of his supporters could not help thinking that his unexpected demise, perhaps, had not been a mere coincidence.[7]

Could it be, that the ever more deepening mystery of the IOR's missing millions had something to do with his "removal?" Another enigma which, like that of "God's Banker," only time could and would clarify.[8]

CHAPTER 32

THE VATICAN MAFIA OPERATORS AND OPERATIONS

After the attentive scrutiny of ambiguous banking transactions, the three Catholic financiers, charged by the Vatican Secretary of State to probe into the Ambrosiano IOR connection, finally came to a somber conclusion. The IOR had had effective control over two of the major Ambrosiano's dummy companies. Indeed, it had manipulated eight more of those mysterious "shell" corporations.

The debacle had been accelerated not only by the Ambrosiano's latest fumblings, but also by the IOR itself, with its refusal, or perhaps "inability," to refund the money which it had borrowed or "lent." The shares which it had bought at "grossly inflated prices" plus Archbishop Marcinkus' "letters of comfort," that had authorized the horrendous borrowing, had done the rest.

The findings remained confidential. "Ugly rumors" about them were swiftly neutralized by official versions to the effect that "the name of the IOR had been used for a hidden project without any knowledge of the IOR" or that "its operations had had the resemblance of regularity" and such like "explanations."

When more explicit comments seemed necessary, these were encapsulated into images of wronged innocence. "The IOR was duped by unscrupulous international pirates," it was said, or of lily-white ineptitude on the part of the Vatican Bank's director, such as that "Archbishop Marcinkus had been the innocent victim of sophisticated cosmopolitan swindlers."[1]

Pope Wojtyla, who knew the true facts, however, quietly set up a committee composed of three members of each disputant. Its task: to reach a compromise acceptable to both Italy and the Vatican. Thereupon, he made it known that he was willing to reach a settlement with Italy's claims about the debts incurred by the IOR.

"The Holy See is disposed to take all the steps that may be required for an understanding on both sides," he said, "provided the entire truth is brought to light."[2]

The announcement had come after the four-day meeting of over 100 cardinals held in Rome in November, 1982, already mentioned during which he pledged his readiness to come to an understanding with Italy over the disputed 1,287 million dollar claim (reduced from the original 1,400 million dollar bill).

The papal admission to settle with a compromise raised more questions than it had answered or appeared to have solved. Since the panel had discovered, among other things, not only that the IOR had been heavily involved in the borrowing of the missing millions via the mysterious "shell" corporations, and equally that it had been their "legal owner," but also that several "letters of comfort" had been issued as early as September of the previous year. And perhaps even more interesting, that Calvi had responded to them with a "letter of discharge" of his own, in which he absolved the IOR of any responsibility for the borrowing.

The close ties between Calvi and the Director of the Vatican Bank, it was further discovered, had gone back years when the two had been involved in controversial activities via another Vatican top financier whom we have already met, Michele Sindona. The trio, Sindona, Marcinkus and Calvi, later nicknamed the Vatican Mafia, had operated together as early as 1972, at a time when they had acquired the Banca Cattolica del Veneto owned by the Vatican itself. The Sindona-Marcinkus-Calvi transactions had manipulated, so it was said, about one hundred million dollars.

When, following the Sindona crash, the official liquidator of the Banca Privata Italiana, one Giorgio Ambrosoli, presented his report to the American judiciary, Ambrosoli testified that "at least 6.5 million dollars had been paid, probably as a commission to an American bishop (Marcinkus at that time was a bishop) and to a Milanese Banker." (Calvi, at this period, was at the Ambrosiano as a Sindona ex-protege.) In his will, written days prior to his report and published in 1981, Ambrosoli, aware of the risk he was courting, wrote prophetically, "I might have to pay a very high price for what I have undertaken to do."

Interested parties, disconcerted at his findings, agreed with him. They decided to prevent the document from reaching the authorities. The day before he was to present his papers, they simply killed him.[3] The true perpetrators of the murder were never discovered.

The close cooperation between Calvi and the IOR continued in later years. This was proved by the fact that in 1975, the IOR wrote an official letter trying to cover Calvi's operations dealing with financial transference to the Banco Ambrosiano's Overseas of Nassau. Calvi and Archbishop Marcinkus, at that time, were President and Adviser, respectively.

In June, 1982, however, Marcinkus denied having had anything to do with it, although the letter of patronage written by the IOR of which Marcinkus was then President, was dated 1975 as seen by the facsimile of the same letter on the pages of this work.[4]

Even more curious, however, was the fact that both Sindona and Calvi had therefore, by association with Archbishop Marcinkus, been closely connected also with the notorious P2 Lodge. One of their friends was not only Lucio Gelli, the Grand Master of the Lodge, who we have already met, but also another influential Mason, one Umberto Ortolani. The latter had always been so close to the Vatican inner circles that he had been made a "Gentleman of his Holiness, the pope," also "Knight of the Holy Sepulcher."

The three Catholic financiers, in short, had dug up a past full of intrigues, many of which were still being spun by the same individuals still heavily involved with financial-Masonic-political activities and long range equivocal operations in which international banking, the Vatican, the U.S. and Soviet Russia had participated, even if by remote control.

The most striking confirmation of the latter was that the missing millions began to vanish into a seemingly bottomless pit, mostly since 1979. That was the year when Karol Wojtyla, the newly elected Polish pope, had forced himself into Poland, under the guise of a pastoral visit as Pope John Paul II. The result of his eight day trip was the launching of a fiercely political revolutionary syndicalism known as Solidarity.

The movement, conceived by Pope Wojtyla, and patronized by the C.I.A., needed and received large sums of money. A good portion of it came from the special section of the C.I.A.; the rest, it was asserted, from the unlimited generosity of the Vatican Bank. Many of the missing millions, it was suspected, were funnelled directly into Poland by the IOR itself and its lay and ecclesiastical agents. The even wider financial "hole" in the Ambrosiano-IOR partnership had been caused, not only by the personal misappropriations of professional mafiosi, but mostly by the large, secret subventions of the IOR.

As late as June 30, 1982, more than ten days after Calvi was found dead in London, the loaned capital and interest due by the companies in Luxembourg, under the code name of the IOR, that is, of the Vatican Bank, was exactly 1,275 million dollars, of which the first payment, 50 million dollars had been due that same June 30, 1982.

The equivocal operations of the IOR, and thus of the Ambrosiano Bank, directed at the furtherance of ideological objectives of a religious-political character in which the Vatican, Freemasonry and tangently, the U.S. had all been involved, had been under suspicion long before the crash came. The suspicions had been fostered by a number of Catholic bankers, who had been monitoring the unorthodox activities of both. Their criticism and fears produced a determined group from Lombardy, north Italy, the very region in which the Ambrosiano was operating, whose specific purpose was to prevent the inevitable forthcoming Ambrosiano-IOR disaster.

To that effect, they prepared a written document meant for Pope Wojtyla. They had prepared it, they said, to save the Ambrosiano, not so much because it was the most prominent Catholic bank, but equally because of its close association with the IOR. They regretted, they added, that the two were co-responsible with Calvi's operations, and dealt with a degenerate Freemasonry in contact with the Vatican itself.

The close association of the Vatican with Sindona, Calvi, Gelli and other Freemasons during the ten previous years, plus their dealings with the IOR, they told the pope, had involved the Vatican in such "imbroglio," the like of which had never been seen before.

In view of that, they asked him to dissolve the IOR link with its current associates. The dissolution was the more urgent, since the Vatican Bank had become, not only a partner of the Ambrosiano, but also because the IOR was a "very active associate," adding by way of an extra warning that the IOR Director, Archbishop Marcinkus, was as active. Indeed, that the archbishop had been considered by none other than the Bank of Italy to be "in the top management" of the whole dangerous Ambrosiano-IOR affair with their sundry phantom corporations.[5]

Pope Wojtyla did nothing. The involvement of the Vatican Bank had already gone too far. The papal machinations, supported by their financial subventions to the counter-revolutionary worker movement in Poland, by now had become unstoppable.

As the crisis of the Ambrosiano was reaching a climax, however, the Vatican began to consider various steps by which to prevent it from turning into a total disaster. The first of such steps was to prevent the Ambrosiano crash. Its postponement would have saved the IOR. The key to the move was Calvi.

Calvi was asked to have a secret encounter with Pope Wojtyla, something which was hotly denied by the Vatican after Calvi's "suicide." The move was aborted because events, meanwhile, had forced Calvi to flee from Rome. Prior to that, Calvi had arranged also a secret meeting with the IOR top administrator subsequently indicted by Italy. The meeting had been arranged for 17th of June, the day before Calvi fled to London to meet his Freemason "brother" Carboni.

That there had been "serious" moves to save the Ambrosiano, and therefore the IOR, was proved also by another top disclosure. Twenty-four hours before Calvi's "suicide," a consortium of bankers from the U.S. had made a definite offer to save the Ambrosiano-IOR with a prompt 1,250 million dollars.[6]

The financial problem, therefore, although of the utmost seriousness, basically was "solvable." The more so since in addition to the providential offer from the U.S. consortium, there had been another monetary rescue move. Calvi, it was disclosed, had flown to London also to strike a deal with a super-Catholic organization, the Opus Dei.

The Opus Dei is a semi-secret religious lay order whose paramount objective is total support of the papacy and of the most conservative principles of the Catholic doctrines. Its devotion to both is unequalled. Its members have dedicated themselves, with their personal and corporate wealth, to be the blind instruments of the Church.

Owing to such religious totality, the Order considered its duty to help the Vatican Bank, and thus the pope, to extricate themselves from the Ambrosiano-IOR impasse. This could be done by filling the "hole" created by the missing millions, with millions of their own.

To the Opus Dei, P2 Lodge was not only a simple Masonic lodge. It was an evil body with powerful political interests, reaching the most recondite nooks of national and international illegality; an entity which had specialized in labyrinthine conspiratorial operations, into which it had drawn the Church, the Vatican and the pope himself.

In their view, members of the Lodge were the instruments of the IOR's involvement in the disaster. Calvi had been one of them. As a director of the Ambrosiano, he had accelerated the tragedy by pressing the IOR to pay back to his bank what, according to him, the IOR owed the Ambrosiano. Calvi, according to such interpretation, had asked the IOR to retrieve the millions of dollars which, according to him, the IOR had deposited in certain numbered Swiss accounts. This he did to save the Ambrosiano from the impending crash, prior to his flight to London.

The disaster occurred when the IOR refused to do so, because either it could not or was ordered not to, or because the money had been "locked" into numbered accounts to which others had the key. The Grand Master of P2 Lodge, Gelli, knew the secret number of the accounts of the Union Bank of Switzerland, as later on (September, 1982) Attorney General of the Swiss Cantonticino, Bernasconi, revealed when stating "that large sums of the Ambrosiano had been secreted into several numbered accounts."

The speculation seemed to have been substantiated, although not the identity of the depositors, when top members of P2 Lodge tried to withdraw, one 60 million dollars, and the other an undisclosed large sum from Swiss banks, as we have already seen, and were arrested as a result.

Calvi's flight to London and his aborted attempt to negotiate a deal with the Opus Dei to prevent the impending Ambrosiano-IOR disaster, therefore, seemed to have been an attempt on the part of the Opus Dei to provide the money, in order to save the Vatican from the inevitability of a major financial scandal.

Also, to prevent the disclosure of the Church's involvement with shady operational partners like a notorious Masonic lodge, and equivocal associates suspected of dealing with political and social subversion, not to mention with arms traffic and even drug smuggling.

That such speculations were not mere idle suppositions seemed to have been supported by Calvi himself. A few weeks before, Calvi, referring to the impending Ambrosiano crash, in fact, gave a telling warning. "Should anything happen to me," Calvi had stated, "the Vatican would find itself in such a scandal that it would have to leave St. Peter's Square."[7]

Thereupon, acknowledging his fear that he might even be killed, he went so far as to imply that the disclosure which might follow, had not a solution been found in the meanwhile, could be of such perilous nature that "the pope himself would have to resign."[8]

It was obvious that a man who could make such ominous allusions must have had factual evidence of a most alarming nature at his disposal. Since it was clear that he was referring to operations that by-passed mere financial transactions, such as the fermenting of political unrest, the sale of arms, and the promotion of ideological subversion.

The sum of such activities, promoted simultaneously by the Mafia, Freemasonry, the Church, and the IOR, would have amalgamated their forces into a monstrous consortium of secretive, if not illegal, activities.

Calvi, who it seemed was ready to accept the Opus Dei's offer, was warned "not to accept their financial assistance."

This warning given at the last moment, had come, it was said, from certain prominent individuals of the P2 Lodge.

Un'alleanza tra la tradizione cattolica e laica

Questo il testo del pro-memoria che un gruppo di tradizionalisti azionisti, appartenenti a vecchie famiglie cattoliche lombarde, aveva cercato di far pervenire all'inizio dell'anno nelle mani del Papa.

① Il Banco Ambrosiano ha sempre avuto una forte caratterizzazione cattolica che ancora oggi è viva nell'immagine esterna del Banco.

② Tale caratterizzazione cattolica non è però solo un retaggio storico o una semplice questione di immagine esterna. Essa ancora oggi si basa su fatti precisi:
● Lo Ior, con 1.991.000 azioni, è il maggior azionista conosciuto del Banco.
● Ancora oggi lo statuto recita: «Il Banco Ambrosiano è una banca fondata da cattolici».
● Il gruppo controlla una banca che porta addirittura il nome cattolico nella ragione sociale: «Banca Cattolica del Veneto».
● Ancora oggi lo statuto prevede: «Nell'esercizio della sua attività il Banco Ambrosiano, secondo la sua tradizione, avrà particolare riguardo per le istituzioni e le iniziative aventi finalità cattoliche».

③ Ma ciò che più conta è che lo Ior non è un socio normale; è un socio fortemente attivo; è un corresponsabile.

Lo Ior ha partecipato in modo assai intenso come associato e corresponsabile del presidente del Banco, dottor Roberto Calvi, alle più spericolate operazioni finanziarie degli ultimi anni, per molte delle quali il Calvi è già stato condannato in sede penale o è o sarà indiziato di reati. Il profondo coinvolgimento dell'Ior nelle operazioni più discutibili di Calvi è provato da una copiosa documentazione risultante da una verifica della Banca d'Italia e già da tempo al vaglio della magistratura milanese.

A semplice titolo di esempio:
● Paul Marcinkus viene dagli ispettori della Banca d'Italia addirittura incluso nel «top management» della banca.
● L'operazione più scandalosa della gestione Calvi è stata realizzata attraverso la società Suprafin. Attraverso questa società, che operava con finanziamento intestato al Banco. Questa società, con fondi del Banco, comprava azioni dai piccoli azionisti e le rivendeva, in blocco, a delle società estere controllate da Calvi e dai suoi associati.

Questa operazione racchiude una serie di violazioni di legge gravissime, oltre che essere l'espressione della più spregiudicata forma speculativa: usare i soldi dei risparmiatori per comprare la proprietà della banca stessa. Esiste la prova scritta che la Suprafin è dello Ior.

● Lo Ior non è solo socio dell'Ambrosiano. E' associato e corresponsabile di Roberto Calvi. E' documentato da un crescente numero di procedure penali che Calvi è oggi uno dei maggiori crocevia della più degenere massoneria (P2) e di filoni mafiosi provenienti dall'eredità di Sindona che Calvi ha ricevuto, ancora una volta con il coinvolgimento di personaggi ampiamente nutriti e coccolati dal Vaticano, come Ortolani, a cavallo tra il Vaticano e potenti circoli della malavita internazionale.

Essere soci di Roberto Calvi vuol dire essere soci o corresponsabili di Gelli e di Ortolani, dato che entrambi lo guidano e lo condizionano fortemente. Il Vaticano è quindi, che piaccia o meno, attraverso la sua associazione con Calvi anche socio attivo di Gelli e di Ortolani.

Se quanto sopra è vero, e lo è incontrovertibilmente, vi sono due alternative.
A. Che lo Ior resti associato e complice di Roberto Calvi, e allora, per almeno dieci anni, rimarrà coinvolto in uno scandalo di proporzioni non inferiori a quello di Sindona.
B. Che lo Ior resti socio del Banco Ambrosiano ma che, insieme ad altri soci laici perbene e in ogni caso non coinvolti nei giri della malavita internazionale, lavori per formare una nuova aggregazione di soci che realizzino un rinnovamento al vertice del Banco. Si può pensare alla presidenza di un cattolico serio come Lazzati e alla immissione nel consiglio di persone di spicco sia del mondo cattolico che laico, realizzando una saldatura di estremo interesse, tipo quella che si è realizzata al S. Paolo di Brescia.

Una scelta in questo senso comporterebbe:

● Un'azione difensiva.
Sciogliere gradualmente e ragionevolmente i complessi intrecci tra Vaticano e Ior, evitando i riscli di una deflagrazione che sarebbe pressoché inevitabile in caso di commissariamento della banca o comunque in caso di uscita del gruppo De Benedetti.

● Un'azione positiva.
Poter esercitare un'azione positiva su una istituzione bancaria che potrebbe avere un ruolo estremamente positivo e intorno alla quale si potrebbe realizzare una saldatura tra la migliore tradizione cattolica e la migliore tradizione laica, di estremo interesse anche sul piano culturale e, in senso lato, politico.

12 gennaio 1982

The above article from IL GIORNALE, August 22, 1982 presents a document drafted by Catholic shareholders and meant for Pope John Paul II. It condemns the close partnership of the Ambrosiano and the IOR. It accuses the Ambrosiano and the IOR of dealing with Freemasonry, and with the international Mafia. The most striking part of this accusation, is that such activities are conducted via a society called SUPRAFIN. The society SUPRAFIN, the writers say, belongs to the IOR. The IOR and the SUPRAFIN, plus the Ambrosiano, are all operating closely with the P2 Lodge and with Sindona, also with Freemasons, all of whom are protected by the Vatican itself. The Bank of Italy, furthermore, has ascertained that Archbishop Marcinkus is operating at "the top management" of the Banco Ambrosiano itself. The writers ask the pope to detach the activities of the Ambrosiano from those of the IOR and of the Vatican before it is too late.

During the crisis of midsummer 1982, after Calvi's "suicide," the Vatican denied any involvement with the Ambrosiano. Yet, the above letter was sent to the pope and read by Marcinkus, January, 1982. The document was dated 12th January, 1982.

Since 1978, that is since the election of a Polish pope, the Vatican had been openly motivated by a strong social interpretation of the gospels. During his sundry peregrinations, Pope Wojtyla had invariably created unrest by encouraging subversive Catholic movements, who had accepted his socialist ideas. Their acceptance, however, was not a mere verbal one. It trespassed into insurrectional fields. These necessitated monetary help, given via local secretive Church channels and more often than not, directly via the secular associates of the IOR.

Financial grants, often through religious organizations, sympathetic with left wing insurrections, meant the involvement, even if tangently, of the Vatican Bank whose financial bulk derives from deposits of religious organizatons. Hence Catholic priests, being involved in actual armed insurrections in Latin America, the Philippines and Poland would automatically have spelled the potential traffic of clandestine sales of arms and, therefore, the involvement of shady banking concerns such as the mysterious "shell" companies of the IOR, and as a result, indirectly of the Vatican itself.

Calvi's Masonic associates, and later many of his Masonic accusers after his death, fled to South America where they had monetary funds, "friends," and made use, it was alleged, of the Ambrosiano's branches in Peru and the Bahamas. The background to the Calvi operations, prior to his flight from Italy, assumes an additional significance, if we were to add yet another facet of what had been going on, prior to the final collapse.

The head of the anti-terrorist police, General Roberto dalla Chiesa, had repeatedly warned Calvi of "impending danger" to his life. The General had hinted, however, that the peril was of a more intangible nature than he suspected. "Look behind your back," he used to tell him. Calvi's wife, who at this time had to be guarded by the police, later insisted that her husband's life had been endangered by the "priests." Calvi, it appears, had also become convinced that those who wanted him out of the way were in the Vatican, a suspicion which was never proved. Prior to leaving for London, he warned his wife that, yes, the danger came "from the priests."

Whatever he might have meant by such an emotive accusation, the fact remained that General della Chiesa, the head of the anti-terrorist police, must have known of some definite plot directed at getting rid of Calvi; or at least he suspected that some elements were determined to silence him for good, lest he should name names, since many of such names could have been found in the highest pinnacles of the political, Masonic, and even ecclesiastical life in Italy, at even the Vatican, itself. After Calvi's "suicide," his briefcase, which he always carried with him, disappeared mysteriously — the only item which was missing. It contained secret documents connected with P2 Lodge and the IOR.

The General's hint to Calvi must have provoked grave apprehension amidst those who were planning his demise, since the General knew about the whole affair, more than it was safe for him to know. The ring, operating the invisible web round the Ambrosiano-IOR-P2 Lodge, decided to act. General della Chiesa was sent to Sicily. While there, he and his wife were riddled by 100 bullets in plain daylight in the center of a Sicilian town (September 22, 1982), ostensibly by the Mafia. In reality, however, it was by the same forces which had already liquidated several other individuals connected with the Ambrosiano-IOR-P2 Lodge.

Calvi's death under Blackfriars Bridge, marked by its macabre ritual, was the climax of something which had been brewing behind a colossal conspiratorial wall of equivocal operations and plots, many of which had penetrated very deeply within the Vatican's citadel. Subsequent events proved this to be so. The Secretary of the IOR itself, Msgr. Donato De Bonis, directly under Archbishop Marcinkus, had his passport withdrawn February 10, 1983 when he was accused of tax evasion in petroleum products. The incriminating operation dated back to the years of the Sindona-Calvi-Marcinkus financial junta. Also involved was a general, the former head of the Ministry of Finance's own police. He was sentenced to several years in jail for tax evasion involving fraudulent handling of some $300 million.

Other prelates were arrested February 7, 1983 including Msgr. Simeone Duca of Rome and Dom F Quaglia. Others had their passports withdrawn including Msgr. Mario Pimpo, director of the department known as "Confidential Affair," the office of Cardinal Poletti, the pope's own vicar of Rome.

The financial activities of the IOR and of its lay partner, the Ambrosiano, while the primary promoters of the great monetary scandal, had uncovered the tip of a submerged iceberg whose magnitudinous proportions had reached the darkest recesses of a twilight world of global intrigues, religious corruption and financial banditry, seldom equalled even in our present century.

CHAPTER 33

RIDDLE OF AN ENIGMA, THE VATICAN BANK

The Institute for Religious Works, the IOR for short, gives the impression of a corporate body, wholly dedicated to pious operations and charitable activities. It is nothing of that kind. It is, or was, one of the richest banks in the world.

As a semi-autonomous entity, it was officially charged with the handling of deposits and investments of hundreds, indeed of thousands, of millions of dollars, most of them the legal property of Roman Catholic lay and religious orders, trusts, legacies and the like. It acted, and still acts, also for many of the Church's own holdings, monetary funds, and multi-million securities portfolios, many of which are or were, secreted in sundry vaults in the U.S. or in numbered accounts in Swiss banks.

As a financial power-house, it was, and is still, an ecclesiastical subterfuge created to by-pass national barriers, international regulations, and to carry out monetary evasions via subterranean semi-diplomatic channels. Because of this, it operates within and outside the boundaries of ultranational legality.

Its wealth has always been reputed to be immense. That this was no mere speculation was substantiated by the prosaic assessments of level headed international financiers. One of these, none other than the Annual Report of the Bank for International Settlement of Basle, Switzerland, lists the foreign currency position of the banks in the ten largest industrial countries of the world.

According to it, in 1977, the IOR had foreign deposits of 100 million dollars, and no debts. That was only one of its current sundry diversified accounts. By 1983, it had about 2 billion dollars in net assets, 6 billion in deposits, and an active relationship with over 200 banks all over the globe.[1]

Its operations have been so secretive and labyrinthine that it is almost impossible to know where and how, or by whom, the money is used or is employed, as the Ambrosiano case has so amply demonstrated.

Because of its ramifications and mystery of its many activities, or rather of its true objectives, the IOR became the major financial power house of the Vatican. From the very beginning, as such, it acted on its behalf during official and semi-official operations, many of which trespassed, very often, from the mere financial into religious, diplomatic and ideological fields.

It is an axiom that financial considerations will corrupt religion and religious institutions. But while it is true that religious considerations can corrupt finances, it is no less true that when religion is supported by finance, and finance is supported by religion, religion will be corrupt simultaneously on two fronts. The result is that it will be rendered the ancillary instrument to both.

When religion happens to be the Catholic Church, by virtue of the fact that she has given herself a uniqueness which is peculiar only to herself, then the same Church will use and abuse her financial might to maintain her own uniqueness, cost what it may.

Money is power. Power is linked with politics. Hence political problems are interlocked with the financial influence of the Vatican in monetary administration. The case of the Ambrosiano-IOR scandal was typical of the double nature and of the double objectives of the IOR itself. It could not have been otherwise since Vatican financial activities have seldom been confined to simple monetary operations.

Whenever activated, they are activated because of some ulterior goal. Besides immediate targets, ecclesiastic or otherwise, their true motive is consistently the expansion of the influence of the Church, as a church, as well as an idealogical crusader.

Under Pope Paul VI, for instance, large sums of money were syphoned, via the IOR, into feeding left-wing orientated movements in many parts of the world. These were also sponsored by another financially mighty power, that of the Jesuits, who shared Paul VI's left wing views. The Vatican-Moscow Alliance, although never officially accepted as such, was a de facto reality. What made such a political reality active were the secret financial operations of the Vatican Bank and its subsidiaries.

The IOR with its vast resources derived by the funds at its disposal, thus, could financially feed Catholic orientated subversive movements in Africa, Latin America, the Philippines or even Eastern Europe.

The advent of a Polish pope changed nothing as far as the use of Vatican finances were concerned. The contrary was the case. Since it accelerated the outward flow of the monetary reserves of the Vatican towards fostering vigorous ideologically motivated activities.

Pope Wojtyla, unlike Paul VI, whose ideological horizon was the world itself, manipulated millions to finance narrow nationalistic subversion in his own country. Following his "pastoral" visit to Poland in 1979, only a year after his election, he became the Godfather of a Catholic-Polish left-wing hybrid called "Solidarity," disguised under the innocent banner of a trade union. In reality it was a naked political disestablishing ploy against the Polish Government.

Catholic workers were openly encouraged by priests, bishops and cardinals, not only with holy water, but also with vast sums of foreign currency and abundant C.I.A. subsidies of millions of dollars. Large sums of money reached the revolutionary priests and workers with regularity worthy of a multinational banking apparatus.

The coffers of the IOR were activated in dispensing their funds eastward. It was not a coincidence that some of its funds began to diminish at an alarming rate since 1979, the beginning of Wojtyla's Godfathering of "Solidarity." The Calvi-P2 Lodge-Ambrosiano-IOR syndicate helped to syphon additional sums also to certain Central American republics.

The financing of Catholic subversion is often camouflaged behind the screen of missionary or charitable operations, hence their undetectability. The IOR, as their official agency, sponsored, approved, and distributed their monetary funds under the political inspiration of the Vatican Bank. The activities of the Ambrosiano, and of the IOR with their "shell" companies and the cooperation of certain "brothers" of the P2 Lodge were meant to subsidize political objectives which they all had in common. Calvi, for instance, although a practicing Catholic, supported left-wing publications, sympathetic to Catholicism. Masons like Gelli and Carboni instead helped right wing junta in South America to fight Russian orientated communism as long as they advocated Catholic-inspired socialism of the type advocated by Wojtyla.

From its inception in 1942, the IOR has consistently acted as a screen meant to conceal activities inconsistent with financial matters. Namely, it was used to by-pass, that is to cheat, the monetary legislation of the national and international community, such as in the initial transference of Vatican assets to the U.S. by invoking equivocal by-laws, or by misusing the diplomatic immunity of the Church to the best advantage of the Vatican Bank. The operation necessitated a smooth machinery, as well as powerful allies in the financial world.

The financial world, more often than not, is motivated by political inducements. These, very often, are inspired by the ideological or religious beliefs of the bodies they represent. The curious exertions of the Vatican with Freemasonry, as in the Sindona-Calvi-Marcinkus case, was by no means unique. Their relationship, although due mostly to the personal amity of individual members of the Masonic brotherhood with individual members of the Vatican, nevertheless was also cemented by their opposition to one major enemy they all wished to destroy — *Russian* inspired communism.

This goal was as powerful as the other one they all had in common: the manipulation and multiplication of legally and illegally acquired wealth.

The close relationship of money with political power, and of religion with both, has always been a characteristic of the Catholic Church. What today is called the IOR, or the Vatican Bank, or Prefecture for Economic Affairs, or Congregation, or such other like euphemisms, has consistently played a paramount role in all papal administrations. Because of the duality of its nature and objectives, it has always had an official side of its monetary operations, and a secret one. The latter known only to a few, as a rule is run by the pope himself.

This dual tradition, which originated long before the birth of the IOR during World War II, goes back to the early Middle Ages and became the traditional policy of, to mention only one notorious name, Alexander VI, the Borgia pope. Alexander, for all his legendary debaucheries, was a sound administrator and believed that money could help run the Church more practically than the Holy Spirit.

The best proof of his belief was himself. He became pope simply by using money, an immense amount of it. He bribed whichever cardinal he could. He did so by giving them sackfuls of golden florins in order of their voting importance. From the lowest, the Cardinal of Venice, 95 years old, and whose vote, therefore, was worth comparatively little, to Cardinal Ascanio Sforza, a potential papal candidate. Cardinal Sforza accepted an immense bribe, and let Borgia become pope. Borgia managed to bribe nine out of a college of less than forty cardinals.

Although openly accused of simony, before and after he became pope, Borgia masterminded the Vatican Treasury, or what now is called the IOR, or Vatican Bank, but which in those days was known as the Apostolic Chamber, or the Department of State, responsible for finances. Papal revenues then, like now, were in two forms, spiritual and temporal, a reflection of the dual nature of the papacy.

The first income took the conventional form of gifts, Peter's Pence, and the like, crowned by such customary payments as the "annates." The annate was one year income from each occupant of a benefice whether a cardinal, a bishop, or a humble parish priest.

Later on, however, since the revenues were not sufficient, a more lucrative revenue came into prominence; the sale of indulgences and of ecclesiastic offices. The sales increased the revenues to such an extent that a sub-department of the Apostolic Chamber was created specially to deal with them. This was called the Datary.

The Datary thus became a kind of secret section of the official Apostolic Chamber. Whereas the finance of the Apostolic Chamber, what today we would call the Vatican Bank, was controlled by sundry financial officials whose task was to supervise the money investment and expenses of the Church in general, the money of the Datary was turned into a secret fund. This was managed directly by the pope without any public supervision or official control. The Datary precedent, in due course, became a tradition and was incorporated into the IOR ever since it was first established.

In other words, the Vatican Bank, past and present, had a dual purpose. The official one, the minding of the millions deposited by Catholic institutions and the unofficial one, the secretive operations which its money permitted the Vatican to conduct in fields which had little or nothing to do with financial matters.

The Vatican has used its secret funds for decades. In the fifties, Pope Pius XII did so with the fostering of the Cold War, supported by Cardinal Spellman and the U.S. State Department, headed by John Foster Dulles.

Pope John XXIII used official and secret funds to finance the Vatican II Council. His successor, Pope Paul VI, the inspirer of the Vatican Moscow Alliance, although a careful administrator, spent most of the IOR money to sustain his secretive diplomatic policy meant at bringing about a rapprochement with Soviet Russian and the eastern communist bloc. His policy necessitated money, most of which came from secretive sources that were never accounted for.

The election of a Polish pope, far from slowing down the process, accelerated it from the beginning. The IOR provided most of the money budgeted for the purpose of carrying out disruptive activities favored by the political line subscribed by Pope John Paul II. These secret operations needed funds. A recent Director of the Vatican Bank once put it, "the Church cannot be run only with Hail Marys." In other words, she needs more millions of dollars than those who run her care to admit.[2]

As Pope Borgia, and successive popes knew well, the more active their policies, the more money needed to carry them out. But whereas the Borgia pope, for instance, spent colossal fortunes on his family, contemporary popes spend even larger ones to foster their pet ideologies, or individual forms of pontifical administration.

More often than not, such extra expenditures are greater than the official annual income of the Vatican. It is a curious fact that in Borgia's days, the Vatican's budget was often as unbalanced as that of the Vatican of today. The complaints of Pope Paul VI and of Pope John Paul II concerning scarcity of revenues, strike a familiar note in spite of the gap of centuries.

In modern times, the Vatican has dissipated thousands of millions of dollars in conspiratorial adventurism, mostly of an idological subversive character. It was these which led it to its unwise association with unscrupulous financial adventurers such as Sindona, Calvi and their supporters. Associations, the like of which brought the Vatican to the brink of political and indeed, of financial disaster. And more than once, even to the very brink of war.[3]

The Ambrosiano-IOR-P2 Lodge saga, in itself, was of a minor political character. As a crisis, however, it became one of truly magnitudinous financial dimensions. This Vatican monetary adventurism, sustained by international lay financial banditry, depleted its bank of vast sums, a large portion of which was used for the launching and supporting of the Polish Solidarity and of subversive movements in Latin America.

The tragically large depletion of the bank's funds was of such an unprecedented character that the pope decided to take an unexpected step to replenish its emptied coffers. He "invented" a fictitious Holy Year. His objective, the collection of millions of dollars via the extra worldwide influx of Catholic pilgrims to Rome, as we shall see presently. No Borgia pope had ever shown such mundane cynicism under direct financial duress. Perhaps because the Borgian eyes had been constantly fixed upon the approaching Jubilee of the year 1500.

A Holy Year is characterized by mass piety, but even more telling, by mass offering. In other words, it is a colossal money maker wrapped in the mantle of religion. Pope Pius XII presided over that of 1950, Pope Paul VI over that of 1975. The next one should have been celebrated in the fatidic year of 2000. The IOR disaster willed otherwise.

Almost 500 years ago Girolamo Savanarola of Florence, referring to the approaching Holy Year of 1500, summed up the true expectation that the pope of his time had concerning the monetary gains of the event: "They ring their bells for coins and for candles," he thundered. "They sell their benefices, sell the sacraments, traffic in masses...no one needs to keep up appearances anymore...."

Savonarola said that to condemn the greed of the Borgia pope. Had he lived now, he would have condemned an institution with which contemporary popes have played with the multiplication of fabulous sums of money, that is, the IOR, better known as the Vatican Bank.

Besides pointing an accusing finger at its bishops and cardinals, he would have done so also at the Bank's depositors, that is, at all the religious and lay orders and institutions which, after accumulating their vast fortunes, had put them into the Bank's vaults, regardless of their vows of poverty. Even more telling, was the pope's daring to "invent" a non-existent Holy Year with the specific objective of collecting millions from the pilgrims eager to gather indulgences while discarding their coins in the Roman coffers.

The Vatican Bank and all that for which it had stood, to him would have been more of an abomination than a Borgia pope himself. The purpose for which that same bank had been created — retention and the multipication of more and more wealth with its equivocal manipulations and political subversion, would have seemed a blasphemy not to be tolerated by any genuine Christian worthy of such name.

Before Savonarola, an ancient chronicler, when referring to similar events could not help saying a truth which had consistently been ignored by Christians of all ages beginning with ours, "Truly we cannot serve God and Mammon at the same time," he wrote. "Truly we cannot stand with one foot in Heaven and the other on Earth."[4]

This is an equally appropriate comment about the Vatican Bank of today, an institution activated by continuous financial operations, incessant monetary activities, and the feverish accumulation of ever more wealth, in open contradiction to the teachings of Jesus Christ, who the pope claims to infallibly represent.

CHAPTER 34

1983-84: THE UNHOLY HOLY YEAR, INDULGENCES, CASH AND POPE-IDOLATRY

The sudden proclamation of Easter 1983 to Easter 1984 as an "extraordinary Holy Year" stunned everybody from the Papal Vicar General and sundry Vatican Congregations, to the Sacred College of Cardinals on the last of their four-day meetings to discuss the IOR's finances.[1] There were two exceptions: Pope John Paul II, who had suddenly discovered its sacredness, and the Shopkeeper Association of Rome. Both expected to treble the 300 million dollars earned during the previous Jubilee of 1975. Indeed, perhaps to quadruple it.

Although none of the cardinals had ever had even a hint of it, they guessed at once its true objective: the collection of as much money as possible within the shortest time possible, and with the least effort possible, to replenish the coffers of the IOR, of Vatican City, and of the Church, in that order.

Rome's Communist mayor called an emergency session. "Our city is not prepared to deal with the enormous number of visitors at such a short notice," he commented. "The oncoming influx of between 10 to 15 million pilgrims will add to our already unmanageable difficulties," he then added, referring to the debt-ridden Roman Council, overburdened with the payment of more than 800,000 dollars a day in interest alone on recent bank loans.

Many judged the promulgation one of the most cynical exercises and abuses of piety for mercenary objectives ever undertaken in recent times. Catholics, in general, although surprised, passively accepted the explanation that 1983 had been earmarked to commemorate the 1950 anniversary of the death of Jesus Christ. Many theologians, however, regarded the date with deep suspicion. Prominent biblical scholars scoffed that the 1950 anniversary of the crucifixion was not 1983 as Pope Wojtyla had announced, but Good Friday of 1986.

Those in the know acknowledged the unpalatable truth that the Jubilee had been a brilliant, even if a most unscrupulous excuse, to recoup part of the money lost by the Vatican during the 1982 debacle; a brazen effort to replace the missing millions with those it hoped to collect during the "extraordinary Holy Year". Nobody had overlooked the fact that the announcement had come on the same day when the pope had said that he was willing to repay some of the Ambrosiano-IOR missing millions. Also shortly before that, Italy's Treasury Minister had sent to the Vatican another threatening reminder that the IOR still owed the shareholders of the Ambrosiano more than one thousand million dollars, not yet paid.

The discreet but relentless pressure of the 200 world banks involved in the IOR's debit-credit "imbroglio," although in the background, was no less effective. A global boycott by the international banking community could have had a most disastrous result upon any future activities with the Catholic Church in general, and with the Vatican financial activities of tomorrow, in particular. A vigorous mobilization of the Catholic world, therefore, had become not only a useful ploy to meet the double pressure, but a most urgent necessity.

When, as a result of it all, therefore, Pope Wojtyla announced the unexpected Holy Year without any warning, indeed without bothering even to consult Rome's civic authorities, the Communist Mayor, Ugo Vetere, exploded unamusedly by saying that "this is no time for jokes." Rome found itself face to face with a practical problem of bewildering complexity: how to prepare the city for the "unholy Holy Year." It was recalled with outrage that the previous pope, Paul VI, had given at least 18 months advance notice prior to the Jubilee of 1975.

When the Holy See, to add insult to injury, urged the Council that Rome had better gear up her touristic resources as briskly as possible, Rome's Mayor was even less amused, knowing that the Shopkeeper Association came only second to the true main beneficiary, the Vatican. Most of the tourists were going to be the "pilgrims" who would have arrived in church-organized packages, billeted and fed in convents, monasteries, and other of Rome's 1,500 religious institutions at good sound profits, all of which were exempt from taxes. Tax exemption, of course, spelled at least double, if not treble profits for the Church money gathering lay and religious agencies.

The mercenary objective of the extraordinary "Holy Year" became even more crystal clear with the brazen reminders from cardinals and even from the pope. The duties of the pilgrims, said Cardinal Casaroli, was not only to seek for indulgences, but also to give "with generosity."

When he opened the meeting of the College of Cardinals to debate the Ambrosiano-IOR collapse, Pope Wojtyla wrote a letter reminding Catholics that the basic sources of the Holy See's finances were "the offerings" by the world's believers. Thereupon, after referring to his "increasing monetary anxiety," Wojtyla pointedly referred to the mutual generosity of the early Christians. He hoped, he then commented, that today Catholics would be no less generous.

While this was going on, steps were being taken to whitewash the IOR for the losses suffered. Cardinal Krol of Philadelphia, a member of the papal commission of fifteen cardinals, who had discussed the IOR's finances and debts "very secretly" and allegedly a member of the inner Polish Mafia at the Vatican, declared that Marcinkus had been virtually cleared of all suggestions of financial "impropriety." The Vatican Bank also had been absolved "of any blame," he commented. The fault had been that of the Ambrosiano.

Another additional but significant disclosure of Krol's was that the Vatican Bank had been used by the Ambrosiano operators to finance dubious "schemes" in Latin America. What he meant by the word, "operators," was never clarified. The facts, however, were there for all to see. Most of the Ambrosiano's operators had been good practicing Catholics and good practicing Freemasons supported by an international outlandish sprinkling of cosmopolitan mafiosi dealing with arms traffic and drug rings. Also financial "filaments" of sundry intelligence apparati had been at work with them, and thus, even if tangently, with the IOR. There had been activities, not only in

1983-84: THE UNHOLY HOLY YEAR

Latin America, but also in Eastern Europe in the pope's own country, communist Poland.

The word "Solidarity" had loomed large in the secret discussion of cardinals and the "three wise men" since it had absorbed vast sums of money. Also, because another justification of the pope for "inventing" the Holy Year of 1983-84 had been, besides the spurious commemoration of the crucifixion, the 600th anniversary of the arrival in Poland of the most sacred Holy Icon, the Black Madonna Czestochowa.

The Black Madonna, according to Polish tradition, had repelled the invasions of semi-pagan enemies such as the Swedes, and above all, the Russians. As a thank-you for her help, she was declared a General of the Polish armies. She had also been crowned Queeen of Poland.

According to Pope Wojtyla, the Madonna was still protecting Catholic Poland against her current enemies; hence her having been acclaimed as the protector of Solidarity. "Our strength is not only in numbers, for we are also a streak of lightning sent by God to uproot a tree whose bark has turned rotten," proclaimed the plaque in the monastery wall of Jasna Gora.[2] "Let's pray that miners and shipyard workers find common cause under the protection of the Black Madonna," Polish priests thundered in the Polish churches.[3]

The belligerent fervor engendered by the Madonna, and the pope's sponsorship of Solidarity cost money more than envisaged by either the IOR or the pope. The preliminary funds, some from the "shell" companies, had turned inadequate. Solidarity became a voracious devourer of dollars. Prior to his death in June, 1982, it had been reckoned that Calvi and associates, had already transferred to Solidarity at least 12 million dollars from the Ambrosiano-IOR combined fund. By the time Pope John Paul II visited Poland again in June, 1983, the sum was reckoned to have reached 16 to 17 million dollars.

La Stampa, one of Italy's most respected newspapers suggested in its June 15, 1983 edition that the pope himself had approved the operation of his entourage, when, during the same papal visit, they secreted into Poland funds worth over two million dollars under the collective protection of their diplomatic immunity. (See also The Daily Express, June 16, 1983.)

Monetary subsidies derived from priestly episcopal, congregational and papal sources, directly and indirectly, (The Congregation for the Propagation of the Faith, and the Institute of Religious Works, for instance), although dedicated to the objectives indicated by their names, were active foci for ideologically motivated activities inspired directly by the pope, who had promised that, had Russia invaded Poland, to suppress it, Pope Wojtyla would have gone there personally to oppose the Soviet action.

Whenever motivated by religious national goals, the Roman Catholic Church becomes a vast political machine dedicated to the proposition that it must help, not only with Hail Marys, as the Director of the Vatican Bank is supposed to have commented, but also with money.

Besides the established ecclesiastic channels, the providers of money are the cults, starting with the Marian ones. These have always been and are still, the surest money spinners of all. The Black Virgin of Poland is one. There, the pious who want intercessions, write out their wishes on pieces of paper that are put in a box, later opened by the priests. The priests then read the notes and take the money, since the pieces of paper are seldom put into the box without coins or banknotes.

A companion Black Madonna, that of the Virgin of Monserrat in Catalonia, is even more successful. She collects ten of thousands of pesetas daily. Other Virgins located in Italy, France, Spain and Portugal, are also active sources of abundant revenues. Those of Lourdes and of Fatima lead the league as described in other chapters.

Recently, another no less successful cult has appeared on the scene: pope-idolatry. The phenomenon of the travelling popes has created a new semi-ecclesiastical apparatus, specifically dedicated to the spending, collecting and the making of money, with the full cooperation of civilian and religious authorities. The image of a travelling pope was originally initiated by Pope Paul VI, and since then, has developed into a veritable ecclesiastico-touristic travel agency, centered at the Vatican.

The pope decides which land to visit, and immediately, far flung operations are set in motion. The ecclesiastic machinery is geared for the reception, theatricality, and management of the papal visitor. Civic authorities are mobilized and coordinated with the papal movements. The whole thing requires money, often millions.

The faithful glimpse the pope, hear his platitudes, and then are made to pay for it all, regardless. Collections are taken from the pews before his Holiness arrives, and even more often, after he has gone. During the papal 1982 visit to England and Scotland, for instance, the pattern was repeated, to the surprise of those who, until then, had been convinced that papal visits consisted exclusively of spiritual abstractions.

In Scotland, Pope Wojtyla's visit cost the thrifty Scots more than three million dollars. After his departure, they were asked to find another million dollars for the privilege (500,000 pounds). They gave it behind subdued Celtic grumblings via additional collections during church services.

In England the same year, the expenditure aggrieved the faithful. In the province of Westminster alone, the debt came to 870,000 pounds sterling, almost 2 million dollars. In Liverpool, 2.5 million pounds; 5 million dollars; in Spain, in November, 1982, between 8 and 10 million. The pope left, wholly unconcerned at the extra millions of dollars debt to be paid by the parish church and by the grumbling civic authorities.

Besides such expenditures, there are the collateral financial transactions in small and large scale, activated by religious authorities, merchant and business people prepared to make money from such visits. In Ireland, the red carpet on which the pope had walked was considered as a relic and sold as such per square yard. In Nigeria, the water in which he washed himself was sold as a healing liquid. In other African countries, anything which had been touched by the pope became saleable, at inflated prices. Even in sober Scotland, pope-idolatry reached unheard of depths. A piece of ground upon which the pope walked became holy ground. It sprouted in front of the garden of a Scottish cardinal (Cardinal Gordon Gray). When Pope John Paul II made the traditional ground-kissing on his arrival, instead of kissing the tarmac, he planted his lips on the grass of the turnhouse instead. The men of the RAF, thereupon, dug up the piece of hallowed turf, and took it to the cardinal who put the sacred papal relic in his front garden.

Pope-idolatry, since John Paul II, became big business wherever the new cult was promoted. While a business enterprise, from which many have and are profiting, it has certainly profited the Vatican itself with millions of dollars of additional revenues.

The sum of all such papal mass exposure is that the annual gift of Peter's Pence has increased considerably since the commencement of pope-idolatry. From the poor 2 or 3 million dollars under Paul VI, to the 20 to 25 million dollars of John Paul II.

The monarchical character of the latter with his theatrical behavior, by appealing to the masses, produced an abundant harvest of monetary offerings in the pews of thousands of Roman Catholic Churches, most of which, ultimately ends up in the Vatican coffers. "What saved the Holy See," commented a Catholic paper approvingly, "were offertories by hundreds of millions of Catholics throughout the world via Peter's Pence and private donations."[4]

The amount of private donations was never disclosed. But it was known to have been substantial. Some Americans gave millions of dollars. This type of income is seldom acknowledged because it becomes part of secret funds. Papal peregrinations thus can produce unpredictable profits, even if at the time the pope can experience slight disappointment. Like when, for instance, during his visit to Coventry, England, after having been presented with a golden chalice, the Lord Mayor immediately asked for it back.[5]

The "invention" of a Holy Year to raise money for the Vatican Bank was imitated, even if on a minor scale, by others. Ecclesiastics auctioned church property for mercenary goals, like that bishop, for instance, who put on sale his episcopal throne dating about 1400 AD at a price of 500 dollars, plus his title of Baron, and another two nobiliary deeds, pertaining to his See.[6]

But if the mercenary behavior of humble hierarchs at times can be justified, that of the papacy cannot. Since by affecting the supposed spirituality of the office, it abases its status to the level of secular concern, buying and selling for reasons which are anything but of a religious character.

Pope Paul VI, for all his monetary problems, never came as low as Pope John Paul II, with the latter's brazen exploitation of religion for mercenary gains. Although some might think him justified, perhaps in accepting the monetary benefits derived from his personal popularity, such as the increase of Peter's Pence, for instance, and other procured from the new cult of pope-idolatry which he had cultivated so assiduously, his invention of the Holy Year of 1983-84 to raise money was most objectionable. Many Catholics were mortified, others condemned an action which had made the papacy adopt practices of the popes of a lurid past. The papacy of today has still the power to fix ecclesiastical calendars, as proved by John Paul II's spurious crucifixion commemoration.

The insidiousness of its result is not only the religious aggrandizement, the magnification of the aura of the papacy and the fostering of papal political bias, but also the collection of vast sums of money under pious pretences. The perils of the mercenary nature of such operations are carefully hidden by the spiritual imponderability of an office, which to many is, or should be, above all earthly considerations, beginning with the monetary ones.

Contemporary papacy, for all its modernization, basically is not different from that of the past. Besides having remained dogmatically unchanged, individual popes are identifiable with their personal idiosyncrasies. It cannot be otherwise because a pope cannot divest himself of his habits, prejudices, outlook or bias. History is crowded by popes who have proved this. One of the most striking examples, in connection with the unscrupulous use of the prestige of the papacy for the purpose of raising money, was that of Pope Benedict IX.

Early in the eleventh century, a local potentate, supported by immense wealth, "bought" the papacy for each one of his three sons. When the first son, after becoming pope, died, the father bought the papacy for his second son. When the second son, and second pope, also died, the papacy was bought for the third time, and the third son also was made pope. He was crowned in the autumn of 1032 as Pope Benedict IX.

One of the most remarkable features of Benedict IX was not only that he had had two brothers who had been popes, but also that he himself had been the youngest pope ever. Benedict IX, in fact, became pope when he was only 14 years old. The buying of the papacy for a 14 year old boy set in motion several plots to kill him. One of the first failed because of a most extraordinary coincidence. This is worth relating.

Plotters decided to execute the deed in St. Peter's Basilica itself. Since they were not permitted to enter with their swords, they carried a length of rope each. At a given signal, they would seize the young pope and strangle him before any guard could intervene.

Providence, or the devil, as it was said later, however, saved him. For, to quote an ancient chronicler "about the sixth hour of the day, there occurred an eclipse of the sun which lasted until the eighth hour; all faces were as pale as death."[7]

The phenomenon saved Benedict, the plotters having lost their nerve. Benedict fled at once from Rome, the first of many such flights. The young pope, after several years of depravity among other misdeeds, set up a brothel in St. Peter's, where he himself and some of his young cardinals raped women pilgrims. He then decided suddenly to marry. The bride's father agreed provided Benedict resign the papacy. The real reason, probably was the young pope's growing fear of assassination.

Before deposing the tiara, however, Benedict decided to amass as much money as he could. He despoiled St. Peter's of whatever gold and precious metals there were. Since the result, however, had been disappointing, (his two other brother popes, having already done so themselves), he decided to sell the most valuable asset still in his hands: the papacy itself. That he brazenly put up for sale on the open market. He found a willing buyer immediately, an archpriest of a local Roman church.[8]

The money required for the purchase was immense. The priest, who had amassed huge funds with the excuse that he wanted to use them to repair the ruined churches of Rome, on hearing of the pope's offer, instead decided to buy the papacy. The bargain was struck. Pope Benedict received the price he had asked for — 1,400 weight in gold. In May, 1045, the archpriest became Pope Gregory VI.

As in the Dark Ages some contemporary popes have abused their authority to collect large quantities of money and satisfy their personal ambitions. Pope Pius XII, for instance, (1939-1953) made princes of his brothers and nephews. Pope John Paul II dared to proclaim a Holy Year to extract money from the believers to save certain Vatican lackies from jail or disgrace.

The "sacredness" of 1983-84 would have never been discovered by him had not the hundreds of millions of dollars been missed from the coffers of the IOR, the Ambrosiano and their other lay and religious associates. Pope Benedict had put the papacy on the market to obtain 1,400 pounds of gold. Pope John Paul II had put on the market the global ecclesiastic machinery of the papacy to get 1,400 million dollars, or its equivalent, from the pockets of the pilgrims allured by his promises of indulgences. If the simony of Pope Benedict IX had been an insult, the proclamation of the Holy Year of 1983-84 by Pope John Paul II was no less reprehensible.

Although a thousand years apart, both popes had abased their Church for monetary gains: one to satiate his personal greed, the other to amend the extravagance and fraud incurred by the financial and ideological misadventures of the IOR-Ambrosiano. In the past, Catholics were shocked by similar mercenary papal promulgations. "The Court of Rome is insatiable, and its appetite for money bottomless," complained a 13th century Flemish Delegation when Pope Boniface first invented the Holy Year in 1300 specifically to collect as much gold as he could.

Later Edward of England referred succinctly to a pope who had also "invented" convenient religious commemorations to extract money from the believers: "The Apostles were commissioned to lead the sheep into pastures, not to shear them." A more appropriate summation of the spirit of the Vatican of today would be almost impossible to find.

CHAPTER 35

THE INTANGIBLE BILLIONS OF THE CATHOLIC CHURCH

The Catholic Church has another type of wealth which, although it cannot be reckoned in with what so far we have called business assets, is nevertheless as real, concrete and as valuable as any ingot or soft or hard currency. These are the intangible, invisible and spiritual riches at her disposal. Some of these grow daily in value just by the reason of their existence. Others are exploited through religious emotion and the hope and fear of believers.

The Catholic Church is the largest owner of historic, architectural and artistic buildings in the world. Some go back to the ancient cultures or the first centuries of Christianity. Besides their "historicity," the sites upon which they are erected — as a rule within the precincts of ancient cities — are as valuable, and in addition the artistic, religious and national patrimony attached to them is incalculable, not easily defined and consequently not easily assessed in terms of contemporary currencies. Thus, for instance — to confine ourselves to Italy alone — what would the Florence Cathedral, the Pisa Cathedral in the Piazza dei Miracoli, the Basilica of St. Mark's in Venice, or the four main Roman basilicas of the Holy See — i.e. St. Paul's Outside the Walls, St. Mary Major, St. John Lateran and St. Peter's itself — bring if they were put up for sale? Considering that the Catholic Church owns hundreds — indeed, thousands — of such historic and artistic buildings throughout Europe, it can be imagined that the wealth they represent in actual dollars is, to say the least, out of ordinary calculation.

Their actual intangible value, however, is not all. Very often they house ecclesiastical objects which, because they have been accumulated along the centuries, have acquired a considerable antique value in addition to their intrinsic worth. Thus a gold chalice, in addition to its actual gold, is worth ten, one hundred or one thousand times more than the precious metal itself, because of its historicity. The treasures of famous cathedrals, basilicas and churches throughout the western world are actual treasures in the most prosaic, concrete and business parlance. Anyone who has seen those of the Cathedral of Valencia, of St. James of Compostella in Spain, of St. Anthony of Padua, St. Mark's in Venice, St. Peter's and similar others, will have no doubt that the Church which owns them is a multi-multi-millionairess in her own right.

Add the numberless statues of saints, angels, martyrs, which adorn most Catholic churches everywhere. Some of them are beautified with crowns of solid gold, silver and precious stones, rare pearls, diamonds and other valuables. The prices which such items would collect at any contemporary antique auction would run into hundreds of millions of dollars, at the lowest possible estimate.

But that is not all. The Catholic Church is the oldest, largest and most impressive art collector of all times. The most celebrated painters, sculptors and artists of the western world, from the first centuries of the Christian era down to our times, have all worked for her or have contributed to the beautification of her edifices. Mantegna, Piero della Francesca, Botticelli, Raphael, Michelangelo, Leonardo, Titian, to mention only a few, have all left many of their masterpieces to her.

In November 1969 the Italian Press reported that three "small and medium-sized" paintings had been stolen from the private apartments of Pope Paul VI in the Vatican while the pontiff was at his summer residence at Castel Gandolfo outside Rome. They had been conservatively estimated at 65 million lire or about two million dollars.[1]

In 1972 a painting by Titian, a Madonna and Child Between two Saints, was stolen, the eighteenth art theft from an Italian church during that year, from Pieve di Cadore, in Northern Italy. The commmercial value of the painting was half a million pounds sterling or one and a half million dollars. The year before, a painting by Velasquez was sold in England for 2,310,000 pounds sterling, or more than seven million dollars.

Again in 1972 another painting by Titian, The Death of Actaeon, became the subject of a tug of war between the National Gallery of London and an American Museum. The price was two and a half million pounds sterling; again over seven million dollars. Not long before, a tondo by Michelangelo which had been put up for sale by the Royal Academy of London, received an immediate offer of almost one million pounds sterling (nearly three million dollars). The British, outraged by the fact that the offer came from the U.S., promoted a public subscription to keep the sculpture in London. The sum was collected within a few weeks.

The present author has calculated that paintings worth at least a million dollars exist in perhaps over 600 churches, cathedrals, monasteries, convents, basilica and the like in Italy alone. If we add France, Germany and, above all, Portugal and Spain, at least another 400 masterpieces worth one million dollars each are in existence. The monetary value of these one thousand pictures is, to say the least, startling: 1,000 million dollars.

Consider the masterpieces the Church owns throughout Europe. Consider the ones it houses at the Vatican itself, or in the churches of Florence and Venice. If one single small work by Leonardo was priced at three million dollars, what would the other masterpieces by Raphael, Michelangelo, and the others be worth? Can any art dealer or museum value the Sistine Chapel for instance? In an open market this would be worth, at a modest estimate, between 250 and 500 million dollars. Then what about the Roman and Greek sculptures of the Vatican galleries?

Some years back the British Museum of London paid more than one million dollars for one ancient manuscript. In 1972 Hans Kraus the New York bookseller, put on sale a Gutenberg Bible, known as the Shuckburgh Gutenberg for a million pounds or almost three million dollars. The Vatican owns hundreds, indeed thousands, of ancient manuscripts, some of them unique. Their sale would bring into its coffers an unknown quantity of millions of dollars.

It is a well-known fact that works of art are to be found in every major and even in minor Catholic churches and monasteries all over Europe. By the mere fact that they exist they render the Catholic Church a billionaire in her own right. And since the value of such masterpieces, far from devaluing, increases each year, the Church becomes *ipso facto* the greatest billionaire concern in the world on account of her artistic possessions alone.

That this is not mere speculation was proved by the Vatican itself when in 1971 it ordered a world census of all the Church's art treasures. The bishops were instructed to see that all parish priests drew up accurate inventories of the works of art in their respective churches, with the help of experts, describing each object and estimating its *financial* value. The Vatican furthermore warned that "any priest selling art treasures of his church" without permission would lose his office and, indeed, be excommunicated.[2]

That the Church had become aware of the immense riches at her disposal was proved also by the fact that bishops and even cardinals openly advocated selling such riches to raise funds to help the poor. Witness Cardinal Heenan, Archbishop of Westminster and Cardinal Primate of England. During the World Synod of Bishops held in Rome he proposed that the pope "should encourage Roman Catholic churches to sell their treasures and possessions to help the world's poor." "I suggest," he said, "that the churches, monasteries and convents should see what treasures they can sell. There must be thousands of chalices, monstrances and other sacred objects which are rarely used. They should be sold to buy food for the hungry." He went so far as to say that the Vatican itself should give a lead. "There would be great value in the example of the Holy See selling some of the masterpieces of art in the Vatican."[3]

The intangible wealth which the Church possesses in all this, therefore, makes of her an intangible and yet potentially concrete billionaire, since the artistic treasure at present in her possession is a capital asset which is not only increasing with the passing of time, but which is and could yield far more profits than any investment in the contemporary stocks and shares of the most prosperous trusts and corporations of the world.

But if the intangibility of her historic and artistic patrimony is a concrete asset, the most profitable investment in her multi-billion portfolios is the imponderability of her religious attributes. These are most valuable capital since most of her members are ready to acknowledge her as their spiritual mistress, mother and dispenser, and as a result are eager to part with their money, valuables and earthly riches to gain her favor, or to gain through her intercession the favor of Heaven.

We have glanced at the past, when multitudes congregated from every corner of Europe to Rome during the first Jubilee in the year 1300. We have seen how the pilgrims from England, Saxony, Scotland and Ireland went to pay homage at the tomb of the Blessed Peter. Those seeking indulgences gave their money to the Church. Times have changed. But to think that the practice has gone with them would be incorrect. For the practice has remained. And although no longer given such spectacular agglomerations of mass piety as in the middle ages, nevertheless it is yielding as spectacular a yield in money as those of yore. Indeed, more.

For the fields have been enlarged. The believers, the pilgrims have multiplied and their peregrinations to holy places are promoted with the frequency, efficiency and profit-yielding characteristic of the mass tourism of our century, where instead of the mule cart, trains or walking tours of the past, the family saloon car, the fast train, the transatlantic aircraft and the intercontinental jet plane are the means which transport the multiplying millions of contemporary pilgrims.

Shrines, the contemporary Catholic scenes of alleged miracles, apparitions and portents, are functioning with the same efficiency as the belt conveyor of a Ford factory, and with the same profitable results for the Church. The consumers, i.e. the believers, will congregate upon these towns and cities to pray, to hope, to be satisfied that they, too, have trod the ground upon which St. Francis of Assisi walked, where the Virgin appeared and spoke. Who, upon glancing at the glossy advertisements of any travel agency, has not been offered a cheap voyage, return, to Lourdes or to Fatima, to mention only two of the most celebrated shrines of our times? Lourdes, for instance, a Pyrenees town of barely 16,000 people, boasts more than 600 hotels. Of 710 businesses, no less than 600 deal exclusively in religious objects and souvenirs, which range from washable plastic Virgins to hourglasses in the shape of Bernadette telling the Virgin how to time eggs. The water of the Grotto is sold in plastic bottles, while perfume, soap and candy are advertised as having been made "from water blessed by the pope and by the Mother of God."

The Shrine receives between three-quarters of a million and a million dollars a year in its collection boxes alone, and during 1958, when Lourdes celebrated the first centenary of the Virgin's appearance, the pilgrims who went there spent over 200 million dollars. Since then the donations and the spending of the pilgrims have increased by leaps and bounds. Lourdes is only the most celebrated Catholic money-producing shrine of our times. Fatima, Monserrat, Assisi, and Rome itself, are not far behind; in addition to which there are the legions of shrines and holy spots, holy waters and the like here, there and everywhere, all receiving gifts from the devotees.

Rome, of course, is still a place of tremendous attraction for Catholics and non-Catholics alike. St. Peter need no longer write letters in gold or sell filings from his chains, for the gifts, in most of the world's coinages, now currently surpass anything which the popes of the eighth or ninth centuries could ever have dreamed of. In addition to the collecting boxes placed strategically everywhere in the Roman churches, there are the many devices which bring an ever-increasing income to the Vatican. There are certificates, indulgences, blessed formulae, all capped by the Roman Rota, by the would-be divorcee. All these are up-to-date, subtle and persuasive means which Holy Mother Church is enriched.

The author recently noticed, while staying with a Spanish friend in Tarragona, a framed photograph of the pope in his bedroom, adorned with golden arabesques, and bearing impressive signatures. When he asked about this, he was told that it was a "preventive absolution," in case the recipient should die without receiving the sacraments of the Church. It had been obtained in Rome that year, and had cost several thousand pesetas, plus an undisclosed offering. This document had been printed in all the major European languages and was being sold by the thousand.[4]

Then there is the sale of holy medals, scapulars, images

and, yes, even relics of ancient saints. The last-named practice is not a colorful relic of the past, but a prosaic reality of the present. Although kept relatively obscure, it is nevertheless a flourishing trade within and outside the Vatican. Whether the relics are endowed with peculiar, mystic or miraculous attributes is for the believers to say, but they certainly continue to bring in cash. It must be remembered that a relic must be sealed within the altar of every church; and since churches are consecrated every week in some part of the world, it follows that a steady monetary trickle continually reaches the Vatican. Add to this the acquiring of indulgences, some which run into millions of years. Nothing is given for nothing. To acquire them one has to pray or to visit the right altar or church but one had better also leave a few coins. Multiply these holy spots by the hundreds and the seekers offer indulgence by the millions and by the end of the year the Church will have collected additional vast sums of money.[5] Such transactions are carried out all over Europe, from Rome to the lesser holy places of Assisi, Padua, Compostella, Montserrat, Fatima, Lourdes and hundreds of others-all bringing money in.

The believers are apt to remember the Church in their wills, so that very often monasteries, convents or other Church institutions become the beneficiaries of small as well as large legacies, large or small real estate, lands, bonds and shares; and this steady accumulation of wealth is far more rewarding than is generally believed, as any bishop or primate could testify. Paul VI, prior to becoming pope, was a specialist in legacies, and in that capacity he handled millions of dollars left to the Church by the faithful. The habit has become so widespread that even in the U.S. more than one diocese has come to rely upon Divine Providence in balancing maladjusted budgets or for dispensing further bounties to outdo the bishop next door.

It is perhaps worth relating, how, in many countries but particularly in the United States, the practice of legacies collection has become a concrete system yielding vast sums. In the U.S. the Catholic Church, in common with other churches, has tax-exempt foundations whose business it is to solicit systematically for large donations and bequests. Catholic groups as already mentioned actively solicit wills. They send letters to lawyers, reminding them that a good Catholic is expected to put his Church in his will, for at least 10 per cent of the corpus. The wealth accumulated by such means is remarkable. One example should suffice. An Associated Press dispatch reported that Mrs. R. T. Wallace of Saratoga Springs, N.Y., bequeathed $2.5 million "to the pope" and another $2.5 million to the Redemptorist Fathers of New York. In this manner the Catholic Church netted $5 million tax free from one single will. Money collected in the U.S. alone, runs into hundreds of millions. The Vatican has never disclosed how much it gets from legacies, wills and bequests. But the sum must be a very large one, since a special body is engaged upon the collection of the wealth received via such channels. The practice is widespread with the result that small and large legacies are continuously putting money into the coffers of the Vatican, all the year round.

The most obvious source of money is, of course, the Sunday offerings. This form of monetary tribute is not to be dismissed as unworthy of mention, if nothing else, because it is a steady and regular habit of the believer and of the happy recipient, Holy Mother Church.

Catholics have to go to mass at least once a week, and on the whole they do. Assuming that of the 800 million Catholics only half go to mass, that would give us a least 400 million attending every week. Assuming that each gives a mere five cents, that comes to $20 million each Sunday, fifty-two times a year. We said five cents, the very minimum, but very often the offering consists of dollars, and even in the poorest countries the generosity of the most indigent parishioners is amazing.

But an even more profitable and regular source of revenue for the Catholic Church is the wafer — more valuable than any gold mine or oil well. Catholic priests, friars and monks are obliged to say mass at least once a day. The mass is a sacrifice, and a Catholic may have this sacrifice, that is, the mass, offered for his particular benefit, or for a dead relative, for the liberation of a soul from purgatory, or a thanksgiving, and the like. The Church fixes a minimum tariff for any believer who wishes a mass to be celebrated for his or her intention. In England, for instance, the fee is a pound sterling or more. With about four thousand priests saying mass daily, that yields over one million dollars a year. Each year. In the U.S. the minimum fee is a dollar, although many priests now charge five or even ten dollars per mass, and the yield has been calculated at about thirty million dollars a year. Add to these two countries the Central and South American republics, the European lands and all the Catholic communities the world over, and the annual revenue to the Church from masses alone will run into fifty or sixty million dollars.

Last but not least, the Vatican's main source of steady, regular income is Peter's Pence. This orginated during the great pilgrimages at the height of the Cult of Peter, the Turnkey of Heaven, which we have already described at the beginning of this book. King Ina enforced a tax of one penny on every family in the Kingdom of Essex to help the pilgrims who went to Rome to do homage to St. Peter. The tax-or, rather, Peter's Pence-had come into existence. Eventually it was called the Romscot, which meant the scot to be paid to Rome. The romscot was ratified by the English King, Offa II, King of Mercia, and others. King Ethelwulf sent to Rome yearly a sum of money for "the lamps of St. Peter's basilica ," for "the oil used in the basilica of St. Paul", and "one hundred mangons for the personal use of the universal apostolic pope". The Emperor Charlemagne made Peter's Pence compulsory to all owners of houses and lands throughout his empire. King Canute did the same in Denmark, the Normans in Sicily (1059) to indicate the end of the Arab occupation. It was introduced in Spain in 1073, in Croatia and Dalmatia in 1076, in Bohemia in 1075, in Portugal in 1144. It was imposed also in the Ukraine, Poland and other countries.

Peter's Pence was a mixture of spontaneous offering and tax. In England it was terminated by Henry VIII in 1534. It was re-established by Queen Mary, but finally abolished by Queen Elizabeth in 1558. It continued or was suppressed in sundry countries according to the political vicissitudes of the times. It almost dwindled away in the eighteeth and nineteeth centuries as a voluntary contribution to the papal coffers. However, when Rome became the Roman Republic in 1848 and the pope had to flee, Catholics came to his help. In 1849 a committee was formed in Paris to collect the Denier de Saint-

Pierre, or Peter's Pence. Bishops all over the world asked for money to help the pope. Ireland became the most enthusiastic collector. From then on, Peter's Pence was revived all over Europe and the Americas. The funds became so impressive that in 1860 the Vatican established a special body to administer them. When in 1870 the pope finally lost all his temporal domains, Peter's Pence became the financial saviour. In Germany and particularly in Ireland parish priests turned into the zealous collectors of money for the pope.

Peter's Pence, having thus been re-established, has continued to this day. In fact, it has become one of the minor sources of papal wealth accumulation. It is collected regularly all over the world in all Catholic Churches. As a rule on St. Peter's Day, June 29th. In Italy the money is given to the bishops, who send it to Rome. In other countries as a rule it is given to the Papal Nuncios. The most generous contributors are Germany and the U.S., the latter the most generous giver of all. American bishops and cardinals, in fact, are considered the bulwark of contemporary Peter's Pence. We have already referred to Cardinal Spellman, who used to bring the pope the minimum of one million dollars.

Various estimates have been made of the total of Peter's Pence, but the Vatican has never given even a hint of it. The present writer, however, has estimated by a simple arithmetical calculation that the sum runs into millions. Assuming that the average contribution of each Catholic is 25 cents, a quarter of a dollar, and as there are at present more than 800 million Catholics, that makes 200 million dollars. The claim that many Catholics give less or even nothing is matched by the fact that many Catholic individuals, beginning with Americans, Germans, Dutch and English, give double or treble this, to compensate for those who give less than 25 cents in poorer countries. It must be remembered that this is not a forced taxation. It is given out of religious zeal, and it is a surprising feature that very often the most backward countries are not only the most devout but also the most generous.

The humble dime of Peter's Pence, when reaching Rome, can, and in fact does, multiply into millions of dollars. Peter's Pence has many imitators — e.g. the Catholic Primates of sundry nations. The dioceses of American bishops and cardinals, for instance, have their own individual collections. To be sure, they are not called Peter's Pence, and the funds are not sent to Rome. They are meant to fall into the coffers of the dioceses. Nevertheless, the contributions are at times very substantial. Since they are integrated with the ecclesiastical machinery of the universal Church, they become *ipso facto* an integral part of her financial imperium. No wonder that certain dioceses in the United States, thanks chiefly to their financial puissance, have been called The Little Vaticans.

But if Peter's Pence is a concrete even if an intangible gatherer of millions the huge Catholic aid and relief network is even more so. The official total estimate is over $1,000 million per annum, at a conservative estimate. The immensity of this sum can better be appreciated if it is remembered that it is larger than the budget of most of the United Nations organizations in the same field. Indeed, it is larger even than the official overseas aid program of the U.S. The $1,000 million dollars a year aid and relief network became financially so overwhelming that finally the Vatican had to create a special body called Cor Unum which met for the first time in 1972 in Rome the better to co-ordinate this self-multiplying Catholic financial octopus.

The dilemma of the Catholic Church and her preoccupation with wealth has become increasingly disturbing to Catholic laymen and clerics alike, since the reconciliation of the doctrines of unworldly values which she preaches with the mounting accumulation of the world's wealth at her disposal is becoming increasingly evasive. That the Church herself in recent years should have become aware of this was proved by the sporadic and yet multiplying protests against her wealth by many of her most sincere adherents. Witness Cardinal Francois Marty, the Archbishop of Paris, who put up for sale part of the furnishings of the Archbishop's house in Paris "as a symbolic gesture." Cardinal Marty explained that he had done so following the appeal of the Archbishop of Recife, Brazil, since both had agreed to "eliminate marks of wealth and ostentation incompatible with the poverty of Christ."[6]

Even the pope began to mention the ancient concept of "a poor Church existing largely for the poor." Of course, the concept was not new.[7] Many popes of the past had said the same, in contradiction to the fact that the Church, notwithstanding their words, had continued to grow and has become richer and richer ever since. The papal declarations were always taken with a great deal of cynicism, especially in Rome. The reaction of the Roman populace has always been a good indicator. A current comment on the last papal admonitions concerning the poverty of the Church, besides being typical, is telling. It refers to the cardinals' slick black limousines going to and from Vatican City. The initials on their plates read: S.C.V. This means Stato Citta del Vaticano, Vatican State. The Romans, however, interpreted the three letters differently: "*Se Christo vedesse*," If Christ could only see this.

It might be said that the Church needs her billions to carry on her multitudinous activities. This seems plausible and indeed, partially correct. The words of St. Gregory the Great can even be recalled: "We have no riches belonging to us; but to us are entrusted the custody and the distribution of the substance of the poor." Since St. Gregory's days, however, the concrete historical reality is that the Church, notwithstanding periodical disestablishments, many of which we have mentioned in the work, has grown into one of the greatest worldly potentates in terms of material wealth, as has her Protestant counterpart. The latter, for instance, has a gross of three billion in the United States alone. The exact figure is: 2,741,307,015 dollars — a worthy rival of the Catholic Church, indeed, her financial peer, if one should consider the total material wealth of the Protestant churches represented by church property, hospitals, schools and the like. This by 1970 amounted to a colossal total of $40.6 billion;[8] by 1980 to $60 billion.[9]

Organized Christianity in this manner has turned into an immense accumulator and user of financial, commercial and industrial wealth, the like of which has never been equalled in past ages.

Almost one thousand million Christians are still the willing contributors to the already fantastic wealth of their denominations. Over 800 million Roman Catholics[10] belong to a Church which, because of her unity, purpose and zeal, has, even more than the Protestant denominations, become a peer of the mightiest financial potentates of the earth.

INTANGIBLE BILLIONS OF THE CATHOLIC CHURCH

The one thousand million Christians, in their eagerness to gain heaven, have not minded putting an extra coin, or an extra million dollars, into the Protestant or Catholic coffers. It is their inalienable right, not only to believe whatever interpretation of Christianity they prefer, but equally to help their own church, financially or otherwise, in whichever form or with whatever amount they wish.

The question which Protestants and Catholics alike should begin to ask themselves with mounting urgency, however, in view of the global tremors at present shaking contemporary society, is a very pertinent one. What would Christ do with all such colossal ecclesiastical accumulation of wealth?

Upon their answer will hang, not only the right or wrong interpretation of Jesus' gospels, but equally the future of organized Christianity itself.

CHAPTER 36

ARBITER OF THE WESTERN WORLD

It has been calculated that were the billions of the Catholic Church to multiply in proportion to their recent growth, and that were all her visible and invisible assets, local and global, to continue their acceleration in monetary value, in addition to a parallel increase of the Catholic population, the Catholic Church would by the close of the present century own, control and have a say, directly or indirectly, in at least one-third of all the sources of wealth of the western world.

The prospect would be a frightening one as a mere abstraction. As a speculation it is alarming. As a prospective reality it is, to say the least, terrifying to non-Catholic and to Catholic alike — indeed, for the very safety of the Catholic Church herself as she is at present constituted.

The process is inevitable, because all the characteristics of past days remain with us-with one new and fearsome feature, their immense acceleration. For whereas in the past the accumulation of the wealth of the Catholic Church, no matter how large, was limited to the confines of one single nation or group of nations, it now straddles the hemispheres, and embraces the two most progressive, vital, energetic and wealthiest continents of the earth: Europe and the Americas.

Her steady accumulation of temporal riches, beside corrupting her, has always brought her to inevitable disaster. We have seen examples of this on earlier pages. Once she became a temporal power by means of Pepin's gifts of Rome and Central Italy, the Church went through the most reprehensible period of her history. Some of her pontiffs were the most gross and execrable villains of an already villainous era; this because most of them wanted Peter's throne not only to rule the Church but also to transform themselves into earthly kings; that is, to exercise temporal dominion, to use temporal riches, and thus, to be led astray by temporal wealth.

The furore which accompanied the closing of the first millennium laid the foundation for the Church's claims of equality with kings and emperors, and in the subsequent centuries she became so top-heavy with spiritual and temporal arrogance, that the Reformation burst upon her with the potency of a natural cataclysm, almost burying her in the ruins. For, having had too much, she lost more than half Europe. The earthly wealth of Northern Europe was taken from her, in addition to the unequivocal allegiance of hundreds of millions of Christians.

Following her recovery she used the Counter-Reformation to bring herself into tune with the novel times. But also to continue with the accumulation of yet more temporal riches.

The French Revolution came, and while the monarchy and the aristocracy were overthrown, the Church, as the possessor of immense parcels of land, real estate and the like, was treated as the most redoubtable earthly potentate of them all. She lost much of her wealth, together with the allegiance of many who had looked at her in anger and hunger for decades.

The revolt of Spanish America repeated the process, and one of the first acts of the newly born Latin Republics was to dispossess her. After 1870, France followed in their footsteps as a result of the Franco-Prussian debacle. The Mexican Revolution during the first decades of the present century did the same. To cap these repeated losses of accumulated earthly riches, there came in 1917 the Bolshevik Revolution. Her counterpart, the Orthodox Church, also insatiably greedy for temporal wealth, shared the downfall of the Czarist Empire with which she had identified herself.

The process which led the Church to such disasters continues now, although not so blatantly, throughout the Christian western world. We have already noted the incredible accumulation of wealth being carried out in our day by the Catholic Church at all levels. The inevitable result will be her ultimate dispossession. This is not gloomy speculation. It is a factual assessment of something which, having repeatedly occured in the past, will occur in the foreseeable future. If historical instances are not sufficiently convincing, then simple elementary reasoning should be.

When a church acquires or is given a real estate asset, a parcel of land, a million shares, or any concrete valuable item, she will keep them for all time, since the church as a corporate body does not perish or go out of existence. In reverse, when a benefactor or donor or private individual dies, there follows as a rule a redistribution of his wealth. The same applies to any business, commercial or financial concern, including the giant trusts or corporations of the twentieth century. With the Catholic Church such a rule does not work. Her individual members might die. The 500 million believers of one generation and their popes might pass away. She, however, as a corporate body, that is, as the possessor of all her wealth will remain. Her billions will continue to multiply. The next generation will add more billions. And so on *ad infinitum.*

By this means, the Church will aggrandize herself with each succeeding generation, until finally, as happened so often in the past, she will find herself the dominant possessor of most of the temporal wealth of the society in which she is active. The process is already visible in many countries, and it is glaringly evident in the most dynamically active land of the western world, the U.S.

The situation is fraught with immense perils, since there is bound ultimately to be an irresistible demand for ecclesiastical expropriation. This will lead to violent commotion, namely, to religious and civic catastrophe.

Today the Church, notwithstanding multiplying disturbing omens, is feverishly engaged upon the accumulation of yet more wealth. In a world torn by tumultuous social unrest, the visible expression of tremendous individual and collective uncertainties, her exertions in the economic structures of contemporary society, more than unwise, are provocative, since the concreteness of the widespread atavistic apprehensions of the masses is becoming increasingly menacing to most of the traditional establishments. That includes the most venerable of them all, the Catholic Church.

The darkening horizon seems to be heralding the potentiality of approaching global holocausts and space incineration. Such terrors, far from dissolving with the passing of the days, are becoming ever more concretised by the unabashed accumulation of the economic omnipotence on the part of a few super colossi, nurtured by a soulless giant technocracy and increasingly materialistically inspired Western ecclesiasticism.

The condominium of the two could generate ultimate individual and collective despair. Despair can trigger explosion. Were this to occur, the conflagration would be such as would endanger the very foundation upon which the Christian fabric is erected.

Potentates, then, could be made to topple from their pedestals. Because of her unlimited financial puissance, the Catholic Church would inevitably be identified with them, with the result that her possessions would once more become the cause, not so much of her humiliation, but of the drastic curtailment of her activities in the spiritual dominion, where she claims to be the only source of verity.

Should that come to pass, she would be judged as the accumulator of immense material possessions, in total disregard of the lament of her Founder: "Foxes have holes, and the birds of the air have nests, but the Son of Man has nowhere to lay his head."

Who then shall testify on her behalf, since the very Gospel will indict her? "Go, sell whatever thou hast, and give to the poor, and thou shalt have treasure in heaven." These are the very words of her Master, He who commanded her to seek, not the riches of this world but those of the Kingdom of God.

NOTES

Chapter 2
1. *The Times*, London, June 26, 1968.
2. St. Gregory, Letter 65.
3. Willibald, *Vita Bonifacii*, 14; also *Liber Pontificalis*.
4. St. Gregory, Letters 12 - 17.
5. *De Gloria Martyrum*, 1.28.
6. Bede, 5.20.
7. M. 151.1181. See also *Historia Ecclesiastica*.
8. Migne M. 89, 1004.
9. *Ibid.*
10. See *The Times*, London, November 29,1969.

Chapter 3
1. A canon of the Church of St. John de Latran, named Lorenzo Valla, proved that the Donation of Constantine had been a clever deceit by the enterprising Hadrian.
2. See Dollinger's *Fables and Prophecies of the Middle Ages*.
3. G.H. Bohmer, art. "Konstantinische Schenkung," Herzog, Hauck, *Realencyclopadie*.

Chapter 4
1. *Summa de Ecclesia*, 94.1.
2. Clementia, 9 *de jur. ej.*
3. Agostino Trionfo and Alvaro Pelayo, theologians of the Papal Court.

Chapter 5
1. Rolls Series, Edition v. 318.
2. Ed. Hearne, 1774, i. 42, 48.
3. Hutton, *Cardinal Rinuccini's Embassy to Ireland*, pp. xxviii-xxix.
4. Milman, *Lat. Christ.* viii, c. vii.
5. Of the Papal Bull made to Castille, touching the New World. Given at St. Peter's, Rome, in the year of the Incarnation of our Lord 1493. The fourth day of the Nones of May, the first years of our Popedom, Englished and published by R. Eden in 1577, to be found in *Hakluytus Posthumus*, printed by William Stansby for Henrie Fetherstone, London, 1625. For further details see also chapter 11 of the present work.
6. For more details, see Avro Manhattan, *2,000 Years of World History*, chapter "The Popes and the Discovery of America."
7. Ap. Martene, ampl. coll. ii, 556.

NOTES

Chapter 6

1. *Fundationis Eccles.*, M. Magdal. 1422, Ludewig I. xi, pp. 457-69.
2. *Ibid.* c. 10.
3. Ordun. Ann. 1228.
4. *Establissement*, Liv. i. chap. 123.
5. *Jur. Prov. Alaman.*, cap. 351, Ed. Schilter, cap. 308.
6. Haddan and Stubbs: *Councils of Great Britain*, 1. 207-8.

Chapter 7

1. See also Infessurae Diar. Urb. Roman. Ann. 1484—Eccard. Corp. Hist. II, 1940.
2. Aquinas, *Summa*, 2a, 2ae, q. 87. Pupilla Oculi, pt IX, c. 18 sec. am. *Summa Angelica*, s. v. Decima para. 7, Lyndwood, ed. Oxon, p. 195b.
3. Johann P.P. VIII, Epist. 127
4. Pastor IV, par. 1-589.

Chapter 8

1. Chron. Astens. cap. 26, Muratori S.R.I.V. 191.
2. P. de Herenthale Vit. Clement VI, ap. Muratori S.R.I. III, ii, 584-7.
3. Raynald, *loc. cit.*; Van Ranst, *Opusc. de Indulg.*, p. 75; Ricci, *Dei Giubulei Universali*, pp. 613.

Chapter 9

1. This tribute was faithfully paid until 1789, the year of the French Revolution. This was explicitly set forth in formal legal documents of 1348 and 1592. La Greze, *Hist. du Droit dans les Pyrenees*, Paris, 1867, p. 339.
2. Desmaze, *Penalites Anciennes*, Paris, 1866, pp. 31-2.
3. See Guillelmi S. Theod. Vit. S. Beri.
4. "All destructive vermin—the emissaries of Satan. It is the duty of the Church to defeat the devil in all his manifestations." See D. Martini de Arles, *Tract. de Superstit.*, ed. Francof., ad. M. 1581.
5. Msgr. Guerin, *Vies des Saints*.
6. *Ibid.*
7. *Ibid.*
8. *Ibid.*
9. The Bull is still preserved in the parish church of Avignonet. It was also related that the church doors, which had been locked, barred, bolted and nailed up for forty years, opened of their own accord.

Chapter 10

1. Ferraris.
2. H.C. Lea, *A History of Auricular Confessions and Indulgences in the Latin Church* (London, 1896), vol III.
3. Jo. Gersonis, *Opusc. de Indulg. Decima Consid.*
4. Lavorii, *de Jubilaeo et Indulg.* P. ii, cap. x, N. 28; Polacchi, *Comment. in Bull. Urbani VIII*, p. 116.
5. *Amort de Indulgent*, I. 163.

6. P. ii. PP. IV. Bull. *Inter assiduas*, paras 143-5. Pius V, on his accession, confirmed these privileges, but in 1567 he greatly reduced the portentous indulgences. Bull *Sicuti bonus*, para. 62 (*ibid.*, p. 226).

Chapter 11
1. Bull *Unam Sanctam*.
2. Cardinal Bellarmine, *Opera*, Tom I: *De Romano Pontefice*.
3. *In Clement Pastoralis*, March 1314.
4. Pope Gregory IX to the Emperor Frederick II, October 1236.

Chapter 13
1. L.B. Simpson, *Many Mexicos* (New York, 1941).
2. Valle-Arizpe, Artemio, *Virreyes y Virreinas de la Nueva Espana* (Madrid 1933).
3. Phipps, *Some Aspects of the Agraian Question in Mexico,* (University of Texas Press, 1925).
4. Simpson Eyler, *The Ejido, Mexico's Way Out* (1937).
5. Phipps, *Some Aspects of the Agraian Question in Mexico* (University of Texas Press, 1925).

Chapter 16
1. For further details about the war between the Catholic Church and the Orthodox Church, see Avro Manhattan, *Catholic Imperialism and World Freedom* (New York, Arno Press, 1972) 5th edition.
2. For further details of the rise of Fascism and Nazism, see Avro Manhattan, *The Vatican in World Politics* (New York, Horizon Press, 1952; 47 editions, twice Book of the Month). Also *Catholic Imperialism and World Freedom*.
3. *The Vatican in World Politics*.

Chapter 17
1. Most of these holdings were in the name of various agents. One of these was listed as a director in forty commercial stock companies. See the article "Unknown Facts about the Vatican Billions" by George Seldes, *The Independent*, New York, 1967.

Chapter 19
1. *The Economist*, London, March 27, 1965.
2. *Ibid.*
3. *The Tablet*, November 9, 1968.
4. For more details, see Nino Lo Bello, *The Vatican Empire* (New York, Simon and Shuster, 1969).
5. *The Economist, v.s.*

Chapter 20
1. M. Murray O'Hair, *Let's Prey*.
2. *Ibid.*

NOTES

3. For further details about Vatican gold, see *United Nations World Magazine*, December, 1952; also *The Churchman*, New York, August, 1954.

4. See George Seldes, "Unknown Facts about the Vatican Billions" in *The Independent*, New York.

5. Nino Lo Bello, *The Vatican Empire* (New York, Trident Press, 1968).

Chapter 21

1. Henry Ford was automatically excommunicated by the Catholic Church in 1965 for re-marrying after a divorce.

2. U.S.A. Internal Revenue Code No. 170(*b*)

Chapter 22

1. *Sunday Express*, London, February 27, 1966.

2. See Avro Manhattan, *The Vatican in World Politics; Vatican Imperialism in the Twentieth Century;* and *Catholic Power Today*.

3. Nino Lo Bello, *The Vatican Empire*.

4. See Avro Manhattan, *the Vatican in World Politics; Catholic Power Today;* and *Catholic Imperialism and World Freedom*.

5. Count Della Torre, Editor of the Vatican newspaper *L'Osservatore Romano*.

6. *Time*, August 21, 1964.

7. Prospectus, May 1, 1967.

8. Figures given by M.A. Larson and C.S. Lowell, *Praise the Lord for Tax Exemption* (Washington, Americans United).

9. Statement made by Thomas J. Gibbons.

10. Father Richard Ginder in the paper *Our Sunday Visitor*.

Chapter 23

1. The Knights of Columbus own the land under the Yankee Stadium.

2. *The Times*, London, August 21, 1964.

3. Names, dates and places are from *Urban Takeover* (Washington, Americans United).

4. Avro Manhattan, *Religious Terror in Ireland* (London, Paravision, 1971).

Chapter 24

1. See M. Murray O'Hair, *Let's Prey*.

2. *The Churchman*, New York, February, 1968.

3. *Let's Prey*.

4. Nino Lo Bello, *The Vatican Empire*.

5. *Ibid*.

6. The Mills Committee, Testimony, p. 1465, part 4.

7. M.A. Larson and C.S. Lowell, *Praise the Lord for Tax Exemption*.

8. *Let's Prey*.

9. P.O.A.U., *The Wealth of the Catholic Church*.

10. *Let's Prey*.

11. *Der Spiegel*, August 8, 1958.

12. *The Wealth of the Catholic Church.*
13. *Praise the Lord for Tax Exemption.*
14. *Ibid.*, p. 192.
15. *Ibid.*, p. 244.
16. *The Wealth of the Catholic Church.*
17. *Let's Prey.*

Chapter 25
1. Founded in Italy in 1835, by Pallotti.
2. As reported by Church and State in 1977.
3. Lo Bello - *The Vatican U.S.A.* originally quoted 80 and 12 respectively in 1969-70.
4. Martin A. Larson, *The Religious Empire* - Luce, Also *The Churchman* January, 1980.
5. In 1917, when the Bolsheviks went into power, they deprived the Church of all legal rights, including that of owning property.
6. In 1943 about 23,000 churches were re-opened, with 33,000 priests.
7. In 1983 Leningrad, with a population of 4 million, had only 4 churches. Moscow, however, with 8 million had 50.
8. In 1977 Soviet Constitution Article 52, guarantees citizens freedom of conscience and "the right to profess any religion or to profess none."
9. A church is permitted to function if 20 responsible people can be registered as a parish council and can keep the building and pay the salary of the priest.
10. In 1983 there were 3 seminaries with 900 students, 3 monateries and 15 convents, 7,500 churches with 10,000 priests, as compared in Czarist days with 54,174 churches, 1,025 monasteries and convents, served by 57,000 priests and 94,000 monks and nuns.
11. Its diameter over 3 meters.

Chapter 26
1. *The Economist,* London, March 27, 1965.
2. Nino Lo Bello, *The Vatican Empire.* See also "*L'Osservatore Romano,*" July 22, 1970.
3. Pope Paul VI, June 24, 1970.
4. *The Times,* London, October 11, 1971.
5. *The Times,* October 15, 1971.
6. Oral birth control pill called "Luteolas" manufactured by the Vatican-owned Instituto Farmacologico Serono. See *Vatican U.S.A.*, N. Lo Bello, 1972.
7. See the German magazine, *Capital.*
8. The Interfan and Novaceta.
9. *Wall Street Journal,* September 14, 1960. See also M. Murray O'Hair, *Let's Prey,* and Lo Bello, *The Vatican Empire.*
10. For a well documented account of the Roman Catholic Church's wealth in the U.S.A., see M. A. Larson and C. S. Lowell, *Praise the Lord for Tax Exemption.*
11. *The Economist,* London, 1965.
12. *Ibid.*

NOTES

13. Robert C. Doty, *New York Times*.
14. *Organized Religion and Money*, 1981.

Chapter 27

1. *Sunday Times*, London, June 1, 1980.
2. August, 1971.
3. For more details, see the author's book, *The Vatican Moscow Washington Alliance*, published by Chick Publications, 1982.

Chapter 28

1. The Vatican sold the company as soon as its ownership became known. See also *The Vatican U.S.A.* N. Lo Bello, 1970.
2. *The Vatican U.S.A.*

Chapter 29

1. A public interest lobby, Common Cause, *Time*, November 15, 1982.
2. *Newsweek*, September 13, 1982.
3. See the author's *The Vatican Moscow Washington Alliance*, Chick Publications, 1982.
4. *Newsweek*, September 13, 1982.
5. *Newsweek*, September 16, 1982.
6. See the author's *The Vatican Moscow Washington Alliance*, Chick Publications, 1982.
7. After a Los Angeles investment adviser had accidently "discovered" them amidst sundry other Vetco shares.
8. The Vatican's subdued filtration with Freemasons, after World War I, was due to their common objective to keep the Communists from power. In 1974 the Vatican gave permission "in particular cases" to join a Masonic Lodge. The permission was widely used by U.S. Catholics.
9. February 11, 1980. See also *The Times*, May 29, 1981.

Chapter 30

1. *Time*, September 13, 1982.
2. *Time*, August 3, 1982. Also Newsweek, August 2, 1982.
3. *Time*, September 13, 1982.
4. Sindona himself, in September, 1982, hastened to declare that the money was given to Calvi's wife, but not to Marcinkus. (*Newsweek*, September 13, 1982).
5. September, 1982.

Chapter 31

1. Nino Andreatta, Treasury Minister, *The Times*, August 7, 1982.
2. As first disclosed by the *London Financial Times*.
3. In an ABC TV interview. See also *The Times*, London, October 1, 1982.
4. Published in Il Giornale, 8/22/82.
5. See the author's *The Vatican Moscow Washington Alliance*, Chick Publications.
6. *El Periodico*, October 29, 1982, Barcelona, Spain.

7. The following spring (1983), Archbiship Marcinkus, far from having been compelled to resign, headed the list of the 18 new cardinals who were elected on February 2, 1983 to the Sacred College. The pope wanted to give him a cardinal hat but did not do so under heavy pressure and protests from senior cardinals who feared further scandals in which the pope himself might have become personally involved.

8. The sudden "demise" of personalities, via "induced" heart attacks, has played an important role in recent decades in major political crises, some of them diverting the course of Vatican's activities. The last three or four pontificates experienced more than one of such demises, the most striking having been that of Pope Wojtyla's predecessor, Pope John Paul I, whose reign lasted only 33 days. For details, see the author's *The Vatican Moscow Washington Alliance*, Chick Publications.

Chapter 32
1. *Newsweek*, September 13, 1982.
2. *The Times*, November 2, 1982.
3. July 12, 1979.
4. Published by *Il Giornale* August 20, 1982.
5. See the photo document below. Il Giornale, August, 1982.
6. Pasienza, December 20, 1982, in a BBC interview.
7. Calvi to his wife, May, 1982.
8. *Il Giornale*, December 12, 1982.

Chapter 33
1. *Newsweek*, September 13, 1982.
2. Archbishop Marcinkus, in 1981.
3. See the author's *The Vatican Moscow Washington Alliance*, Chick Publications, 1982.
4. Giovanni de Musi, 1350 AD, *Cronicle di Piacenza*.

Chapter 34
1. November 1, 1982.
2. Polish poet, Maria Konopnika.
3. *The Times*, August, 14, 1982.
4. *Universe*, December 2, 1982.
5. It was later explained that Coventry had planned to give a set of four.
6. The Bishop of Cassano Ionio, South Italy, August, 1982.
7. *Liber Pontificalis*.
8. Giovanni Gratiano, of St. John at the Latin Gate.

Chapter 35
1. The paintings included works by Perugino, Weyden and Mino da Fiesole. See *The Times*, London, November 5, 1969.
2. *The Times*, May 19, 1971.

NOTES

1. *The paintings included works by Perugino, Weyden and Mino da Fiesole. See The Times*, London, November 5, 1969.

2. *The Times*, May 19, 1971.

3. *The Times*, October 21, 1971.

4. The document was in the apartment of Professor J. Ibaiz, Prat de la Riba, Tarragona, Spain, 1972.

5. E.g. 30,000 years at the Nativity of the Virgin and 100,000 at Epiphany. See also the article by Avro Manhattan, "How to Become a Saint Without Even Trying," *The Independent*, New York, 1969.

6. *The Times*, June 22, 1970.

7. *The Times*, July 21, 1970.

8. M.A. Larson and C.S. Lowell, *Praise the Lord for Tax Exemption.*

9. *Finance and Property*, January 15, 1980.

10. In 1978 Roman Catholics numbered officially 765 million. (See *Operation World*.) 1984 projections are 800 million.